PRAISE FOR *WHEN THE GAME*

"For sports leagues and their franchises to be success   ...vate
partnerships need to be created across a wide spectru   ...ivities. When it
comes to public-private partnerships relating to sports facilities, Rick Horrow
knows the terrain and has helped bring many of these projects to fruition for
the benefit of fans, teams, and communities."

—Paul Tagliabue,
Commissioner of the National Football League

"I've known Rick Horrow for many years, from our work together within Jack
Nicklaus's organization to our efforts to bring professional baseball to South
Florida. At no time since I first shook his hand have I seen his passion for
sport waver, nor his determination to champion a cause diminish. He is a true
sportsman to the end."

—Mike Schmidt,
National Baseball Hall of Fame, Philadelphia Phillies

"In West Virginia, Rick Horrow was instrumental in introducing televised
professional sport—in our case, golf—to a state hungry for top-level modern
competition. In *When the Game Is on the Line,* Horrow brings professional
sport, in all of its drama, to readers hungry for a behind-the-scenes look at
how their favorite sporting events came to be. Horrow's business experiences
and applied expertise are also valuable learnings for civic and corporate
leaders everywhere."

—Bob Wise, President, Alliance for
Excellent Education, Washington, D.C.,
Governor, West Virginia, 2001–2005

"I've seen firsthand what Rick Horrow can accomplish by developing
consensus between teams and their communities. He is truly an ally in
business, and in his dedication to providing a unique entertainment
experience to sports fanatics everywhere. Whether you're a lifelong season
ticket holder or casual fan, you'll enjoy reading the stories behind the jerseys
in Rick Horrow's true-to-life book."

—Jeff Lurie,
Owner and Chief Executive Officer, Philadelphia Eagles

"Rick Horrow's endless expertise and insights bring a unique perspective to sports talk radio. We worked together to pioneer the first national sports talk radio show devoted exclusively to the sports business—*Fox MoneyBall*. Rick has helped take this critically acclaimed program to millions of ears each week, plus he appears on all our other shows on a daily basis, to help make even the most complex sports business stories understandable for our hosts and listeners. With his latest book, Rick inks the stories he voices on air, providing yet another resource for those hungry for insider sports information. It's an awesome read."

—**Andrew Ashwood,**
VP/GM–Executive Producer, Fox Sports Radio

"Rick Horrow was one of the Founding Directors of CBS SportsLine, and worked with me as we created a media company from scratch to its current position as one of the top sports Internet services in the world. His book and Ten Horrow Principles illustrate the dynamic examples of how these traits can be applicable to every business and deal-making situation."

—**Michael Levy,**
Founder and Chairman, CBS SportsLine

"The business of sport is a very specialized niche in the world of news coverage, and no one covers it better than Rick Horrow. In person and on air, he embodies his nickname 'The Sports Professor,' providing an in-depth education and firsthand perspective on all the sports stories that transcend the field of play and become water cooler and dinnertime chatter every day. He is a real asset to our CNN news team."

—**Jim Lemay,**
Executive Producer, CNN

"Through his fascinating tales of deal-making in the big-leagues that read more like fiction than fact, Rick Horrow shares a set of profound principles that anyone can apply. . . as long as you can think 'What if?'"

—**Pat Croce,**
author of *I Feel Great and You Will Too!* and *110%*

"Rick Horrow is one of the foremost experts in sports facility development anywhere in the world. *When the Game Is on the Line* showcases his visionary deal-making at some of the biggest sports deals ever struck."

—**Paul Weiler,**
Friendly Professor of Sports and Entertainment Law, Harvard Law School

"You cannot stop Rick Horrow. Maybe you can slow him down, but only if you find a way to confiscate his plane ticket and cell phone. Otherwise, he is everywhere at once, it seems, maneuvering behind the curtain of professional sports like the man making the marionette move . . . And he isn't about to downshift."

—Greg Cote,
columnist, *Miami Herald*

"Rick Horrow sees beyond narrow interests and knows how to get sparring parties to the table and sell a vision to everyone's benefit. Corporations, public officials, community leaders and voters of all stripes can learn from the stories he tells from the trenches in this entertaining and illuminating book. This is deal-making for the new millennium."

—Ronald J. Norick,
Mayor of Oklahoma City, 1987–1998

"Do not get in the way of Rick Horrow when he's on the scent of a new big deal! Through fascinating, behind-the-scenes stories, *When the Game Is on the Line* reveals his perseverance, moxie, and winning style."

—Lesa France Kennedy,
President, International Speedway Corporation

"Rick Horrow's optimism and perseverance against the odds have paid off again and again. *When the Game Is on the Line* shows that with a can-do attitude, an ability to see the big picture, and an unflinching commitment to see things through, you can overcome the most intractable obstacles."

—Julius Erving

"An eye-opening lesson in high stakes politics, big business and civic responsibility . . . [Horrow's] infectious energy and positive spirit make this a must-read for anyone interested in the sport of business and the business of sports."

—*Publishers Weekly*

"A fascinating examination of the considerable realm where sports and business overlap, a world of big egos combined with multimillion-dollar agreements. The author's credentials are impressive . . . An insightful read on the art of negotiating in any realm."

—*Library Journal*

"Sparks of insight . . . "
　　—*Newsweek*

". . . Refreshingly free of business jargon. It is candid about its author's mistakes and the unappetizing sausage-making of stadium-building. What can you say about Miami officials who paid homeless people to skedaddle while pro basketball officials toured a potential arena site? After reading, you'll have no doubt as to [Horrow's] passion."
　　—*Boston Globe*

"A backstage pass to explosive closed-door meetings involving everyone from Joe Robbie to Jack Nicklaus. Power-dealmaker Rick Horrow tells the stories behind the stories. . . ."
　　—*OverTime Magazine*

"[Gives] even the most disinterested follower of the business of professional sports (and the sleazy politics that goes with it) reason to read on."
　　—*Hartford Courant*

". . . Horrow's single-minded focus comes with an unshakable belief that his work is of clear benefit to each city, with inevitable economic development resulting from these projects."
　　—*Miami Herald*

"An insider's look at sports franchises and the multifaceted funding of their arenas . . . full of lessons on people, power, and politics."
　　—*Akron Beacon Journal*

WHEN THE GAME IS ON THE LINE

From The Man Who Brought
The Heat To Miami And
The Browns Back To Cleveland,
An Inside Look At The High-Stakes
World Of Sports Deal-Making

RICK HORROW
WITH LARY BLOOM

NEW YORK

WHEN THE GAME IS ON THE LINE
RICK HORROW
WITH LARY BLOOM

ISBN 978-1-60037-899-7 Paperback
ISBN 978-1-60037-900-0 EPub Version
Library of Congress Control Number: 2010942733

Published by:

MORGAN JAMES PUBLISHING
The Entrepreneurial Publisher
5 Penn Plaza, 23rd Floor
New York City, New York 10001
(212) 655-5470 Office
(516) 908-4496 Fax
www.MorganJamesPublishing.com

Cover & Interior Design by:
Bonnie Bushman
bbushman@bresnan.net

In an effort to support local communities, raise awareness and funds, Morgan James Publishing donates one percent of all book sales for the life of each book to Habitat for Humanity.
Get involved today, visit
www.HelpHabitatForHumanity.org.

Dedicated to the memory of Benjamin Horrow

CONTENTS

ACKNOWLEDGMENTS

Writing is a lonely enterprise, but publishing a book isn't. As in deal-making, it requires many partners. If you're fortunate, you'll find one like Lisa DiMona, of Lark Productions in Dobbs Ferry, New York, who, with her associates Karen Watts and Robin Dellabough, had the vision for this book and provided great support throughout. It is also important to engage a publishing house that believes in the idea and helps shape the manuscript. David Goehring, publisher of Perseus Publishing, provided critical guidance, as did the book's enthusiastic and tireless editor, Nick Philipson. Others at Perseus who contributed mightily to the effort include Elizabeth Carduff, Lissa Warren, David Tripp, John Thomas, Erin Sprague, and Arlinda Shtuni. As for the encouragement necessary for such a project, it began at home. Thanks to Terri, Katie, and Caroline Horrow for their patience, understanding, and advice. And to Liz Gwillim for similar contributions. Thanks, too, to the following who offered us encouragement, ideas, or vital information: Jim Travis, Roxanne Coady, Bram Alden, Anne Horrow, Raul Masvidal, Maurice Ferre, Xavier Suarez, Edwin Pope, Larry Turner, Eston Melton, David Talley, Steve Muss, Paul Weiler, Rick Moore, Ron Norick, Sandy Seidman, Lon Seidman, Justin Ermler, Sukey Howard, Brenda Carter, Jim Bruza, Laurie Majors, Oscar Majors, William Clay Ford Jr., Amy Coleman, Eric Golden, Joel Levine, Sandy Meyers, Bob Marcusse, Kevin Gray, Lesa France Kennedy, Rick Hornung, John Dorschner, Betty Curbelo, Suzanne Staubach, Maureen Connolly, Bob Herrfeldt, Jeff Olanoff, Mike Woollen, Bryan Trubey, Michael Birkin, Dale Adams, Karen Zahorsky, Stephen Greyser, Ted Killory, Scott Michel, Rick Mercer, Mike

Schmidt, Paul Tagliabue, Roger Goodell, Greg Aiello, Joe Foss, Joe Rose, Evan Shapiro, Greg and Laura Norman, Bart Collins, Dave Hyde, Dennis Wellner, Mike Levy, Bernie Swain, Harry Rhoads, Clyde Echols, Louis King, Herb McBride, Frank Poe, Larry Lemak, John Jones, Ed Quimby, Dale Koger, John DiCiurcio, Bill Blechman, Andy Breslau, Jeff Lurie, Tom Lewand Sr., Tom Lewand Jr., Fereydoun Kian, Peggy Sussex, and M. Horrow.

FOREWORD: BOB GRAHAM

All enlightened civic and political leaders understand that sports and entertainment are critical in the growth and development of a city, region, and state. In a general sense, sports is "community," allowing strangers to become neighbors. This is especially true of South Florida -- over the last 50 years, and today. While the fact that the region is effectively a "melting pot" may draw civic praise, it is certainly difficult to manufacture "community" among those who grew up elsewhere. Therefore, the sports business is especially significant to all of us who grew up in South Florida.

I remember in 1946 watching Johnny Mize when the New York Giants held Spring Training at the old Miami field (near where the new Miami Marlins stadium is being built). In his first season back from World War II, Mize hit .337 and was named to the All-Star team. Who can forget the 1967 touchdown kickoff return by Miami Dolphin Joe Auer, which ushered in the American Football League Miami Dolphins.

Obviously, the 1972 perfect season has been on everybody's mind, as has the two Florida Marlins World Series championships and the one Miami Heat title. While residents may all come from different backgrounds, religions, political philosophies, and beliefs, South Floridians can all remember where they were on January 14, 1973, when the Dolphins completed their perfect season with a 14-7 win over the Washington Redskins.

When Rick Horrow began his stint as Founding Director of the Miami Sports and Exhibition Authority in 1980, the region had a much different landscape. Numerous stadiums, arenas, teams, and leagues had come, gone, or evaporated. The "presumption of failure" was rampant. I believed in the development of sports and entertainment, and believed that the legacy of South Florida deserved no less. *When the Game Is on the Line* describes many of the early travails before the Miami Arena, the Miami Heat, and Wayne Huizenga and the Florida Marlins and Panthers.

The momentum generated in the early 1980's was critical to the landscape that we see today. There would be no Heat, Marlins or Panthers, no American Airlines Arena or Bank Atlantic Center and certainly no LeBron James. While there have been over 350 sports, arts, and entertainment facilities built nationwide since the 1980 Sports and Exhibition Authority commencement (at a cost of nearly $30 billion), it is probable that none were as difficult and controversial than those early South Florida efforts.

The metamorphosis of the Miami Heat, construction of a new facility for the Florida/Miami Marlins, and the new ownership and entertainment orientation of the Miami Dolphins are a necessary next step in the positive and international evolution of the region. *When the Game Is on the Line* provides an interesting perspective and chronology. Further, the business principles outlined in the book provide necessary guidelines on how to succeed in complex, controversial, and difficult situations. The 10 business keys cut across all areas of business and life: vision, flexibility, tenacity, compromise, subtlety, focus, proactivity, optimism, and a sense of history and purpose are all keys to be followed.

While the $750 billion business of sports continues to grow, these lessons are applicable in a wide variety of situations.

Robert "Bob" Graham
Florida Governor, 1979-1987
United States Senator, 1987-2005

PROLOGUE: TAKING THE HEAT

Within the glittery sports snow globe that is the National Basketball Association, July 8, 2010 was pro basketball's equivalent of 9/11. Not in terms, to be sure, of mayhem and anguish, but in the sense that the way the world was perceived before and the way it was observed after are two entirely different things.

On that date in South Florida, the snow globe cracked open to absorb two new points of light, in the forms of NBA superstars LeBron James and Chris Bosh, to join the Miami Heat's star point guard Dwyane Wade. The move changed for a decade at least the balance of power not only among the NBA's elite teams but among the region's pro sports franchises as well. It also created an exciting new landscape for local businesses, broadcasters, tourism, and of course, sports fans.

Professional sports in South Florida really began in 1966 with the award of the Miami Dolphins. That American Football League franchise was originally destined for New Orleans, but racial and financial circumstances caused the AFL owners to reconsider.

On an interesting and synergistic parallel track, the New Orleans Saints celebrate the five-year Katrina history and the NFL world championship while Miami celebrates its veritable sports rebirth with James, Bosh, and Wade leading the NBA Miami Heat in its new era of lofty expectations, beginning October 2010.

The 1972 Miami Dolphins perfect season inspired me to return home after Harvard Law School to become the Founding Director of the Miami Sports & Exhibition Authority. Former Governor and

Senator Bob Graham provided the political leverage and emotional motivation to move the process forward. The first edition of *When the Game Is on the Line* talks about those successes and failures.

The Miami Arena, though economically and physically outdated and outsized, allowed Miami to take its "next big step" with the award of the Heat in the mid-1980's, and the acceptance of South Florida as a "sports region" of its own (not only a place where old sports allegiances come to retire).

Though demolished in 2009, the old Miami Arena gave 30 million spectators a taste of the big leagues, and more importantly allowed the region to overcome the rampant presumption of failure that doomed previous efforts. The Heat thus begat the Florida Panthers, which begat the Florida Marlins. South Florida went from a minor league expansion city (the old AFL in 1966) to the quickest region to go to four major league sports franchises in history (alongside Phoenix, Arizona).

The development of the Miami Arena and the awarding of the Miami Heat were central to that theme. Now that the Marlins have won two world championships and the Heat one, South Florida sports fans take the metamorphosis for granted.

The real hero behind the transformation remains Carnival Cruise Line founder Ted Arison. On April 21, 1987, he in essence founded the Miami Heat by putting community interests ahead of his lack of basketball knowledge and writing a $32.5 million check to NBA Commissioner David Stern in his offices in New York City. With one pen stroke, Miami received its first major league expansion franchise.

The meeting was critical in other respects as well. Commissioner Stern intended that the league welcome three new expansion franchises to the fold in one process. However, Arison's compelling case also focused on a potential Orlando-Miami rivalry. The prospect so intrigued Stern that the result was four franchises – the Minnesota Timberwolves, Charlotte Hornets, Orlando Magic, and Miami Heat -- all to begin play within the next three years.

The road to franchise stability and international awareness of both the Miami Heat and the Orlando Magic took strikingly parallel paths. While Orlando began play a year earlier, both the Heat and Magic played in facilities that were ultimately important for their early successes, but were replaced by larger venues over time.

Under Governor and Senator Bob Graham's leadership, a statewide funding process was created to supplement local and team initiatives -- producing the American Airlines Arena in Miami and the Amway Center in downtown Orlando. That facility, which opened in late 2010, boasts state-of-the-art amenities, infrastructure, and hospitality. What's more, the nearby Disney Institute entered into a new signature relationship with the Magic wherein Disney has provided input on hospitality, transportation, facility access, and the like. The result is a model facility outside (infrastructure and technology) and inside (hospitality "the Disney way").

It is appropriate, and ironic, that Miami celebrated the LeBron/Bosh/Wade "coming out party" the day after Orlando celebrates the opening of its new Amway Arena. The development of the Miami Arena allowed that, and the creation of the new American Airlines Arena created the revenue to sign Wade and Shaquille O'Neal -- leading to Miami's first world basketball championship.

Clearly, this was a long, long way from the 1984 Washington Bullets-New Jersey Nets exhibition game we promoted at the three-walled Knight Convention Center.

Ted Arison's son Mickey has now become one of the most influential owners in the National Basketball Association, working hand-in-hand with Coach Pat Riley to lure James and Bosh to join Wade.

At the same time, Wade, James, and Bosh were thinking about building their own dynasty (that their contracts expired at the same time in the Summer of 2010 allowed this to happen). Together, the efforts of the Heat and the championship desires of the marquee players created a perfect storm that ushered in a new era of South Florida sports.

However, the amalgamation of three superstars (and three multinational corporations) was not easy.

Ironically, two days after "The Decision," the Miami Dolphins took out full page newspaper ads in regional newspapers welcoming the Heat superstar trio -- and truly embracing the idea of a new sports era for the four million people in the region.

New Dolphins owner Stephen Ross – like me, a Miami Beach high school graduate -- brought his own unique vision to the Miami Dolphins. Ross invited such entertainment industry boldface names as Jimmy Buffett, Serena and Venus Williams, Marc Anthony and J Lo to come on board as minority owners. He introduced the cutting edge technology of FanVision, envisioned a covered Sun Life Stadium (now in the planning process), and created a regional water park – to name a few new ideas. Ross has said numerous times that while owning a pro football team is a labor of love, it is also a business based on providing an entertaining experience for all of South Florida and working to build regional consensus at the same time.

The Dolphins continue to pursue their perfect season legacy, the Miami Heat harbors lofty expectations of the Wade/Bosh/James trifecta, the two-time world champion Florida Marlins prepare to move into their new stadium, and the Florida Panthers grow their fan base though creative marketing approaches.

And then there's golf. Florida has long been known as the Golf Capital of the World, and the sport certainly takes its rightful place alongside professional team sports in the South Florida sports pantheon. "South Florida golf has endured over 70 years of professional golf at the highest level," says Ken Kennerly, Founder, President and CEO of IGP Sports, and Entertainment Group Executive Director, The Honda Classic, "and no doubt will continue well into the future. The 'Golf Capital of the World' will always play a major role in the history of this great game."

The 1940 Senior PGA Championship was the first recognized professional golf tournament of any magnitude in South Florida, won by Otto Hackbarth at North Shore Country Club and Bobby

Jones Country Club in Sarasota. The Senior PGA Championship remained in Florida from 1940 until 2000, and boasted such great champions as Gene Sarazen, Jimmy Demaret, Sam Snead, Julius Boros, Arnold Palmer, Jack Nicklaus, and Hale Irwin.

Following the success of the Senior PGA Championship, the "young" guys were introduced to golf in South Florida at the Doral Resort in Miami, whose tenure as a home to the pros began in 1962 with Billy Casper winning the inaugural Doral Country Club Open Invitational. Doral Resort & Country Club today hosts one of the premier events on the PGA Tour, now known as the World Golf Championship, Cadillac Championship. Doral's 50 years of history includes great Champions such as Nicklaus, Billy Casper, Doug Sanders, Lee Trevino, Tom Weiskopf, Raymond Floyd, Tiger Woods, and Phil Mickelson.

Major Championship history began in South Florida in 1971 with the PGA Championship won by none other than Nicklaus, the Golden Bear, at the original PGA National Golf Club. Major golf moved down the street to the new PGA National Golf Club in 1983 where the U.S. team was victorious over Europe in the Ryder Cup; PGA National also hosted the 1987 PGA Championship won by Larry Nelson.

Another great "golfing legend" in the region not exactly known for his golfing prowess was the comedian Jackie Gleason. The Jackie Gleason Inverrary Classic began in 1972 in Ft Lauderdale, with Weiskopf winning the inaugural tournament at Inverrary Country Club. The Jackie Gleason in 1982 became The Honda Classic, which today is also one of the premier events on the PGA Tour, and now contested at the famed PGA National Golf Club in Palm Beach Gardens.

- - - - - - - - - -

We chose to update and release *When the Game Is on the Line* as part of the new "Sports Professor Series" in order to recount and emphasize the business and leadership principles necessary to accomplish big dreams. Our first book in the series, Jerry Colangelo's

Return of the Gold, chronicles his efforts to put together a gold medal-winning basketball team; *Return of the Gold* was followed by my *Beyond the Box Score*, co-authored with Horrow Sports Ventures Vice President Karla Swatek. Other key industry leaders will speak to their efforts in future "Sports Professor" books.

Clearly, the 10 principles outlined at the end of *When the Game Is on the Line* are as relevant today as they ever have been -- Mickey Arison and Pat Riley dreamed of attracting the new Heat mega-superstars before actually implementing their goals; Stephen Ross broke the mold in redefining sports as entertainment; Dwyane Wade became the ultimate consensus builder in helping to shape a synchronized team of interchangeable parts; LeBron James placed his ego behind his teammates in an effort to create a legacy and dynasty — and is in the process of withstanding the inevitable criticism that necessarily followed.

All 10 *When the Game Is on the Line* principles apply to all aspects of complex deal-making, negotiation, and certainly the saga that lead to the creation of the new purported dynasty in the making.

Rick Horrow
February, 2011

INTRODUCTION

A Tale of Four or Five Cities

As the Hornets Swarmed

On November 1, 2005, in the ultimate act of bandwagoneering in the modern history of sport, a sellout crowd of 19,163 screaming new fans watched "their" New Orleans/Oklahoma City Hornets rally to the first home victory of the NBA season at downtown Oklahoma City's Ford Center.

Sitting next to former Mayor Ron Norick, I watched the melee—the first NBA experience ever for more than half the crowd—with a rush of pride and ownership I'd seldom felt in the other cities in which I'd engineered major sports deals. This little city on the prairie was special to me, representing the finest work I'd ever done in helping disparate members of a community accomplish their goals.

In the wake of August's Hurricane Katrina, the Hornets had made a 35-game commitment to play the majority of their home games in Oklahoma City after Katrina rendered their home court at New Orleans Arena completely unplayable. And, behind the scenes as usual, I'd helped make it happen.

More than 6,500 season ticket deposits were secured during the first week of ticket sales alone. Five Oklahoma City–based companies agreed to be presenting sponsors, marking the first time in major pro sports history that five regional partners came together in one presenting sponsorship role.

Though Hornet owner George Shinn was publicly adamant that the team was "going back to New Orleans," Oklahoma City leaders recognized a seminal opportunity to showcase their community and bring major league sports to town, and gave it their collective all.

But the drama actually runs much deeper than that.

On December 14, 1993, under my guidance, the Oklahoma City region passed Metropolitan Area Projects Strategies (MAPS), a $500 million facility infrastructure package. MAPS became the largest public facility referendum in U.S. history, bundling nine projects together in one vote—the new arena, a central library, convention center, performing arts center, baseball stadium, retail canal, and other facilities.

In its first twelve years, the MAPS initiative has created over $1 billion in economic impact, lured seven million tourists annually, and provided an unprecedented feeling of community self-esteem, badly needed after the April 1995 bombing of the Murrah Federal Building, which was, at that point, the biggest act of terrorism in U.S. history.

The MAPS story not only became one of the prominent tales in *When The Game Is On the Line*—from a facilities development perspective, MAPS started a national trend that has now culminated in over 265 sports, arts, and recreation facilities at a cost of nearly $20 billion.

The MAPS campaign for the new arena in Oklahoma City always hinted at the desire to bring major league sports to the region, but it was never the central theme. In fact, the arena was billed as necessary regardless of whether a professional sports franchise came.

The first year of the Ford Center's operations saw over 300,000 tickets sold, placing it tenth in overall sales according to *Pollstar* magazine, just three spots below New York City's Madison Square Garden. Oklahoma City stayed on the national radar as a possible candidate for a professional sports franchise.

At the same time, Charlotte Hornets owner George Shinn was settled in Charlotte in the middle of his tenure at the Charlotte Arena. A few years later, he became disillusioned with the market and made good on his threat to move. The Charlotte Hornets, of course, ultimately became the New Orleans Hornets.

Fast-forward to August 29, 2005, when Hurricane Katrina devastated New Orleans. Oklahoma City Mayor Mick Cornett and City Manager Jim Couch put a deal together with the Hornets in 22 days, guaranteeing $10 million if the Hornets don't reach their $40 million local revenue goal and making a commitment to house the Hornets for the 2005–2006 season with an option for one more season thereafter.

NBA Commissioner David Stern and Shinn were adamant that the Hornets were New Orleans's team to lose. However, pundits predicted that it was the beginning of a long-term relationship. Oklahoma City's median household income of $34,947 was adequate for the NBA, and the Ford Center, with its 19,675 seats and 49 private suites, could also fill the bill.

More importantly, Oklahoma City wanted a major league sports team in a bad way. The Greater Oklahoma City Chamber of Commerce estimated that the 2005–2006 Hornets season would produce $60 million in economic impact, even if the Ford Center was less than two-thirds full for the committed 35 games.

Oklahoma City was not about to let the Hornets fly away.

No N.O.? San Antonio?

The butterfly effect of hurricanes and sports economics reaches even further.

Losses sustained by New Orleans due to Hurricane Katrina have unquestionably been other communities' gains, especially from a sports business perspective. Over forty-three sports facilities nationwide, mostly arenas as far away as Arizona and Indiana, played host to New Orleans refugees in the days and weeks after the storm. Louisiana student athletes found temporary homes on a host of other campuses; many would stay on permanently.

And in perhaps the most economically significant Katrina-related development, San Antonio Mayor Phil Hardberger made it his personal mission to keep the New Orleans Saints for longer than the one year they agreed to play in San Antonio's Alamodome.

Like the Hornets, the Saints lost their home base to Katrina. No viewer was likely to soon forget the dramatic news coverage of the 25,000 New Orleans residents forced to take refuge in the Superdome during the worst days of the storm. But from day one it certainly seemed as though Saints owner Tom Benson was ready to forget about New Orleans.

In the weeks following Katrina's devastation of the city, the Saints signed a parallel agreement with the city of San Antonio to the Hornets' deal in Oklahoma City, committing to playing three "home" games in the Alamodome. The estimated $30 million in economic impact from the three games alone didn't even take into account tickets, merchandising, parking, or concession revenues. Small wonder that Mayor Hardberger coveted a permanent portion of the $6 billion annual total National Football League business.

The remainder of the Saints home games were to be played in Baton Rouge at Louisiana State's Tiger Stadium. Benson, visibly shaken by the toll Katrina had taken on his home state, had publicly expressed doubt about Louisiana's ongoing ability to support the team. He was loudly booed—and he claimed, threatened—at the Saints' Baton Rouge matchup with the Miami Dolphins and vowed not to return to the state.

While the Saints consider invoking their Force Majure ("Act of God") clause, starting a 90-day exit strategy countdown, recent developments indicate that Louisiana Governor Kathleen Blanco and Benson agree to delay the legal deadline to start that exit clock.

Superdome officials indicated that they would pay Benson only a fraction of a $15 million subsidy for 2005 because of games lost to Hurricane Katrina. And no one seems to know how to fund needed Superdome renovations.

As NFL Commissioner Paul Tagliabue preaches patience in regards to the Saints' situation, in San Antonio Hardberger nonetheless prepares to play hardball. He's lined up support from the city's business community and the former mayors who supported adding an NFL franchise to the city.

Now the waiting game begins to see where the Saints will end up marching.

Motor City Momentum

From the game's most memorable moments—Broadway Joe Namath's 1969 victory guarantee, the Dolphins' cap to their perfect 1972–1973 season, Janet Jackson's oft-TiVoed 2004 flesh flash—the Super Bowl is the most watched party for big business each year, just as it is for most Americans.

When I set the scene in the first chapter of *When The Game Is On the Line* in 2003, Detroit's Ford Field had just opened, and the city was only beginning preparations for its 2006 big event.

Super Bowl XL on February 5, 2006, should bring more than 120,000 visitors to the Motor City, 3,000 media, viewers in 230 countries, and $300-400 million in economic impact. (That's the equivalent of 42,918,454 Supremes albums.) The three-year-old Ford Field is part of a $505 million project I was involved in, comprising two stadiums (Comerica Park is the second) and a downtown sports-entertainment shopping complex. Super Bowl XL provides the biggest of international stages upon which to showcase downtown Detroit's rebirth.

By comparison, last summer's MLB All-Star Game at Comerica Park brought $50–70 million in economic impact and 30,000 visitors to the region.

As in all recent host cities, the merchants of Motown will be dancing in the streets. Last year, the successful entertainment village created in downtown Houston was resurrected along Jacksonville's riverfront. The 12-day festival set into motion over 50 concerts, 185 unique events, and the 850,000–square foot NFL Experience, which drew 125,000 people to the entertainment area next to the St. Johns River.

Detroit's Super Bowl has planned a similar downtown festival with a winter theme, complete with ice sculptures, skating, and outdoor concerts.

The other business boon at every Super Bowl can be seen during the game's commercial breaks. Ad spending on network TV was $16.4 billion last year. Fox took in $144 million from Super Bowl XXXIX advertising alone, charging a record $2.4 million for a 30-second spot.

The Super Bowl is a top destination for A-list celebrities and athletes looking to party hop and schmooze. Last year's Super Bowl attracted the likes of Bill Clinton, Paris Hilton, Donald Trump, and Sean "P. Diddy" Combs. The constellation of music superstars, Hollywood elite, and Beltway power brokers expected in Detroit has party planners charging six-figure fees for downtown buildings empty for decades.

If the glitterati enjoy the party, it could go a long way toward changing Detroit's image from poster child for urban decay to hip destination city.

And I'll be there to enjoy the fruits of my Motown labor.

Elsewhere in Sports Town, U.S.A.

Since the publication of *When The Game Is On the Line* in 2003, many of the players have changed, but the end results keep growing and growing.

My Harvard Law School roommate and regular squash rival John Roberts is now Chief Justice of the United States Supreme Court. In those days, when we would watch football together, while my full attention was focused on the games—which would serve me well in my career as a sports business dealmaker—it was clear that John's focus was on a higher playing field.

While I still regularly abide by my ten Horrow Principles of Doing Business (see Chapter Nine), some of the rules of play have changed.

In Miami, where it all started for me, the Marlins won their second World Series in a five-year stretch. With the addition of Shaquille O'Neal, the Heat have become real contenders, and Heat owner Ted Arison's son Micky has been named Chairman of the National Basketball Association's prestigious Board of Governors. (See Chapter Three for more on the Heat.)

NASCAR (Chapter Seven) is speeding forward with a 90 percent growth rate, the most of any sport, and is looking at building new tracks in the state of Washington and near the millions of potential fans in New York City. In Kansas City, where my own NASCAR chapter began, we've started construction on a new downtown arena I helped secure, and the city has just been awarded its first ever Super Bowl—providing, of course, that a needed $500 million of improvements are made to Arrowhead Stadium, including a new retractable roof to keep out the February cold.

In the NFL (Chapter Eight), new stadiums are committed in Indianapolis and in New York/New Jersey. Arizona's Glendale facility opens in August 2006, and Tagliabue has green-lighted the NFL's return to Los Angeles, possibly, even, for two teams—one to play in the oft-renovated Coliseum, and one to play, with the "Los Angeles" Angels, in the city of Anaheim.

Finally, as much as I love the game, it simply wouldn't do for me to end with any other sport than golf. As far as the PGA Tour goes (Chapter Five), they've just announced the FedEx Cup, a postseason playoff fashioned after NASCAR's Nextel Chase for the Championship, and heavily borrowed from my friend Greg Norman's idea for the World Tour of Golf proposed a decade ago.

And fifteen-year-old Michelle Wie has set new standards of sponsorship with her ascent to the LPGA and her $10 million annual sponsorship deal with Sony and Nike. With the signing, Wie becomes the highest endorsed female golfer and third highest endorsed female athlete in the world.

But that story is for another time—and, perhaps, for another book.

—Rick Horrow
November 2005

CHAPTER 1

In the Lions Den

Make no little plans. They have no magic to stir men's blood.

DANIEL HUDSON BURNHAM,
architect of the Chicago Plan, 1909

On the morning of August 24, 2002, I drove a rental car from Detroit's Metro Airport toward downtown and through pro football history. Here was the site of Dinan Field, where for 40 cents, if you had a spare 40 cents in the Depression, you could have witnessed the very first Detroit Lions game. I passed the site, too, of old Briggs Stadium (later renamed Tiger Stadium), where Bobby Layne and Doak Walker led the locals to NFL championships in the early 1950s. Briggs was where the Lions had last played in downtown Detroit, on Thanksgiving Day 1974, before abandoning the decaying Motor City for the Pontiac Silverdome. Now all these years later, in a preseason game against the Pittsburgh Steelers, the franchise would come full circle, back to the heart of downtown, and to its new dome home: the $312 million Ford Field.

I couldn't find a parking place close by, so I settled on a lot a few blocks away. The attendant, wearing a proud smile and a tattered shirt, nodded toward the just-completed stadium that features a retro design and a brick wall saved from the warehouse of the old J. L. Hudson Department Store. He said, "Sure is a beautiful thing, isn't it?"

I agreed, and added, "I helped build it." I thought perhaps that he'd waive the $30 parking fee, but he held his hand out to take the cash. It was only right that I should pay. I had argued, as I always argue in making downtown stadium deals, that such facilities are economic generators, and help restore pride and prosperity to inner-city neighborhoods. My thirty bucks, then, would contribute to an estimated $372 million yearly in economic stimulus. Besides, I could well afford to pay the man. The NFL had paid me handsomely over the course of the last few years to help the Lions and a dozen other franchises to secure new homes or improve old ones. And the league represents only a fraction of my Horrow Sports Ventures business, built during an era of unprecedented growth in professional football, baseball, basketball, hockey, golf, and other sports. It has been a decade when 79 major league stadiums and arenas have been modernized or built, and overall, 256 sports, arts, convention, and entertainment facilities developed at a total cost of about $20 billion.

I didn't get into the details of the Detroit deal with the parking attendant. He had a lot of collecting to do. But I am certain that if he had had the time to listen he would have been surprised by the facts of the case, and how close he and the city came to having to find other ways to make do on autumn afternoons. In the fashion of almost all of dozens of deals over the years, this one was a cliffhanger. The local press captured none of the behind-the-scenes tension. How could it? Reporters aren't in the room when I negotiate with public figures and business leaders, or when owners face daunting decisions, or lawsuits (as in the case of the Lions, when officials in Pontiac tried to save the Lions for that city.) Reporters certainly weren't there when, against formidable odds, we put together the most intense and complex deal in any NFL city in an atmosphere where there were no shortage of "bright" ideas floating around the room. They didn't see the heroic and visionary support of then Detroit mayor Dennis Archer, or when William Clay Ford Jr., chairman of Ford Motor Co. and owner of the Lions, had to decide whether to make the convenient and safe choice of staying in Pontiac or take the risky and more expensive route and come back to the environs where his great-grandfather became one of the world's legendary manufacturers.

I had told Bill Ford I was coming to the opening festivities, but didn't expect to see him until the start of the game. I planned to take my own tour of the facilities. In the buzz of activity, 200 or more officials gathered on the grasslike FieldTurf. I spotted Ford about 30 yards away. He wore a blue and silver tie (the team's colors) and his hair, as usual, was impeccably combed. He saw me, too. When I reached him, I put out my hand. He ignored it, and hugged me instead. I shouldn't have been surprised—he is the rarest corporate bird, a garrulous Buddhist who wears his heart on his sleeve. He said, "I'm so glad you're here, Rick. This is your house, too."

Not long after, we were up in the owner's box (one of 132 skyboxes), sitting on plush Visteon seats (in the style of the Lincoln Navigator), enjoying an inaugural feast of pasta with lobster, spinach salad, fine Bordeaux, and the offerings of an overstuffed dessert tray. We watched as the Lions, coming off a disappointing season, took the opening kickoff and marched down the field to a touchdown. The new stadium seemed to have already made a difference.

I didn't stay for game's end (and, alas, the Lions' eventual defeat) because I had to get on to the next city, the next deal, and my thirty-second car rental of the calendar year. But I did swing by the best seat in the house, the skybox reserved for local public officials. There was gaiety at the 50-yard-line perch—champagne, bountiful food, and any number of politicians eager to take credit for what they saw in front of them. I noticed that Dennis Archer, the former mayor whose tenacity and courage had been a key to the new stadium, wasn't present. This didn't surprise me. I learned long ago about the realities of politics, that the real forces in a success story are shoved aside, and that public figures who put nothing but obstacles in the way of visionary projects show up at the ribbon cutting to take the credit and pop the corks.

In fact, it was such behavior that became part of the impetus to write this book. I learned to make deals in the most unpromising of circumstances. I also learned how to negotiate with caustic egomaniacs who owned football and baseball teams, and to whom collaboration and compromise were fighting words. I had the privilege of being present during negotiations that determined the fate of cities and franchises; usually I was in the position of devising and pushing a plan, and then selling it to voters, often addressing intense criticism of the very idea of public funding. And, in doing this unique work, I built a compelling repository of inside stories of the games.

I was in the room when Art Modell, then owner of the Browns, played his own devious game with the city of Cleveland, all the while knowing his true intention of moving his team to Baltimore; and I carried out an innovative and risky plan to help save pro football for Cleveland. I know the extreme measures taken in a variety of places to make sure our efforts to stabilize franchises worked (including persuading one team owner, Malcolm Glazer of the Tampa Bay Buccaneers, to leave town during our campaign, and offering wine and donuts to the homeless in San Francisco in exchange for registering to vote). I was, uncomfortably, in the room when the tyrannical founder of the Miami Dolphins, Joe Robbie, announced his intentions to stand in the path of every sensible idea for the city; I had to come up with ways around him. I witnessed, firsthand, the heartless leverage game played by the National Hockey League with Oklahoma City in the weeks after the tragedy of the terrorist bombing there—for this is an ugly side to sports and big business. I knew from personal experience how Hall of Fame golfer Jack Nicklaus runs his Golden Bear International business (ineptly) and the details of how he almost became the unlikely owner of the Minnesota Twins a decade before the team was publicly for sale. I know hundreds of ironies and oddities—such as why fairy shrimp, tiny creatures who swim upside-down, prevented Sacramento from being a serious contender for a monumental new NASCAR track. I also know that the state of Missouri could have become home to the track instead of Kansas—if the body language of a governor had been different.

In doing this work, I have compiled what I am convinced are valuable lessons that can be used by anyone who must negotiate. You don't need to be a stadium builder to find yourself up against egomaniacs, unpromising odds, a consuming presumption of failure, a daunting marketing task, or manipulative people who respond, "That's a good idea, but we don't do things that way." These obstacles are common in circumstances wherever there is a need for something new and visionary, or wherever persuasiveness is useful (just about everywhere), whenever tenacity and thinking on your feet are needed (also just about everywhere), no matter the scope or the subject of the prospective deal. I instinctively knew that a recounting of more than twenty years of sports deal-making—which has by necessity included political and business deal-making—would reveal ideas and procedures that I never came across in formal studies at Northwestern or Harvard Law School.

Birth of a Salesman

One final reason to put these episodes and lessons on paper is to honor my father, who, without knowing it, had a great effect on the direction of my life.

Benjamin Horrow was also a lawyer who saw the limitations of the law. He was a member of a large Philadelphia firm, with a closet full of Brooks Brothers suits, when he came home one day and convinced my mother that it was time for them to enjoy the virtues of Florida on a permanent basis. He said the weather would be better for his knee, which still ached from an old sports injury. His true intention was to give up the law and, in the tradition of many before him, head to Miami where life could begin again, and where he could reinvent himself as an entrepreneur. The "Magic City" had drawn this kind of adventurous spirit for a century, ever since pioneer Julia Tuttle convinced Henry Flagler to extend his Florida East Coast Railroad past Palm Beach to her little bit of heaven.

My father hoped to exploit this little bit of heaven; there were enormous opportunities suggested by its subtropical weather. He had the idea of producing and marketing cabanas, awnings, and hurricane shutters, a business that over the years became very successful.

I was born in Miami, the only child of Ben and Anne Horrow. I inherited my father's sense of adventure, and his interest in sports. I did not possess his social skills early on. In fact, my acceptance in the second grade was due entirely to my capacity for detail and sports-page memorization. I wowed classmates during the 1962 World Series by reciting the batting orders and statistics of every New York Yankees and San Francisco Giants player.

My father egged me on in my obsession with sports. We watched golf and NFL football on Sunday afternoons, snuck off as often as we could to spring training games at the ramshackle Miami Stadium. He was amused by the way I scored every game, and kept meticulous records. (I still do. My garage, in something of a departure from its original intent—as my wife points out—is full of boxes of box scores and game programs going back decades.)

My father and I both had dreams of Miami as a major league city. We rejoiced when in 1965 the *Miami Herald* announced that the city had been awarded a new franchise in the American Football League— its first big-league franchise in any sport. There were two Dolphins partners. One name was well known to my father, the comedian Danny Thomas. The other was a Minneapolis businessman, who like Thomas was of Lebanese descent, named Joe Robbie.

Our celebration, however, was brief. One day my mother sat me down in the living room and said, "We're losing your father." That's when I first heard the word melanoma. She explained that the cancer had spread, and that doctors didn't expect him to live much longer. He was 60 years old.

Mount Sinai Hospital in Miami Beach discouraged visits by children but at 11 years old I was becoming the man of the house, and made several trips. My father and I reviewed the Dolphins' first draft picks, and agreed that the new team had done a first-rate job in scouting. We mailed off a check for season tickets. My father, however, didn't live long enough to use them.

I wished, of course, that he could have witnessed that 1972–73 undefeated season from the 50-yard line, as my mother and I did, and watched as Larry Csonka, Bob Griese, Paul Warfield, Manny Fernandez, Nick Buoniconti, Dick Anderson, Larry Little, Jim Kiick, coach Don Shula, owner Joe Robbie (by this time he had bought out Danny Thomas), and others managed to do the impossible. They not only achieved football perfection (17–0) but, in unprecedented fashion, became a unifying force in a city where nothing seemed unified.

In the years following my father's death, I was already following in his footsteps. My mother was something of a strict disciplinarian. She remembers now that on occasion, when I felt the rules were unreasonable, I would say, "We need to sit down and talk." At 11 years old, I would press my points cordially but firmly until she relented. Even then, the deal-maker. "You're just like your father," she would say.

The one thing that made me different from him is that I eventually understood that my love of sports would not simply serve as diversion, but as a living. I suspected this when I went off to Northwestern, and I had even a stronger idea about it at Harvard, where I clearly strayed from the traditional path—to run the bases.

My contracts professor must have been the inspiration for the stern and humorless Professor Kingsfield (the John Houseman character in the movie *The Paper Chase*). I struck a deal with the guy. Just before the start of the first class of the semester, I said, "I'd really like you to call on me for a particular case." It concerned Napoleon Lajoie, a classic law-school case that defined what "specific performance" is. What made it interesting to me was that Lajoie was a Hall of Fame baseball player. That day at Harvard, there were 500 people in the section. The professor, wearing a dour expression, called on me and said, "Please state the facts of the case, Mr. Horrow." Normally you spin a thirty-second recitation of the circumstances. But I had a show prepared. I took out a baseball cap, put it on, went up to the blackboard, wrote down Lajoie's career stats (3,242 hits, 1,599 RBIs, .338 batting average), drew a baseball diamond, and started describing everything in metaphorical baseball terms. When I finished the facts of the case and what the legal holding was, my fellow students cheered as if their favorite slugger had just delivered a game-winning hit in the late innings.

It was a stunt I knew that my father would have enjoyed. It was a stunt that typified what was to come over the next several years as I at first struggled to define my way and then devised methods that would turn indifference or opposition into passionate support. Along the way, I applied the Horrow Principles—inspired by the father, defined by the son.

CHAPTER 2

Miami Game Plan

Good luck is another name for tenacity of purpose.
RALPH WALDO EMERSON

I argued my first and last case in a court of law on October 14, 1980. My "retirement" from the courtroom at age 25, and after only a few hours at the bar, was self-imposed.

The task that morning was merely to ask the judge to delay a trial. Our client, an agricultural conglomerate, had been sued for alleged unfair treatment of workers, and we needed more time for depositions. A senior partner of Paul and Thomson, one of Miami's top firms, was at my side. He was there to lend support, and, no doubt, to see for himself whether the new hotshot from Harvard Law School had something to offer besides a fancy degree.

I used skills I had first developed as a two-time state debate champion at Miami Beach High to argue the motion. But my heart wasn't in the effort. I daydreamed the whole time. As the judge offered commentary on the fine points of civil procedure, I thought instead about a speech I would soon give in Washington, D.C., on sports violence, a subject that had always interested me. I reviewed highlights from the first game of the Miami Dolphins new season (Bob Griese had just thrown the one hundredth touchdown pass of his career in a 20–17 win over the Atlanta Falcons). Mostly, I wondered whether I would fulfill a personal promise to lift my hometown of Miami from a one-sport wonder to major league status in all respects.

Despite all this distraction, my motion was granted. All was well in corporate America. The senior partner pumped my hand and said, "Good job, Rick."

And I thought, "I gotta get out of here."

So began a singular career navigation. I drew my own chart with a certain imprecision, as if on the back of a cocktail napkin. I had no idea of the realities. I told Parker Thomson, the co-founder of our law firm, that I didn't have a moment to waste, and that I had to leave the firm and find a way to help build new sports arenas, and then attract franchises to Miami. He must have summoned every ounce of willpower not to scoff at such impertinence and ingratitude in a new junior associate. In fact, Parker, a generous man as well as a first-rate lawyer, offered to abet my escape. Paul and Thomson had long represented Joe Robbie, owner of the Dolphins. If I could do what I hoped, everyone could benefit.

I set out to create a career as a "sports lawyer," which at the time was almost unheard of. Among the members of the bar who had no idea what the phrase meant was an old hero of mine. I called Nick Buoniconti, former stalwart middle linebacker of the Dolphins' "No Name Defense," at his law office in Miami, with the hopes that he would take me on.

"You don't know me," I said, "but I'd like to tell you what I've been up to." I had assumed—my first lesson in bad assumptions—that a veteran of Super Bowl championship teams would at least dabble in athletic issues. Nick, I learned, represented a player or two, but most of his work was drudgery: divorce and collection cases. I told him I wanted to practice sports law.

He asked, "What the hell is that?"

I explained that I intended to follow through on a plan I developed before I came back home to Miami, when I was a law clerk in Washington, to create a sports authority in South Florida.

He asked, "What the hell is that?"

I said, "Let me come by and drop off my credentials and we can talk."

Buoniconti and the Seven-Minute Rule

The next day I saw my old hero in the pin-striped uniform of a lawyer. But he was still in amazing shape—seemingly ready to pull jersey 85 over an imperceptible neck. Allowing only a few moments for pleasantries, I went right to business. Time is crucial for successful people. I usually ask for seven minutes, and then launch directly into the purpose for my visit—what I want, why I want it, why it's in the best interest of the other party that I get what I want, and why I'm best qualified to be involved. If I ask for seven minutes and haven't been persuasive in that time, well then, show me the door.

I told Nick about the origins of the dream: growing up in South Florida, sitting on the dock at 310 West DiLido Drive, on an island between Miami and Miami Beach, looking out over glistening Biscayne Bay at twilight, and examining the city's skyline. Then its most distinguishing features were the old pink Freedom Tower, downtown's last prominent vestige of the city's formative days, and the architecturally undistinguished Southeast Bank building, the only other skyscraper at the time. I imagined a city with an arena for basketball and hockey, and with a major league baseball stadium.

I reviewed, in abridged fashion, Miami's less than distinguished history in its efforts to lure professional sports. With the exception of the Dolphins case, one empty promise after another, one fiasco after another. The Buffalo franchise in the NBA was about to move to town—and then it wasn't. A developer announced he would build an arena on South Beach, but he never followed through. When the city flirted with the old World Hockey Association, an actual arena wall was built near the airport, but that's all that was ever erected—one wall. A Saudi Arabian sheik announced he would fund a baseball stadium in West Dade, but the promise was soon forgotten. In Miami, you didn't actually have to do anything. You just had to announce a plan, the newspaper would publish an instant profile, you'd be a big shot, and the town would be left where it was. As a result, a general presumption of failure took hold. In this way, it was like so much else in South Florida, which, for all of its natural wonders, always suffered from an overpopulation of big talkers, and worse.

I told Nick of the sports authorities organized by local governments in Pittsburgh and New Jersey to foster the development of teams and tax-supported arenas, and that I had written a 50-page "brief" about how to do it in Miami. I said that by using his firm and his sports reputation as a base, and adding to it my preparation and passion, we could pull this off. I argued that a sports authority would not only lead to new franchises for Miami but be valuable to Nick otherwise because it would open up business opportunities.

After staring at the ceiling, Nick said, "My partner and I can't possibly let you pursue your ideas totally on our nickel." I focused on the word "totally." Clearly he was interested. So I brought out my addendum to the seven-minute monologue: the offer to do anything to make it work. I told him that I would be glad (though I surely wouldn't be) to help him on some of his routine matters if I could spend most of my time laying the groundwork for the new authority. I told him also that I would try to pick up some hours from Joe Robbie, which would be helpful in two regards. Nick wouldn't have to pay me much, and the connection with Robbie would prove beneficial.

Nick said, "I'm not sure how you're going to pull this off. But if you can talk Joe into this, we'll do what we can."

The next day Parker Thomson agreed to give up some of Robbie's routine business so that I could have a base. He said he would recommend to Joe that he meet with me, "but I can't sell Joe Robbie on you. You'll have to sell yourself. Go meet the guy."

He warned, however, that Joe was "difficult" to deal with. He chose the word carefully. He could have used impossible. He could have used any number of terms. He could have said, "Rick, if you learn to deal with Joe Robbie, everything else will be a piece of cake." He could have described the role Joe Robbie played as kingpin, or, as described by the *Miami Herald*'s most influential sports columnist, as rattlesnake.

Looking back on that era and Robbie's influence, Edwin Pope, who in 45 years of writing columns for the *Herald* has always been direct, makes no apologies for the rattlesnake remark, or for the effect Robbie and the Dolphins had on all sports in South Florida.

"We first had University of Miami teams, then big time horse racing, a few golf tournaments—and that was about it. Not much in the way of major sports activity around here. All of a sudden (in the mid-'60s) the Dolphins came. They became The Blob. There was a sci-fi movie of that title about a piece of protoplasm that rolls into town and starts getting bigger—goes through grocery stores, picks up cars, houses, taking the whole town with it. That's what pro football became to Miami—a blob, rolling through South Florida eating everybody's lunch. Now, everyone else had a hard time selling out anything. The University of Miami basketball team folded, and the football team was in danger of cancellation. Pro football was king. And Joe Robbie, as owner of the Dolphins, was in an eternal war with the city—he was against everything the city wanted to do. He was the orneriest and most contentious brilliant man I ever knew. If you couple his personality with the stupidity and ineptitude and corruption of Miami politicians, you had one of the most unhandsome collaborations in the history of sports and communities."

Of course, back then I was plunging straight ahead into the rattlesnake pit. I said to Parker Thomson, "If we can get Joe to feel comfortable with me in this process, then we're on our way."

Parker said, "You mean you'll be on your way."

Meet Joe Robbie, If You Dare

Joe Robbie's office on Biscayne Boulevard was a shrine to the Dolphins. I ogled the Super Bowl trophies, photographs, and signed footballs. Robbie would be the key to everything. As owner of the only major sports franchise in the state, he had authority and influence. It was old news that Robbie had been contentious about the Orange Bowl; he was dissatisfied with it and desperately wanted a new stadium. But I assumed that the Dolphins owner would be sympathetic to the expansion of professional sports to basketball, baseball, and hockey even as we addressed the Orange Bowl problem. It was another bad assumption.

In his inner office, Joe shook my hand without enthusiasm and said, "I've heard about you." The tone was not cordial. It said, "So what is it that you want? Why are you wasting my time?" He gestured forcefully toward a soft couch, and he took the hard-back chair, seeming twice as tall as I was.

I decided to briefly ease into issues. I told him that my father and I bought season tickets from the beginning. He had no warm response to this, and I moved on. As I offered my pitch—similar to what I had told Nick about developing major sports aside from football for Miami—I understood this was a defining moment, and that if I could get through the next hour, the next 50 years would work out just fine.

I said, "I know all roads lead through you, and that I can't do any of this work without your help." He seemed to appreciate his ego being stroked. Yet he didn't let flattery deter him, particularly when I mentioned that I would be picking up support for sports expansion in the business and political communities.

He said, "I'm the only place you can go. And here, you're either a friend or an enemy. I can make you or break you. You can talk to anyone in town, but they will not make any sports decisions without receiving instructions from me first."

Obviously he was not interested in any major league team but the Dolphins, and had the opinion that other teams would simply take attention away from football, from his revenues, and from him. I argued that momentum for other pro sports would make a new stadium possible. The Rising Tide Lifts All Boats Theory—which he deftly sunk.

He said, "I guess you didn't hear me. You won't make decisions on how you are supposed to think without receiving instructions from me first."

If I had made a big display on behalf of principle, the meeting with Joe Robbie would have been over quickly. On the other hand, if I had caved in entirely, and went in lockstep with him, it would have affected my ability to get anything done. I knew I had to stick to the point, and to argue it persuasively.

I said, "I would like to try to make the case that you're going to be much better off if we bring these other sports, and we also focus on your situation at the same time. The community will be better off, too. And the result will be that you'll get your new stadium more quickly." I told him that if I worked for him, I could make all this happen, though I really had no idea how. Instinct is a teacher. And instinct teaches that you will find answers—what I call "the details"—later.

He asked, "What's it going to cost me?"

Aha, the money question! I knew I was in for trouble. Joe Robbie had a widespread reputation as a skinflint. He was often seen in the locker room counting the towels, and he insisted that every expenditure, no matter how modest, go through his office. Bud Adams, owner of the Houston Oilers, once commented that Robbie was "running a $2 million a year business like a fruit stand."

Knowing all this, I simply told him the facts. "I'm currently making $45,000 plus expenses."

Robbie said, "I'm happy for you. I'll pay you $9,000."

I said, "OK. This is a lifelong dream. Thank you for the meeting." I put out my hand, and he shook it.

Robbie assumed that I would be working for him full time for $9,000—that I would be just another person to bully financially. But I assumed no such thing. To me, this was a victory. It wasn't yet a victory, however, big enough to talk to my wife Terri about. I didn't relish the idea of coming home and saying, "Guess what dear. I just traded my $45,000 job in the employ of cordial and enlightened people for a madman's $9,000." Even so, I instinctively understood that a temporary sacrifice of income was the only way to get what I wanted in the long run, and that the risk was no real risk at all because I was committed to my ideas for Miami, and convinced that I could succeed.

I called Nick and sealed a $9,000 deal with him, and then persuaded Joe, who initially balked at the plan, to accept me as a part-time $9,000 employee when I pointed out that by using Nick's office I'd save him tons of money.

I went home and I told Terri, "You're married to a happier guy today than yesterday. The bad news is we've got a lot less money to spend." At the time, Terri, who had majored in anthropology at Northwestern, was the chief curator at the Fort Lauderdale Historical Society, and so we had a little security. She said, "I think we can make ends meet."

The next day Parker Thomson told me that his founding partner, Dan Paul, was indignant and wanted to be reimbursed for the expenses the firm had paid to move our household goods from Washington, D.C., to Miami. Parker said that after much persuasion Paul relented. But after 1980, Paul and Thomson instituted The Rick Horrow Rule, which specified that no moving expenses would be paid until the new employee had completed six months of service.

The Best (and Worst) Place to Deal

In his book *Miami: City of the Future*, T. D. Allman writes, "Practically everything people say about [Miami], both good and bad, is true."

To put it another way, if a young man were to choose a place to begin a career as a deal-maker, he couldn't choose a better and worse place to do it than Miami.

In Miami, nothing is nailed down. In Miami, roots run three inches deep. In Miami, routine (though it occurs) is never newsworthy. It was at first a haven for adventure and fortune seekers from the north, then a retirement destination for the elderly, and then an escape for everyone who had seen enough of Fidel and had the means to get out of Cuba. It has always been a winter escape for Mafia figures (Al Capone, Lucky Luciano, and Meyer Lansky among them.) It became, too, the destination for Castro's criminal class in the Mariel Boat Lift. Miami, in the early 1980s, was attractive to Latin Americans, and to Europeans. Soon it would become a haven for beautiful young women hoping for modeling careers. Everyone comes in search of something.

As the mayor of the time, Maurice Ferre, himself a native of Ponce, Puerto Rico, explains it, "Miami is the end of the line. People here don't have a vested interest. They are not stakeholders, and don't feel a deep-rooted obligation to the city."

Deal-making in the public sector, then, particularly for a young man who had many naïve notions, could be daunting, and there was every chance I could lose my shirt and my house in the process. On the other hand, I was blessed. Miami was the perfect place to begin because as a center of politics and power it has always been a snake pit. If I could learn to prevail in this atmosphere, I could prevail anywhere.

In short order, I would help set a world record for the number of sports authorities established and then disbanded. I would lose and re-gain my job four times. I would face an array of obstacles. Most of these obstacles would be in human form—a backstabbing team owner, a mysterious fat man, an undermining undertaker. I would learn to make use of diverse allies, including a Bay of Pigs survivor, two natives of Tel Aviv, Japanese bankers, and a Puerto Rican–born Miami mayor. Nevertheless, I would be left on many occasions without, it seemed, a chance in hell, and with every reason to quit. Except for one thing. I was determined to succeed.

There's Always a Mysterious Fat Man

I was out of town on the day of my first Miami triumph. I had to re-trieve the good news from an answering machine after delivering a speech at Washington State University on sports violence. I had cam-paigned back at Harvard to digress from the usual curriculum. I made a bet with my criminal law professor, Jim Vorenberg, that if I beat him at squash he would allow me to put aside traditional studies and con-centrate on unprecedented material: the matter of athletes bashing ath-letes and getting away with it. I won the game, became the first-ever sports law student at Harvard, wrote a book on the subject, and found myself traveling all around the country to talk about it.

While I was gone, people in high Florida places decided that my "brief" on establishing a sports authority made persuasive arguments. Legislation was passed that created the Dade County Sports Authority.

Steve Muss, a developer who had renovated the Fontainebleau Hotel, was named chairman. A promising start, I thought. But I still wondered what my part in this, if any, would be.

Then I had a call from a man I'd never heard of who summoned me without explanation to Star Island, a tiny and isolated community of luxury homes between Miami and Miami Beach. I told the guard at the gate that I was visiting an island resident named Stephen Paul Ross. I drove around the circle, beneath the rows of stately royal palms, to an impressive white Spanish-style house. When a man answered the door, I was astonished by what I saw. He was enormous—from side to side. He wore a white shirt that was not tucked in, and it hung over his belly. His trousers were several sizes too small. I thought, gee, this is not the way help should dress. But it wasn't the help. It was Stephen Paul Ross. He invited me in without taxing any instincts for cordiality.

The place was expansive, about 10,000 square feet, with marble floors. But the house hardly had the feel of home. There was barely a stick of furniture in it, and it seemed in desperate need of repair. We sat down near large windows that offered a marvelous view of Biscayne Bay and the Miami skyline, much the same view that I saw as a child from my parents' dock.

Ross said in an authoritative tone, "I represent a group of powerful Miamians who have been watching you for some time. You could go a long way in this town. The group wants you to run the new sports authority, first as acting executive director, and, if you follow the script, executive director." I acknowledged the compliment and opportunity, but it was clear there was more stick to go along with carrot.

He went on, "I'm going to have your home phone number, but you're not going to have mine. I'm going to call you all hours of the day or night and tell you what to do." By this time, I later learned, he did most of his business from his living room (he always boasted, "I give good phone"). Ross said, "You realize this is a once in a lifetime opportunity. If the chairman, Steve Muss, wants to see you about it, he'll call in the next few days. We expect that you'll follow instructions—you might call it blind loyalty."

It's important at such a juncture to indicate in one breath that you're both a team player and an independent thinker—no easy task. To Ross, I wanted to establish my intelligence, not blind loyalty. I said, "I lived my life to this point wanting to bring more sports to South Florida, and anything I can do there is important to me."

When I left, I was pleased and bewildered. I was happy to be considered for the sports authority job but had no idea why I was being tested in this way. Stephen Paul Ross was obviously a secretive guy and, until much later when the *Miami Herald* began to write investigative pieces about him, was strictly behind the scenes. I learned that he was a partner in a political consulting business, and was something of a kingmaker.

He had been a University of Miami student until he was tossed out for some unsavory bit of political activism. With lots of chutzpah, he started his own public relations firm. Instead of calling it, in the fashion of the times, Stephen Paul Ross and Associates, he decided on the more impressive National Projects, though he was involved in no national projects. His business card, in the years when he distributed cards (later he had no need for them—people always knew where to reach Ross), listed him as vice president. He was at first the only officer, and the only employee. But in sticky situations when he didn't know what to say or do, this allowed him to respond, "I'll talk to the boss." Also on the National Projects business card, in the lower left-hand corner, were the words "Southern Division," giving the impression that he was part of an enormous operation. And yet Ross, a man with a strong personality and morbid obesity, needed none of that pretense. He had run the campaigns at one time or another of many politicians of consequence in South Florida. And he eventually became the target of press investigations because of the impression that he arranged unsavory deals for government contracts. None of this was proven, but his reputation had him at the heart of all important matters. Ross met regularly with key government leaders and developers at a greasy spoon restaurant in a Miami Holiday Inn, known to insiders as the Conspiracy Inn.

Two days passed before I got a call from Steve Muss's secretary. She asked me if I could meet the chair of the new authority for breakfast at his Seacoast Towers penthouse on Collins Avenue. That Sunday morning, Muss, an imposing man with a head of graying curly hair, showed me his impressive collection of African art, and all the trinkets he had acquired from worldwide travel. He said, "Before we start, tell me what you think of Stephen Paul Ross." Muss was testing me. He wanted to see if the level of ego I carried around with me would prove an obstacle to his work.

I replied, "He is one of the most eclectic messengers I've ever met. If I'm to go to Star Island to pick up messages, it will be interesting, but something I could handle." Bantering with Muss was not a problem. I could let him believe I respected his ego and development history, yet I wouldn't be a sycophant. I was always close to the edge. I never let any of the egomaniacs think they could control me. I let them believe I could be an extension of their personality or ego drive, and I could be an eloquent spokesman for their cause. But I always leave wiggle room.

Muss's idea, clearly, was to fight Joe Robbie at every turn. Robbie had just announced his intention to build a new football stadium in the northern part of the county. Muss, on the other hand, was determined to build a domed facility for football, baseball, basketball, and hockey at "Buena Vista," property just across the causeway from his Fontainebleau. I had a sense now of what I was facing—two powerful figures, in Muss and Robbie, who clearly despised each other.

Muss asked me what I thought about the Buena Vista site. I said I hadn't had time to study it, but, "If it helps us bring all sports to South Florida, I'm for it."

He studied me, and I knew what he was thinking. "If I appoint this guy as director of the sports authority, I'll have a bridge to Robbie. I'll use this guy." I was thinking about how to sell Robbie on Buena Vista— by convincing him that he was the preferred tenant, and the situation would be much more advantageous, and more profitable, than north Dade County.

Muss said, "You sound like my kind of guy. I'll get back to you soon."

A few days later, I was in the audience at the first Dade County Sports Authority meeting. Muss had told me to come to the old Dupont Plaza Hotel, and not prepare any kind of a talk. "Just be available if someone asks you a question. But you don't have to know anything."

There had been more than a hundred applicants to serve on the Sports Authority board—it was the hottest advisory board going. The afternoon before the Dade County commissioners voted on potential board members, *Miami Herald* reporter Eston Melton called Dick Knight, who had become Stephen Paul Ross's partner in National Projects. Knight predicted the names of the nine who would be chosen out of the more than a hundred, Muss among them. That night by secret ballot, the Dade County Commission selected those nine almost unanimously. Melton, convinced that some deal had been arranged, called Knight back and asked if the outcome had been engineered by him and Ross. Knight admitted that it had. In the years following, when Melton quit the newspaper business and went to work for Ross, he learned how all this worked. Ross and Knight had cozy relationships with the members of the Dade County Commission, having several as clients and, in one case, having their pension money in the bank that was run by one of them. Ross and Knight also had favorites in the business community—people they knew they could work with, such as Muss, whom they could help appoint through their connections to prestigious civic positions. These people would become very useful to them because, when it came time for bidding on the large projects that had to be built, Ross and Knight would represent the architects, engineers, and contractors that offered their services. It was all one golden circle, drawn by the political consultants.

Clearly, I was dealing with an entrenched and powerful process that was well beyond my experience, so, during the first meeting of the authority, I did what Muss suggested and just listened. Muss mentioned my credentials, and told his colleagues that, "Rick Horrow could bring South Florida sports to the next level." That day, I was appointed the full-time acting director, with a salary of $34,000—to be raised to $48,000 when the "acting" was removed from the title.

A week before I was to begin, I gave a speech to the Miami Jaycees. The mayor of Dade County (both the city and the county had mayors) introduced me, calling me "the next pioneer of South Florida sports." It was all heady stuff for me, and I thought I was in. I told the group we'd bring in not only a new stadium for the Dolphins but also attract new or existing franchises for the National Basketball Association, the National Hockey League, and Major League Baseball.

That night, I went to see Joe Robbie at his club, the Palm Bay. By then, I knew something of his reputation for imbibing but hadn't seen the voluminous evidence others had. For example, Edwin Pope told author Dave Hyde (*Still Perfect*) of Robbie's ability, if that is the word, to nearly pass out in midsentence and, upon awakening, pick up precisely where he left off. Robbie's wife, Elizabeth, once told a reporter that a limousine driver delivered them home one night and asked her, "Mrs. Robbie, what should I do when I get where we're going—dump him on the sidewalk?"

On this night at the Palm Bay, Robbie was already completely drunk, but still pounding down one Scotch after another. Sometimes, according to legend, Robbie would recite poetry in such a state, including favorite lines from Matthew Arnold. But there wouldn't be any of that here. He and I stood at the corner of the bar. I said, "Joe, I just gave a speech at the Jaycees about the sports future of Miami and they loved it."

Robbie said, "I don't care about that other stuff. If you don't do a stadium for me, you're going to regret it. If you don't corral that motherfucker Muss, your head's gonna roll."

If It's Tuesday, This Must Be Philadelphia

August 2, 1981, was the beginning of my $681 nationwide tour, to investigate how other cities created facilities for Major League Baseball, and, frankly, to get out of town and focus on something positive.

I planned the cheapest trip possible, wary of creating a potential public relations problem; the *Herald* might have a field day reporting on a baseball junket at taxpayer expense. The *Herald* in those days was more than just a large and profitable newspaper: It was by far the single most dominating social force in the community. The editor regularly sent an emissary to the mayor's office to deliver instructions on public policy. If Maurice Ferre was unwilling to take the *Herald*'s "advice," he would pay the price on the editorial pages. It was important to play the paper properly. As the new director of the new authority, I needed to forge a positive, and frugal, public image.

It would have seemed unlikely, even impossible, to visit 12 cities for so little money. I convinced executives at Eastern Airlines, which was headquartered in Miami, of the enormous potential for local business, especially tourism, if I was successful in luring a major league franchise. Eastern gave me cut-rate airfares.

Of all the major league cities I visited, New Orleans was the most illuminating. The draw wasn't Bourbon Street, with all of its funky style, fabulous music, and hedonistic attitude. Or even the beignets at Café Du Monde. What struck me most was an enormous venue in another part of town—the Louisiana Superdome.

I had always thought of it as merely a field for the games of the New Orleans Saints. But I was surprised when I visited the site, and talked to officials there, by the diversity of events within the place. They showed me photographs of a myriad of events. Sports, of course. But many activities that occur there have nothing at all to do with traditional games. Trade shows, flower shows, rodeo, auto shows, concerts, and many more. In fact, the Superdome was home to 290 separate events, an average of almost one per day, and served as something of a community town green, if in concrete and steel. Up to that point, I had been thinking of sports venues as distinct and limited. Now I saw that I could argue much more persuasively back home in Miami if I articulated the vision of an arena that could host a wide array of events. The supporters of sports teams wouldn't object—they'd still get their place to play. And those who had no interest in sports would find an enlightened self-interest in joining the effort. I was so excited by the prospect, I dreamed of picking up the Superdome and carrying it 900 miles to the southeast.

Yet I was reminded of the mountain of work that lay in front of me when I walked through Texas Stadium in Irving. My tour guide (the stadium manager) asked me, "How old are you, kid?" I told him I was 26. He said, "I'm 66. And you've accomplished more on this stadium stuff than I did in 40 years. I thought I'd get a stadium done here in six years, and then move on. I didn't realize it would take a lot longer." The conversation worried me. I was happy for the compliment, but I would have to remind myself many times that patience is a virtue—if not my favorite virtue—and that obstacles are everywhere. If Texas, where there is a long history of the love of sports, is tough, what about Miami?

The Middle Ground Is Never Safe

The New Orleans revelation came into play in short order. Because very soon thereafter we had a Miami Dome. Or at least we had a drawing of one by the architectural firm that had designed stadiums in New Orleans, Vancouver, and Seattle. Also, the Dade County Sports Authority produced a feasibility study, looking at a number of sites and concepts. Muss's Buena Vista, of course, was one. But so was Lake Lucerne, in north Dade—a place Joe Robbie had his eye on.

I had already seemed to make an enemy of Robbie because of his perception of Muss's influence on me, but I still needed his support. It would be in everyone's interest if he were a team player. But the odds seemed long. *Herald* columnist Edwin Pope, in recalling the Dolphins owner's obstinate nature, said, "Joe Robbie made Steve Muss seem like St. Francis of Assisi." In late 1981, however, I found it hard for a time to distinguish between the two.

In November, I met with the *Herald* editorial board. It had seemed to me that the board was predisposed toward the Muss plan. Wanting to keep the process open, as well as the remote possibility of Robbie's support, I argued that we should do what's best for South Florida, not just Miami.

But if I thought I was playing the game deftly, I soon found I had a lot to learn about real-world connections. Don't ever tell the press—

even at supposedly confidential meetings of editorial boards—things you prefer your boss would never hear. Just three hours after my "private" meeting, I got a call from Muss. He said in a stern tone, "Do you think you're representing Dade County or Miami?" He obviously had a mole on the board, and he clearly thought I was undermining him. I was shocked that Muss had a board connection. But I shouldn't have been. People like him don't get into those powerful positions without making acquaintances in high places. Still, I responded forcefully. "This is the Dade County Sports Authority." I also said, to deaf ears, that we had to stay flexible in order to get buy-ins from as many people as possible. At the same time, his henchman Ross started referring to me as the "Easter Bunny," because I was hopping around the county promising candy for everyone.

A few days later, an editorial (in favor of Muss's Buena Vista) ran and the other shoe dropped. Robbie thought I had orchestrated the piece. He said, "Now you're writing articles in the goddamned *Herald*. What are you going to do next—buy the goddamned newspaper?"

I was still thinking, though, that if I could just get Robbie and Muss in the same room, we'd at least come up with the prospect of civility and negotiation. And I needed to do it fast. The Sports Authority was going to make decisions soon about the site for an all-purpose facility. One of the purposes would be baseball, and the Major League Baseball owners would hold their annual meeting in the area on December 8. It was my intention to sell South Florida as an ideal location for an expansion franchise. This would also be a chance to demonstrate our commitment to teamwork, though we didn't really have such a commitment. In fact Robbie and Muss would not meet, and would not agree to present a unified front. Still, if I could get a high sign from Major League Baseball, it would be just the impetus we needed to get the community to believe in our stadium cause.

Timing is crucial. And my timing was bad. On the very morning the baseball meeting began, the *Herald* ran a piece in which Robbie blasted me as "a puppet of Steve Muss," and said his Dolphins would "never play in the rat-infested" plot of land that Muss favored.

Nevertheless, I arrived at the Diplomat Hotel with reason to be confident. I had a new title. "Acting" had been removed from it, and I'd gotten a handsome raise. I was aware, of course, that every Major League owner had read the morning paper, and that there would be a moment when I'd have to address the controversy. I began with something impressive that they could look at—a model of the domed stadium. I focused on matters that I calculated would intrigue them. Namely, how to make money. "Cubans love baseball," I exclaimed, and the rights for Latin American and Cuban TV would make Major League Baseball a fortune. I anticipated concerns about the subtropical weather, and the threat of rainouts. I presented studies that showed that over many seasons there were fewer rainouts for our longtime minor league team, the Miami Marlins, than there had been in Atlanta, Pittsburgh, Texas, and many Major League franchise locations. At this point, I had to figure a way to diffuse the Robbie controversy. I looked around the room at cordial but skeptical faces. These men were, for the most part, strictly business—men who bought teams and would sell them for a higher price later. Passion for the game did not seem to have a place on the agenda except in one case—that of a former car dealer from Milwaukee. I could see in Bud Selig's comments and attitude an openness and understanding of what I was doing. And so I looked at Selig, smiled and said, "You may have read about this in the *Herald*," referring to the Robbie quote. "He is just naturally concerned because the sports authority had a mandate to bring in other sports, and wasn't just looking out for football. Eventually, he'll be fine with all this."

Selig, owner of the Milwaukee Brewers (and later MLB commissioner), made it a point to acknowledge my presentation, offering congratulations for "thinking on your feet," and said the presentation was skillful and clever, under the circumstances. He said, "Keep up the good work." Selig, as I learned, displayed an enormous capacity for detail. Fifteen years later, when we were on the same panel at a sports law conference, he recalled particulars of my Diplomat presentation as if it had happened the day before. It wasn't hard for me to understand why he had risen from the ranks to become the most powerful figure in the game. He remembers names, and what people do. Key advantages in forging consensus.

At the Diplomat meeting, Selig and the other owners probably didn't give Miami significant consideration, particularly when the city's most powerful sports figure campaigned against it so publicly. I could take solace, however, in the fact that at least we had our process under way. We had the prospect of a new facility and a chosen site that we could present to the voters. If I was going to fight from a foxhole, at least I had Steve Muss in the foxhole with me. I had a speech rehearsed for Muss—a motivational message about how bright the future seemed.

However, Muss had his own message on my answering machine: "This is more than I can handle. I wanted you to know first. I'm resigning from the sports authority." Muss had taken a pounding from the *Miami Herald*. Stories and editorials were ripping him for an apparent conflict of interest because of property he owned near Buena Vista. In the wake of Muss's resignation, the reporters called me, and asked what's next. I said we have to move forward. Though I had no idea how.

The next day the Dade County commissioners met. One of the agenda items was the approval of the 1982 budget for the Sports Authority. It was a perfunctory matter. Or so I thought. The proposed budget was rejected by unanimous vote. In effect, the authority was gone and with it, obviously, my job. Dismissal #1.

One of the commissioners was Clara Oesterle. She came up to me after the meeting and said, "It's nothing personal. But you just don't mess with Joe Robbie."

The Necessary Amigo

I spent the bleak Christmas holiday asking myself new questions. One of them was, should I find a more sensible way to make a living? And I almost did. Steve Muss reappeared long enough to tell me about his plans to get into the casino business, and offered a place for me. Muss, Ross, and Dick Knight hinted, too, that eventually—if I adhered to the prescribed fashion—I might find a prominent life in public service. Maybe even embark on the road to the governor's residence in Tallahassee. This was how a career in public life was often forged—a politician-in-the-making attaching himself to powerful business interests. It was heady stuff, an invitation to be part of a certain in-crowd. And it was out of the question. I could surely do the job—use my rhetorical skills to help Muss in his ambitious venture. But to do it I'd have to give up my dream. I told Steve Ross, "No thanks—my loyalty isn't to Steve Muss or to anyone else. It's to get teams and stadiums for my hometown."

Ross replied, "Then you're on your own."

There was another question I considered during that holiday season: What would happen if, in the effort to restore a sports authority, I used the assets and aspirations of my enemy, Joe Robbie, to my advantage? There is a flip side to everything, even the appearance of utter defeat. I needed to explain the idea to a receptive ear. Raul Masvidal was the most politically connected, resourceful, and encouraging member of the newly defunct Dade County Sports Authority. Just the guy to call.

Masvidal describes himself now as "a classic Cuban refugee." But a classic Cuban refugee, if there is such a thing, wouldn't find himself as a 17-year-old student banished from home and parents. This was Masvidal's fate as a young man when, in 1960, less than two years after Castro seized power, he raised an American flag to protest the visit to Cuba by Anastas I. Mikoyan, the Soviet Union's first deputy minister. It didn't help that his father, though one of the few voices of the people in the Batista regime, was considered an enemy of the revolution. The young man was put on a plane bound for Miami, to make connections that, according to the plan, would ultimately bring him to relatives in Chile.

During the long layover, he called the Miamian who owned the private school he had attended in Cuba. Young Raul was encouraged to stay, to live in the owner's house, and to attend school locally. The owner even paid for the first semester at the University of Miami, and, in the years that followed, Raul finished at the university studying economics while working as a hotel doorman—and for the Central Intelligence Agency. The CIA actively recruited Cuban exiles for an invasion force.

Brigade 2506 trained in the hills of Guatemala. Masvidal was in the intelligence unit. The invasion of Cuba, called Operation Zapata for the peninsula it targeted, became forever known instead by the surrounding body of water, the Bay of Pigs. In the force of 1,500 that landed, more than one hundred were killed, and almost all of the rest captured. Masvidal was one of the handful who came away unscathed. He had been assigned to bring in the communications equipment. But when he saw things were not going well, he escaped on a U.S. Navy vessel.

It wasn't the last time, however, that the CIA came calling. Twice more Masvidal was on their payroll. During the Cuban Missile Crisis, he and others were flown to Guatemala to be trained as paratroopers. He came back to be a full-time student and part-time counterrevolutionary. The CIA connections led him to an operative, a professor at the University of Miami, who recommended him for the International Management program at the American Graduate School of International Management, in Phoenix. Eventually, Masvidal became a "classic Cuban refugee" in the sense that he became successful. He was an executive with a Canadian bank and eventually owned his own bank. In those capacities he became involved in community affairs. Masvidal, obviously, had many connections, and, as I learned, he possessed certain skills useful for invading new territory against considerable odds.

The "Wow" Factor, or When You're in Trouble, Double

Over lunch, I told Masvidal the essence of my plan. We had worked for an all-purpose sports facility in Miami. Political realities prevented this. But we weren't thinking big enough. The "Wow" factor was still missing; that is, the idea that would make people pay attention, even if they wonder aloud, "Is he nuts?"

I argued that we should double the effort instead of let it wither away. Masvidal was amused. "How? There isn't the money or the support."

I explained that we could apply leverage, even though it appeared there was none. Joe Robbie needed help. The Orange Bowl, built in 1932, was falling apart, and as a result he felt financially vulnerable.

Even if the Bowl was refurbished, it would never have adequate parking; fans were obliged to pay opportunistic homeowners in the neighborhood for the privilege of renting their front lawns for three hours. Robbie craved a modern facility with acres of parking, but he still needed public support for all of the permits, the access, and most likely the funding to build.

I told Masvidal that Robbie's trek north could be to our advantage, and at the same time would get us a new arena in downtown Miami. I argued that instead of a sports authority limited to one county we should embrace two. As Robbie's chosen site bordered Broward County, we should invite Broward into our planning, replacing the failed Dade authority with a regional body—thus providing more resources. Broward would support an arena for Miami because it would get a football stadium that could possibly be used for baseball, too, convenient to all of its residents. Dade would support the idea because it would still physically be home to the stadium and allow the prospect for new winter sports franchises, and Broward residents would be contributing funds to the effort. Robbie would go along with all of this because it was in his interest, and his interest was all he cared about.

Masvidal was impressed, but said, "You can't be involved." Joe might even bite off his own nose if he heard the name Rick Horrow. I suggested that Masvidal employ his skills as a diplomat to work behind the scenes on behalf of the idea, and do it without ever mentioning me until the appropriate time when enough momentum has built and Robbie had no choice but to go along with it. Masvidal agreed.

Masvidal, it turned out, had every tool as a negotiator. In the style of the best Latin power brokers, he was a street fighter who nevertheless could disarm with his considerable charm. Though he could speak the language of his adopted country perfectly, he would on occasion employ his "infirm" English to seem humble. But in almost all cases he seemed to know how to get what he wanted.

In the days of our early collaboration, he provided all the support I needed, even when I seemed to go beyond the bounds of propriety. Hoping to gather support for our ideas, I gave a speech at Tiger Bay, a political gossip club, founded by fat Steve Ross. There, staring straight at Ross, I told the group that the failure of the authority rested at the feet of "gutless politicians who lack vision and who crawl in a hole, and then show up at the ribbon cutting." In the days that followed I carried my fight to local television, and there was quite a furor. I was on the hot seat.

Masvidal called and said, "I have been talking to people in Miami and in Broward County who saw you going nuts on TV. I thought we were going to keep this quiet." When I admitted to making a mistake, he disagreed. "No you didn't. That was the most passionate statement about South Florida that I've heard in 20 years." He went on to say that we should convene the new, broader sports authority quicker than we had imagined. "And we'll appoint you as director." He would arrange it.

I asked, "How will you deal with the Robbie problem?" He said he wouldn't bother asking Joe Robbie. And that after my statements of the last few days, I would be seen as a defender of other sports, not as someone who merely served as Joe Robbie's bucket carrier. "The whole process," he predicted, "will be moved up a notch."

In mid-February, the Dade County commissioners approved a new ordinance, with only one dissenting vote (by Robbie's puppet, Clara Oesterle). Dade would extend an invitation to Broward County to join in the efforts to build a stadium for football and an arena for basketball and hockey.

The Idiot's Guide to Football Field Design

Never underestimate the capacity of public servants to make fools of themselves, and, in the process, try to make a jackass of anyone who promotes a vision. Broward's focus was on Robbie's proposed football field, which straddled the two counties in a spot called Lake Lucerne. In a spectacular demonstration of political buffoonery, Broward officials insisted that the new facility be built in such a way that half of it would be physically in their county. That is, 50 yards of the football field would actually have to be located in Broward. It was a loony idea, of course, and made loonier by the fact that the Dade–Broward line runs east and west, which meant the field would have to be built north–south. In football season, the receding sun would be at an angle that would blind receivers, and the passing game would be compromised. And how about the running game? Perhaps a sign could be posted at a critical yard marker, urging the ball carriers to pick up their pace, so that all those Broward retirees, eager to get to dinner, wouldn't miss the early bird specials.

The stadium architects made five or six attempts to arrange a plan that would suit Broward County and the NFL, which had its own guidelines about how to position fields. In the end, the architects were able to shift the field slightly in the design, and everyone agreed to the alterations. Even Joe Robbie was moderately cooperative during the process. Raul Masvidal must have told him, "I don't like Rick, either. But we need him."

The first regional infrastructure sports authority in Florida history was formed—the South Florida Sports Authority. For me and for our movement this was an exciting opportunity: It gave us the best shot for a voter referendum. And so we planned a "Pennies for Progress" sales tax. If Dade and Broward voters approved, there would be a temporary increase in the sales tax (one cent) in both counties to pay for an array of new projects for performing arts, conventions, and spring training facilities—and, of course, for the money to pay for a new sports arena as well as a stadium for Joe Robbie.

But, as always, there is a fly in the ointment. And sometimes a snake. In the middle of September, a Miami city commissioner named J. L. Plummer Jr. called me with the first of many frustrating (and worse) conversations. Plummer, who was also a funeral home director, was not at all enthusiastic about the regional authority. He told me that if the referendum, set for November 2, was successful, Miami would get its arena, but he would see to it that the money allocated for Robbie's Lake Lucerne project would go to Orange Bowl renovations. Plummer was only one member of a five-member City Commission, and had no position with the county, but as I learned in the next few months and years, he was much more than that. Now it seemed that the Dade/Broward collaboration, something that I conceived, was something of a ruse, a well-orchestrated plot by someone else and I was at the back end of it.

In September, the combined County Commission met, and the results were disastrous. Broward put forth its ideas—half of the projected $280 million in revenue raised by the sales tax would go to facilities there. A fair plan. But the commissioners from Dade trumped it. They talked of a new arena, expanding the Miami Beach convention center, a new tennis center—and taking the football money to renovate the Orange Bowl. Typical Miami politics.

The Broward County people stormed out, and the next day they yanked their money away from the commission. The budget that was in place was voided. Broward's participation in the referendum ended. The authority staff—including my position—was no longer authorized. Dismissal #2. But I still had something of an opportunity.

Dade County asked me to spend 30 days, with pay, to study the possible local projects—as the referendum in that county was still in place. So I could count on another month of income. Not a small thing in my circumstance.

Soon, the Dade County Commission would meet, and I had an idea that might grant me, at long last, some job security. Things were happening fast around me. Joe Robbie, through an intermediary, purchased land at Lake Lucerne. And the arena effort in Miami was in clear jeopardy. How could we save it? Who could help? And how, not incidentally, could I gain a better prospect of feeding my family? I had no choice but to go straight to the most influential public official in town.

To Knock on Power's Door

As a public official, Mayor Maurice Ferre was elegant, erudite, and worldly. When the king and queen of Bulgaria, in exile at the time, came to a party at a local developer's house (Miami is that kind of a place), the mayor made fast friends. He developed excellent relationships with politicians and business leaders in many Latin American and European countries. Even now, when asked to review his accomplishments at City Hall over a 12-year period in the '70s and '80s, he ranks the establishment of Miami as an international business city at the top. His curriculum vitae reveals ample evidence of his diverse connections. A partial inventory of his wall of honor: Order of "Isabel La Catolica" (Spain), Order of "El Libertador" (Venezuela), "Honor al Merito de la Republica" (Colombia), Order of "Honor y Merito de Duarte, Sanchez y Mella" (Dominican Republic), Order of "Merito de Lima" (Peru), and "Official Order de Coteaux de Champagne, Medallion" (France). In the early 1980s, he also held the keys to a Miami arena and to a modernized Orange Bowl (never mind Joe Robbie's grand plans).

When I visited him at his home in Coconut Grove, I was something of a stranger. I had met him only once. I was a kid with some big ideas. Now, these ideas held great promise—a real possibility of an arena, and of drawing franchises, if only we could pass the referendum. I needed Ferre's political capital.

His house was splendid and spotless—silk covers on the couches, servants carrying fine china. Coming directly from a racquetball game, I was wearing shorts, a sweat-soaked shirt, and sneakers (wrong!). He was cordial, but he must have thought I was there to take out the trash.

I hoped to press a plan for the Dade County Commission that could bring major sports to the community. Also, I had been measuring my security in weeks, or in days. This plan could change that. I told the mayor that I was confident that the arena process would eventually make Miami a pro sports city. It wouldn't stop at basketball and hockey. Tennis would be included, and maybe even the Olympics. I hoped Ferre would go before the County Commission and help arrange all of this.

He said, "Don't worry about a thing. I'll make one phone call." I knew instantly who would be at the other end of the line—fat Steve Ross on Star Island. I had just called Ross a gutless politician at Tiger Bay. But I had nothing to fear. The way it works is you call the guy who can do it. Ross was doing a professional job for Ferre, and he would do what he was told.

So, the briefest sports authority in the history of the United States was created—and our third one. A budget was approved, with me as director, but by law it would terminate on November 3 (less than a month later) if the vote didn't come out favorably, which it didn't. The referendum was dead on arrival—defeated 64 percent to 36 percent. I had been more than a bit naïve. I thought the pundits who predicted failure hadn't taken the pulse of the community. The community would certainly share my vision. Now, I was crushed. And so was my third sports authority directorship. Dismissal #3.

Quit now? Of course not. Maurice Ferre and I worked out another plan. According to local law, if we acted within four days of the election we could get an ordinance passed by city council for a special election, in this case to apply a sales tax vote just in the city limits.

Ferre worked his magic. He always said, "To succeed in Miami politics, all you need to do is count to three." This was a reference to the five-person City Commission. He had one vote, and he sought two others for majority. In the early part of his tenure as mayor, this was no problem. So on November 10, 1982, the city created yet another sports authority—this one called The Miami Sports Authority—authorized a sales tax vote on December 14, and gave me another month of job security as director. Not precisely what I had in mind.

At home, Terri asked, "When is this all over?"

I replied, "When we get this deal done."

On December 7, 1982, I was speaking at Eastern Montana University. Another Pearl Harbor Day with bad news. I got word that back home Robbie was campaigning strenuously against the new tax proposal, saying it was "stupid." He said he would build his stadium anyway, and that he didn't require anyone's help. Never mind that our various authorities had already given him plenty by helping to create the site and arranging for interest-free public bonds to finance the project.

But on December 14, Robbie won again. The referendum went down 81 percent to 19 percent—four out of five voters against us! Dismissal #4.

If Terri had asked me then how I felt, I would have had to tell her something neither of us wanted to hear. I was angry and frustrated. I was clearly being whipped, and couldn't understand why nobody, other than Ferre, was coming to my rescue. Miami was run by a bunch of sissies, to use a respectable word. And at the time I had nagging doubts that anything positive could happen. Until once again I called on Maurice Ferre.

What would he say if I were to ask him for a staff position for a year's time to work specifically on bringing pro sports to Miami? Would he risk his own political capital to invest further in what seemed to many like a lost cause? I pleaded, "Find a way to pay me to work with you and to pick up the pieces. I'm in too deep now. I believe in this vision."

I pointed out an emerging sports phenomenon. Expansion was now permanently on league agendas. Of course, there were dreamers and schemers in other cities. We'd be up against them, certainly, and we'd be doing it from the "fraud capital" of America. But I was confident, and knew that above all else I had to demonstrate that confidence.

I told the mayor, "Miami will get a basketball franchise. If Milwaukee—Milwaukee!—can get one, we can, too. I promise you we'll do those things and make this happen. Just a year. That's all I need. I'll be absolutely loyal to you."

He asked, "Are you sure we can get the NBA?"

I replied, "Of course we'll get a team. I'm certain of it."

Ferre said, "OK. I'll do it." He was willing to deal with what would certainly be political fallout, and I'd have a paycheck once again. More than that, I'd devise a plan that would, at last, succeed.

Strange Bedfellows Celebrate

Within a few months, we had the money, $40 million, to build a Miami arena. I got it because I was able to push two new ideas. First, I understood that no matter how much I believed in sports and in sports facilities as valuable assets for the community, the reality was that we couldn't build them until I expanded my vision, and I invited parties who had no interest in sports to the table. I had to build a coalition of people who had a lot at stake in the community—the Chamber of Commerce, tourism officials, developers, arts leaders. Individually, we were powerless to get what we wanted, but together we could sell a package of civic improvements that was irresistible. My second idea: We could sell it not to the skeptical voters but to the state legislature, which was always looking for ways to raise revenues without burdening taxpayers.

I told Ferre, "Let's let the tourists pay for this. They don't vote." We'd just get the legislature to extend the existing hotel tax by three cents. Then we'd divide the proceeds between sports, cultural, and tourism initiatives. I lobbied hard in Tallahassee, and, with the support of such a variety of constituencies, it wasn't hard to get political backing. In fact, the legislature passed the measure, the "Convention Development Tax," easily. And we were home free. So it seemed.

I was now a full-time employee of the city, director of the new Miami Sports and Exhibition Authority—note the addition, for the sake of diversity—and approved by the City Commission by 4 to 1. The lone dissenter was J. L. Plummer Jr., who looked directly at me when his turn to vote came. He smiled and said, "No." It was a cold-blooded smile, as if he were playing a game. I knew I hadn't seen the last of the undertaker.

CHAPTER 3

The Heat Is On

*There is no such thing as a soft sell or a hard
sell. There is only a smart sell and a stupid sell.*

CHARLES BROWER,
advertising executive

The Miami years and the struggle to lay the groundwork for major
league sports yield one persistent image: the steps of City Hall. The
building itself is not at all imposing. It is of art deco design and of
modest proportions. But it was the place where every key question was
debated and decided, and it is where the roots of the Miami Heat, the
Florida Marlins, and the Florida Panthers can be traced. You can find
their beginnings under the debris of political warfare.

Miami City Hall was where, in desperation, I camped out for three
days and nights in the effort to convince an unsympathetic new mayor
that he held the future of Miami in his hands, and where I had to rely
on every ounce of energy, intuition, leverage, political savvy, and passion I could summon, or once again Miami as a sports landscape
would become parched earth for another decade. But I am ahead of
myself.

December 7, 1983. For the third year Pearl Harbor Day came with
bad news. Fat Steve Ross had told J. L. Plummer Jr. that building an
arena and luring professional sports to Miami meant the world to me.

Armed with that knowledge, Plummer warned that unless I gave him what he wanted, "I'll make life miserable for you."

He demanded public funding to expand convention space for Coconut Grove, the trendy and chic Miami section that he represented. The idea was absurd. In the Grove, Mercedes-Benz convertibles jockeyed for spaces near expensive sidewalk restaurants, and trophy wives wore furs to the theater. I told Plummer that the enlightened solution to our problem was to invest in Miami's downtown, and that if Coconut Grove wanted ballroom space the people there ought to find it themselves. He said, "Fuck the enlightened solution. Coconut Grove gets what it wants, Miami Beach gets its convention center improvements, and if there's any money left over for your sports crap, we'll talk."

I already felt squeezed. We could count on a lot of money coming in, but $40 million wouldn't be enough to do everything. My vision was to create a first-class arena in a redeveloped urban area—an idea that would require many partners.

Plummer was pulling the rug out, and we were aware that downtown was generally a hard sell. With the prominent exception of bustling Calle Ocho, the heart of "Little Havana," neighborhoods were deteriorating and acquiring a reputation for danger. Also, I had little reason to believe that the NBA would be sympathetic to our cause. In public statements, league officials were openly cynical, or at least skeptical of Miami ever winning a franchise—new arena or not. Commissioner David Stern had talked publicly about the emerging markets of Charlotte, Minnesota, and Orlando. He said, "Miami is where people go to retire. My mother lives there."

Mastering the Finesse Game

I needed a persuasive sales pitch to convince the NBA that Miami was worthy of an expansion team. But I would have to answer all of the commissioner's questions, and assure a total community commitment to a new franchise. The news media was savvy. As soon as I indicated the interest of the NBA—I planned to announce this at a press conference—reporters would certainly call the league and ask for comment. If an NBA official said, "I don't know anything about it, and we've never heard of Rick Horrow," my credibility would vanish in the time it took the *Herald* to print its first edition.

I called Gary Bettman, then the league's number three executive, and said, "You don't know me, but . . ." I explained the delicate politics, and that we already had money for an arena. We merely needed a commitment from a developer. I pleaded, "When the press calls, please don't say anything negative that will kill the process."

Bettman replied, "I've gotten a lot of calls over the years from Miami people who were full of shit. It's refreshing that at least you're honest." And, after my press conference, reporters called Bettman. He said warm and fuzzy things about Miami without ever making a promise. He also said he'd spoken with me. To the reporters and the reading public, it seemed as if the NBA had embraced the project. In reality, I had only asked Bettman for the gift of enthusiastic vagueness, which he delivered brilliantly.

With momentum building, city commissioners and other insiders quickly proposed sites for a new arena, intent on advancing their own interests. But I had a different, simpler plan. I would approach developers first, then see what sites they brought with them. There was no precedent for the idea and it quickly inspired skepticism, but I prevailed by arguing that it would make the lives of public officials easier. The developer would take on the financial and architectural reports. I hadn't the foggiest idea if this process would succeed. But I figured we'd advance the project, and, as always, worry about the details later. The vision would reveal answers.

Public and Private and Promising

The traditional method of funding projects was to determine how much public money was needed for a new facility, and then ask the voters to cough it up. If the project helped revitalize the neighborhood, so be it. But I could make the prospect of costly new infrastructure more appealing if the public didn't have to go it alone. I would seek private investment, so the burden would be shared. The developer would invest in the facility itself, become property owner, and acquire an equity interest. In exchange, it would develop the area around the arena, creating an array of new activity. The arena itself would bring in a million people a year—so it would be a prime site for restaurants and other businesses that would need to hire local workers. Again, it was an unprecedented idea, but opposition soon dissipated amid a buzz of activity.

Though we already had local interest, I sent RFPs (requests for proposals) to more than 100 developers around the country. The idea was to stir up interest and create as much leverage as possible. I also put together a "developer conference." I sent invitations to everyone I knew, and many people I didn't, and more than 400 people showed up. In my speech, I portrayed the NBA as solidly behind Miami. I said I was comfortable that we could build an arena for $40 million and entice private money.

Everybody in the industry seemed well aware of the hazards of Miami politics and the historical lack of commitment to public projects, but I downplayed all of that—it was something in the past that could be overcome with vision and persistence.

As time went on, I told the developers they had a chance for a new kind of deal, and that they stood to make a ton of money. I pledged, though I was in no position to do so, a trouble-free process and the support of community leaders. What I didn't know, however, was that the community leader I was counting on most was about to deliver unexpected, and discouraging, news. On the other hand, I was learning that in this business the unexpected was the only thing I could count on.

Raul Masvidal, my rock and ally, the unshakable veteran of the Bay of Pigs and the toughest of Miami infighting, explained his impending resignation as chair of the Sports Authority this way: "I'm getting too much grief from the City Commission about what you're doing. I can't help you anymore. You're in for some trouble. Watch yourself."

J. L. Plummer Jr. was livid about the RFPs, which made no mention of Coconut Grove. Plummer obviously had complained to Masvidal at the same time Robbie was complaining about me and our plans for new sports franchises.

Robbie and his fellow rascals had won another battle. Still, I managed to lobby successfully to replace Masvidal as chair with bank executive Larry Turner, who was experienced at difficult negotiations and who supported my ideas about Miami as a sports capital. And I decided that, no matter the political turmoil back home, it was time to make a personal appeal to the NBA.

Gary Bettman was studious and prepared, even as he offered coffee and rolls in his New York office. He knew about the infighting, the lack of commitment on the part of key people, and the odds in general that I faced. He said, "Be serious with me. How the hell are you going to pull this off?"

I said the market, the demographics, the national interest in Miami were positive indications, and that the political infighting was the natural consequence of the prospect of big change. All would be well, in time. It would be inevitable. The forces were aligned. "We have a lot of transplanted New York Knicks fans. And, of course, Cubans love basketball." I argued the last based on my memory of the Miami Floridians, who played briefly in the old American Basketball Association, and featured "the world's tallest Cuban," a 7-foot center named Al Cueto.

Bettman smiled. He figured I was a glass half-full guy with unbridled optimism who can get things done. He said, "Stay in touch with me. Don't promise anything. I'll put you in with the owners groups. They can get to know you." He acknowledged that an expansion process was at least being considered, and that we ought to be in the game. He warned, however, "Don't mention it to the local media. I'll deny anything's going on."

When I got back to town, there were three formal proposals waiting. The most appealing was from Decoma (Development Construction Management), formed by Hines, a company from Houston. It was the only proposal that had a tangible commitment—$7.1 million of its own money—so it appealed to me. But whereas the other proposals focused on upscale areas, Decoma's was for Overtown, seemingly the least likely neighborhood on which to stake a city's sports future. Still, I figured it could be a demonstration of the power of investment, optimism, and urban enlightenment.

To Sell the Unsellable

Overtown was one of the oldest neighborhoods in the city, and traditionally home to a large African-American community that in the first half of the twentieth century was, by law, segregated. The neighborhood retained some of its historic architecture, including the Lyric Theater, described in 1915 by a local newspaper as "Possibly the most beautiful and costly playhouse owned by colored people in all of the southland." The village also contained the D. A. Dorsey House, home of Miami's first African-American millionaire, and the historic Greater Bethel AME Church. But by 1980, and in the wake of race riots in nearby Liberty City, the place had become notorious as a center of homelessness and crime. And when Michael Browning, a *Herald* reporter, was stabbed under a highway overpass in Overtown and then, after his recovery, wrote about the attack in *Tropic,* the *Herald*'s Sunday magazine, the neighborhood seemed doomed. And yet from our point of view it had possibilities. Property, as a result of the natural order of commerce, was cheap. The location was central. The planned city monorail, the "People Mover," would stop there. And urban restoration and revitalization were, in a sense, what this idea was all about. As time went on, Overtown seemed to us the right choice, and the choice that, in the end, I knew we'd have to fight very hard for.

We got a psychological boost when the *New York Times* wrote a piece about Miami—how it should be considered for an NBA franchise. This helped maintain momentum. But I needed something else. Something dramatic. Something more than talk. I needed the game itself.

If I could have an exhibition game, the locals would see for themselves the heat that NBA competition generates. And, at the same time, if we drew a big crowd at whatever venue I could arrange, I could demonstrate to the league that Miami was an inevitable destination.

So I produced the first NBA exhibition game in the history of the city. I lined up the Washington Bullets and the New Jersey Nets. I convinced the Bank of America to underwrite the expenses by arguing that it would be both good public relations for the bank and a chance to get in on the ground floor of arena development. I commissioned a logo design for our fantasy franchise. It featured a sun, a basketball, and some palm trees. To be sure, it looked like a sumo wrestler's belly with a trunk coming up from the gut. But it was a start. I organized a media blitz that resulted in a sold-out Knight Center. Of course, in true Miami style, the place was unsuited for the occasion. Because of the way it was configured, there were seats on only three of the four sides, and on the fourth side, right behind the basket, there was a brick wall. If the players ran too hard on a fast break, they could be injured. Fortunately, nothing untoward happened, and the game came down, in theatrical fashion, to a nail-biting conclusion. The Bullets nipped the Nets, 94–92. The crowd got into it, cheering loudly for both sides, as if orchestrated by me. It was a glorious evening all around. Even David Stern's mother enjoyed it. We sent a car to her condominium and picked her up. We were confident she would call the commissioner in New York the next day and tell him what a good time she had.

The general thrust of the effort had awakened everyone, and I was getting calls from skeptics who suddenly wanted to be a part of it. One of them was Hank Goldberg, then an overbearing local sports talk show host and now an overbearing national sports commentator. He called and said, "I've been an admirer of yours." I thought, "Horseshit, Hank—you've never been an admirer of anybody." But I said, "Thank you." He said he was working with a local public relations firm and wanted to make the sports authority a client. He was apparently working both sides of the street, as PR man and as independent sports commentator.

I said, "We don't need PR. You'll just have to cover us the way you want to cover us, and I'll hope you'll do the right thing."

He said, "That's not how I thought this call would go. You're making a big mistake." I would, of course, hear from him again.

Take Me Out to the Crab Game

If you were to examine my appointment books for this period (or actually for any period in the last couple of decades) you would see that in no case was my attention focused entirely on one pursuit. In the midst of the effort to build an arena and to lure an NBA team, I continued the effort to bring Major League Baseball to town. I was certain that quite apart from compromising my focus and energies, a two-sport effort would call greater attention to the possibilities and help overcome the presumption of failure. People would begin to see things my way, and say, "This *is* possible." I hoped to stir up baseball enthusiasm without worrying about details such as if we were going to have a stadium to play in or not.

To that end, I put together a group of interested parties that we called the South Florida Baseball Corporation. It had no offices and no significant pot of money, but it had instant respect because of the people involved (including a judge and the longtime University of Miami baseball coach, Ron Fraser). Its primary purpose was to market South Florida as the ideal baseball location and to become the coordinator of any perspective ownership groups.

As emissary of that body, and as director of the authority, I played connections wherever I could. John McMullen, then the owner of the Houston Astros, was one of those connections. We knew that he was also involved with the Hines Company, which had formed Decoma, the company that offered the investment in Overtown. McMullen, then, would be a key target in the upcoming meeting of the Major League Baseball owners in Houston. He had already offered to invest in Miami, and would be sympathetic to our cause.

In December 1984, I took an entourage to Houston—though we were unofficial visitors to the baseball meeting. Our intention was to sell our ideas informally and to use McMullen, a respected owner, as our entree. Of course, he didn't know this yet. We rented a suite and arranged for stone crabs to be flown in from the legendary Joe's Stone Crabs on Miami Beach, where diners line up for hours waiting for a table.

John McMullen was cordial but irascible. As I introduced myself in the suite, about to make the Decoma connection, he interrupted. "Never mind the sales pitch. Where's the food?" We showed him the big tray of stone crabs, complete with Joe's special sauces, and the implements required to crack open the hard shells and to extract the meat. I said, "We flew them in just for you. I assume you know how to eat them."

He said, dismissively, "Don't tell me how to eat stone crabs. I was in Florida before you were born." He then bit into a stone crab as if he were eating a ham sandwich. We heard an unappetizing crunch. Almost immediately, two of his caps fell out of his mouth. I figured the future of Major League Baseball in Miami was on the floor.

McMullen, apparently, thought he was eating soft-shelled crabs. I said, "These must be particularly hard-shelled stone crabs." He sensed my attempt to save face, if not expensive dental work, and smiled an imperfect smile. He assured me that his dentist could repair the damage. And, indeed, he introduced us to several colleagues. Though we didn't make it onto the agenda, we had never expected to. It was our intent only to show the seriousness of our purpose. In this regard, we were successful.

Word soon spread. In short order, we began to harvest calls from a variety of entrepreneurs interested in cobbling together enough investors for a baseball franchise. Commissioner Peter Ueberoth began to talk about expansion and the need to identify "worthy regions." He considered South Florida one of them.

Back home, momentum continued to grow and important people in the community were impressed. Except for one.

Joe Robbie called Larry Turner, the new sports authority chair. He warned, "Stay away from baseball. Or else."

So You Want to Be an NBA Owner?

Robbie, as it turned out, used every opportunity he could to return the focus to football and to publicly discredit our efforts—even on celebratory occasions. The Dolphins' owner decided to build the new stadium for the Dolphins at the Lake Lucerne site, and to fund the construction privately. But when he announced this grand plan at a press conference, he also used the opportunity to blast all the things we were doing, as well as all of the diverse sports negotiations that were taking place without his approval. Among other things, he argued that a downtown Miami arena would be a waste of taxpayers' money because "the city will never get an NBA or NHL team."

I knew that I couldn't let Robbie stop our momentum. I had to keep baseball on track. And, most significantly and timely at that point, I had to be sure we had a bead on professional basketball. So I finally met with NBA commissioner David Stern in New York. Stern was impressive and, well, stern. This is not to say he doesn't have a bit of P. T. Barnum in him. But he's so smart that any astute promoter who comes into the room knows instantly to leave the bullshit in the briefcase. I promised him—because I didn't think it was bullshit—that by year's end we'd have a site and a developer chosen.

Stern was not one to announce his intentions, so I can't say for certain what the direct consequences of this meeting might have been. But within seven days, I needed a scorecard to keep track of the people who called and presented themselves as prospective owners of a new Miami team. Sidney Schlenker, who had co-produced an Arthur Miller revival, *A View From the Bridge*, said he wanted to buy the Denver Nuggets and move them to town. I barely had a moment to consider this prospect when Alan Potamkin, a Miami Cadillac dealer, said he wanted to get into the game by applying for an expansion franchise. I didn't know Potamkin, but, growing up in South Florida, I had seen the television commercials from the time his father owned the dealership—a lot of screaming, red balloons flying all over the lot, and other unsubtle sales methods. Then, a third figure appeared. Les Alexander, a Boca Raton stockbroker, called with the magic words, "You don't know me, but . . ." So now I had hungry entrepreneurs competing against each other.

If prospective owners were birds in the bushes, money was a bird in the hand. The Sports Authority received a check for $3.5 million, the first installment of the Convention Development Tax. I made an enlarged copy of the check and carried it around with me. But if I thought we were in the clear, I was wrong. In Miami, you must be prepared for anything. You must expect April Fool's Day to stretch into April Fool's Month.

J. L. Plummer Jr., the undertaker, was undermining arena plans; he attacked my ideas at commission meetings. Plummer was the last vestige of the old Anglo political influence, a cross between playboy and down-home guy. He wore gold chains and slicked-back hair, and rolled his "Rs" as if he were pontificating. In the middle of the City Commission meeting, he turned to me and said, "You're going to have a short career if you tell us what decisions we should make."

Plummer was not alone in his criticism. Clara Oesterle, Robbie's puppet, blamed me for the slow pace of arena negotiations. Radio commentator Hank Goldberg, still smarting from my refusal to sign the Sports Authority up with the advertising agency he worked for, awarded me, on the air, the distinction as the biggest fraud in South Florida. The County Commission made noises about its own dissatisfactions, and though that body was not directly connected to the arena process (the city was at the heart of it), it could make trouble, particularly now when delicate negotiations with the most attractive developer, Decoma, were beginning; it wouldn't take much to produce a successful campaign against investing in a troubled area of town.

Squeeze Play

In the situation I faced in early 1985, it was important to overcome the carping and criticism with acts that had the prospect of yielding positive results. I madly made calls to everybody. I assured Gary Bettman we'd have a deal soon. I told Decoma we were obliged to finish lease negotiations quickly to beat new competition outside the city; it was important that Decoma emerge the victor because its $7.1 million contribution to the arena project was the only real commitment we had. And with our focus on the Overtown site, we had every expectation of attracting federal housing funds to augment our efforts to revitalize the district.

But Overtown remained a hard sell. Some people exploited fears of the white establishment that had concerns about the neighborhood but didn't want to say them aloud. It was infuriating to listen to political code words such as "inaccessible" and "lack of parking" when people really meant, "There are too many blacks in the neighborhood." At a meeting of the Chamber of Commerce, I took the pragmatic path. I argued that we could philosophically debate the right location for the next ten years, and be back where we were in the mid-1970s, without teams or prospects. Or we could make a financial deal with a real commitment from Decoma, and hope that it renovates the surrounding area. Pounding on the podium as Nikita Khrushchev once did at the United Nations, I shouted, "We've been talking too long. Let's get this done." People twice my age stood to applaud. The sports authority quickly approved the Decoma business plan. And then the next day, the City Commission blessed the particulars. However, when I was leaving City Hall, J. L. Plummer Jr. said, "Don't think you're home free. You still have to sell the bonds." Then he started to laugh.

Somehow he knew that the usually routine selling of bonds would be anything but in our political banana republic. In stadium financing, revenue bonds are sold by bankers and are paid off by, in some cases, the revenue from the facility or, in other cases, the taxes that are approved for the projects. In our circumstance, we had $3.5 million a year from the bed tax, plus the Decoma investment. And that, together with a 20-year bond, like a mortgage payment, added up to $48 million. But, in banana republics where bad deals and criminal indictments dominate the public record, nothing is what it seems. Bankers know this. And they know enough to stay away. Every bank that we turned to said no, until we found, across the Pacific, sympathetic ears.

Two Japanese banks couldn't help but be impressed that encouragement was coming from the NBA offices. Gary Bettman said the NBA was willing to consider expansion, though there was no timetable. He listed nine cites "worthy of application." Miami was one of them. This was a big deal—the first formal discussion of expansion, and the first time Miami had been mentioned in any positive way by NBA officials. The word Miami even started appearing in Duluth sports pages.

In August, Terri and I were at the gate at the airport, about to head off to the Caribbean on a well-deserved 10-day adventure. Just before leaving, I checked my phone answering machine. There was a message from J. L. Plummer Jr., which said, in effect, "Give me $10 million for Coconut Grove. Or you'll be very sorry." We visited Martinique, Antigua, and St. Thomas, but I couldn't enjoy a thing. I kept thinking about Plummer, his high-blown attitudes and his hypocrisy. He seemed so protective of his precious Coconut Grove. But if he cared so much about it, why had he tossed McDonald's wrappers from his silver sedan onto the pavement? (I witnessed this misdemeanor in the Grove while driving behind the silver sedan with PLUMMER on its license plate.) Now he seemed willing to trash the city's welfare by making the arena deal impractical. He would take that risk because he was experienced at politics and knew that, in the end, one of the two of us would cave in, and it wouldn't be him. I was dealing with a man who played every angle. During our "vacation," I called consistently from the islands, hoping to convince him that his plan would only leave us with a white elephant downtown. But he never took my calls.

When we returned, the news wasn't any better. In fact, the whole enterprise now seemed in doubt. A new federal law had passed that would eliminate tax-exempt financing of certain kinds of bonds for arenas and stadiums—our kinds of bonds. The law would take effect on January 1 of the following year. This meant that unless we finished our deal with the banks by the end of December, it would collapse, because the three percentage points that would be added to the interest would make the project too costly. I didn't know if, as a funeral director, Plummer was a math whiz, but I suspected that this news delighted him. As it turned out, he made trouble wherever he could.

He stuck his nose, for example, into the baseball negotiations. As the preparations for meeting the bonding deadline proceeded, I invited George Argyros, the Seattle Mariners' owner, to visit and to see for himself what Miami had to offer. We arranged this quietly, without informing the press; it was our intention to merely lay groundwork and not risk complications, or not to overpromise anything that we couldn't deliver. I introduced Argyros to Maurice Ferre and Larry Turner at the Grand Bay. Later, we took a helicopter tour to showcase downtown Miami by air. I told Argyros that the city was willing to fund a baseball stadium, though I had no evidence of this. It occurred to me that if we could demonstrate the interest of a real Major League owner in Miami we would be presenting an entirely different proposition to voters than in the past. It wouldn't be speculative. We'd have an owner on the hook.

By this time, Ferre was no longer mayor. The new man at City Hall was Xavier Suarez, a Cuban immigrant and something of a political newcomer. Suarez, like Ferre, was intellectual and instinctive. His father had been a university dean, and Suarez himself held a law degree and master's degree from the Kennedy School of Government at Harvard. In his effort to stay afloat as a City Hall novice, he was more pragmatic and less idealistic than his predecessor. He forged alliances of convenience, and this allowed Plummer even more prominence. Suarez was out of town during Argyros's visit, and that left an opening for Plummer, the official with the most seniority, to invite himself.

Over a lobster lunch, which the sports authority paid for, Argyros allowed me to sketch out the path and the timeline to a new stadium in South Florida. Plummer kept quiet until the critical moment when I could see that Argyros was really getting into the spirit of it. With impeccable timing that in another venue could be labeled coitus interruptus, he said to me, "Not only are you not going to get a baseball stadium built, but you're not going to get your arena funded." Then he turned to our guest and said, "Frankly, Mr. Argyros, I don't know why you're here, because we're going to build a stadium over my dead body." It was an amusing comment from a funeral director but, at the time, I couldn't see any humor in it at all. After the meeting, I explained to Argyros that Plummer's opinion was certainly the minority opinion. "He's not that important," I said. Privately, of course, I was seething. I seldom let such emotion show, and only those closest to me ever saw any evidence.

Larry Turner, reflecting on his years at the Sports Authority, now tells the story of calling my office afterward. My secretary told him, "Rick is in the hallway." Turner asked, "What's he doing out there?" She replied, "Banging his head against the wall."

I knew that opposition to Overtown was brewing, that Plummer was contriving, that we were heading toward a possible blowout.

Praying at the Altar of Momentum

Still, when you press forward on every front you can hardly go a day without some promising developments. And soon after the disheartening lunch with Argyros, Gary Bettman called from the NBA offices to say he was sending down expansion criteria in the hopes that "We'll move along your process even more." Bettman was playing the leverage game, too. He hoped to choose new franchises from a great variety of viable candidates, so he was helping each prepare, ratcheting the stakes. Nevertheless, we'd eagerly take the help and the compliment that came with it and use this to our advantage.

In October, we hosted another NBA exhibition at the Knight Center. The Utah Jazz beat the New Jersey Nets, 113–96. Afterward, Lew Schaffel, general manager of the Nets, told me he had learned that Alan Potamkin was about to file an application to the NBA. He asked if I was committed to Potamkin. I wasn't, of course, unless he played by our rules. But I couldn't say that. I wanted to keep, as always, the process moving along. Schaffel wanted to get into the game, too. So I said, "I'm committed to whomever gets the NBA franchise." He said, "I'll call you next month. I want you to meet a friend of mine." Clearly, Schaffel had a partner in mind.

I went to Philadelphia to talk with Schaffel's man, Billy Cunningham, the Hall of Fame forward of the 76ers and also a successful former coach. Billy said he had been "promised a franchise by David Stern," and was shopping for a place to put it. He said, "Tell me why I should put a team in Miami." I was dealing, I understood, with an arrogant man. I seriously doubted that he had any such guarantee from Stern, who always played every angle. Still, I pushed straight ahead, and gave my best Miami spiel.

Cunningham and Schaffel, of course, had competition. Just a few days after our meeting, Alan Potamkin, the Cadillac dealer, sent a $100,000 check and an official application to the NBA, saying they pledged publicly to work with me and with the Sports Authority. But, when I pressed Bettman a few days later, I learned that though the application from Potamkin prominently mentioned the Overtown site, it also said other sites would be explored.

It was important, of course, to keep any internal difficulties from our bankers. We faced a real deadline now, and so I put a great deal of time and energy into these negotiations. In early November, we met at the World Trade Center with Tseuo Makabe of the Long Term Credit Bank of Japan. The session lasted 12 hours. The banker spent most of the time revealing what he had learned about Miami, and he wasn't in a happy mood. He asked: "Why is your city government so unstable?" I replied, "This is a new Miami. We now have enlightened leaders." J. L. Plummer Jr. enlightened? At crunch time, and with success just around the bend, a negotiator can find himself abundantly charitable.

A month later, the bank agreed to sell the bonds. I was delighted. Another Pearl Harbor Day was on the horizon, and this time the Japanese were coming to the rescue. But of course I was too optimistic. On the afternoon of December 6, a political reporter from the *Miami News* called and said that Plummer was so upset about this bond issue that he announced he was going to New York to officially represent the city. Plummer was hoping to manipulate the process, and to secure what he saw as Coconut Grove's proper portion of the windfall. It wasn't orthodox or legal. But it was classic Miami.

Knowing When to Compromise (to Be Precise, Cave in)

On Pearl Harbor Day 1985, the *Miami News* article came out, quoting Plummer and me. The next day, authority chair Larry Turner met with the recalcitrant city commissioner to try to negotiate. Turner called me and said, "Here's the good news. Plummer is willing let us keep $38 million if he can have $10 million for himself. He says unless he gets that amount for a convention center upgrade in Coconut Grove he'll scuttle the deal." Turner also observed that, "If Plummer had to get on a plane to Tokyo to ruin this he would do it." I was appalled. The arena needed every penny it could get.

At the next Sports Authority meeting, I asked the directors and the developer if it was possible to build a proper arena for $10 million less than what we had the week before. It could be done, everyone agreed, with fewer skyboxes, and by making the arena smaller than planned. Instead of 16,800 seats—a representative building for the NBA and NHL—it would have about 15,000, making it one of the smallest facilities in the league, but still acceptable (at the time). I said, "Give me an hour to make calls." I reached the remaining competitors for the franchise—Lew Schaffel, Sidney Schlenker, Alan Potamkin, and Les Alexander. I told them we'd be meeting in the next hour. If any of them would like to put up an extra few million in exchange for the right to build more luxury seats in the arena, and collect the revenue from them, now was the time. "If not we don't think we can hold off slashing $10 million out of our budget and still make the end of December deadline to do this deal." None of them bit. They argued that Miami was an unproven market, that they didn't know if there would be a demand for skyboxes, and other nonsense. And I was fuming. I felt I had almost single-handedly gotten us to this point—on the verge of a new arena—and these gutless people were going to get the equity and the glory with none of the risk.

I could have called Plummer's bluff, of course. But I also knew that with Suarez as the new mayor and with Plummer's influence at City Hall, our 5–0 vote in favor of selling the bonds could quickly turn to 1–4. Also, Plummer could call the underwriters in Tokyo and havoc would result. Plummer could have also appointed all new members of the authority, including Turner, and replaced him with a hack. My choice was to take on Plummer and possibly lose the authority and the bond deal and the NBA, too, or to make the best deal I could. I had no leverage—the last time I would ever go into a negotiation without leverage. I would have to take the money—less money—and run.

The authority voted to alter the bond arrangement. Now $30 million would go to the arena, and a $10 million subordinate issue would benefit Coconut Grove. It passed 9–0. The next day, the vote made headlines in the *Herald*. The report explained the new financing and I was quoted. Here's what I wanted to say: "Plummer, that asshole, hijacked the money, and now we've got to skimp on the arena." What I said was something right out of Plummer's script—that this will attract conventions to our city. I said this because it was important to give the impression that we were working together. It was inaccurate, of course, but sometimes you've got to camouflage the bullshit.

The last business day of the year, December 27, we were in New York. We signed the papers with the bank in the Edwardian room of the Plaza Hotel, just as if it was routine business, and nothing untoward had happened. Yet Overtown was still hanging in the balance, and a showdown was coming.

Find the Producer

Potamkin held a press conference and expressed doubts that the arena could be done on time. In fact, there was no real agreement on when it had to be done, and no pressing need for it to be done "on time." We had no teams, and no schedule. But he was making trouble, and saying that construction delays and red tape caused by the downtown location and inevitable obstacles would dissuade league officials from ruling favorably on the city's application. Privately, we had all agreed to keep sensitive issues such as this one among ourselves. But Potamkin was looking out for his own interests.

Over dinner in Coral Gables, he said, "I'm just telling you right now. I'm not going to play basketball in an arena that has no parking. You've got to find parking for me." As dinner went on, he got more and more contentious and demanding. Almost always, I am able to put such behavior aside, and to stick to the primary issues. But that night my emotions got the best of me. Before we could order our after-dinner espresso, I said, "We're going over the same arguments we resolved five months ago. If you don't want to be a partner in this, just tell me, and we'll deal with someone else." I got up and walked out.

I shouldn't have done that. But, on the other hand, I didn't want Potamkin to think he could use me. And, in this negotiation, I had leverage. We had a viable process going on, and, though Potamkin to that point had submitted the only formal application to date, we also had a variety of potential investors.

A few days later, Raul Masvidal, still looking out for my interests though no longer chair of the Sports Authority, called. He asked, "Do you know who Zev Buffman is?" Buffman, a Tel Aviv native who had lived in the Miami area for many years, was a theatrical producer. Over two and a half decades on Broadway, he has produced nearly 30 plays and musicals, including *Jerry's Girls, Joseph and the Amazing Technicolor Dreamcoat, Little Foxes* (with Elizabeth Taylor), *Brigadoon* (a revival), *Requiem for a Heavyweight,* and a play that won him a Tony Award, the revival of Arthur Miller's *A View From the Bridge* (coproduced, interestingly, with Sidney Schlenker).

Buffman, in fact, produced the last play Terri and I saw, which was in early January 1986, in Miami Beach. To be accurate, Terri witnessed the whole play. I spent the second act in the men's room, listening via portable radio to the NCAA championship football game between Brigham Young and Michigan. (Brigham Young won.)

Masvidal painted a picture of Buffman as a producer not just of plays but potentially of big-league sports. (Also, he turned out to be a producer of "Fs"—at the time he spelled his last name Bufman, but recently changed it to Buffman.) I met Zev at the Grand Bay on March 5 for lunch. He was a gregarious man who articulated his visions with something of an Israeli accent. I told him that we've got the arena dollars, but, in regard to potential ownership of a team, that we didn't have an exclusive arrangement with anybody. We needed to have people who would focus on the arena first, and not try to play all different sites off against each other. I said, "We think downtown Miami is the best place for the NBA and so does David Stern." I suggested that Zev meet Cunningham. I called Billy and told him about the idea. I also introduced Buffman to Potamkin. Buffman, it turned out, had a trump card. He was always the producer—with other people's money. He had the interest of Ted Arison, owner of Carnival Cruise Lines, and fellow Tel Aviv native. Buffman could provide the showbiz that would help sell all of this, but Arison was the deep-pockets guy we'd need.

Pick and Roll Politics

In May 1986, I met with Gary Bettman and Russ Granik (the NBA's number two man) in New York for a routine progress report. But nothing important is ever routine. The NBA expressed concerned about Alan Potamkin's willingness to pull the trigger. Bettman said Potamkin didn't seem to him to be the type who would commit to the ups and downs of franchise ownership.

Then the *Miami News* reported the complaints of a new political player—Cesar Odio, who had just assumed the city manager's job. The city manager, in Miami's form of government, has more influence over day-to-day affairs than the mayor, even if he doesn't have as much visibility. Odio complained that arena negotiations were going too slowly, and he wanted to take them over. People around me thought I should be offended by this, but I was flattered. Latecomers were lining up to be identified with a project that was clearly succeeding.

Zev Buffman called when I returned from New York, and told me he had made a deal with Billy Cunningham. Buffman, who still knew little about basketball, was aware that he needed to attach himself to an NBA name, and so they worked out an agreement where Cunningham would be a suitable "rent-a-citizen" and Schaffel would be the expert executive. Both would earn part of the new team. This was unsettling news. I harbored fantasies (well-earned I thought) of having some role in the franchise, and had worked hard to put myself in that position. Harder, by far, than Cunningham. Still, I had to put such personal ambitions aside and stay focused on the larger issues.

In a few months, the NBA would make franchise recommendations, so it was important to do everything I could to get our application ready. I urged Buffman to strike quickly and publicly. The NBA had its concerns about Potamkin. Schlenker, who had purchased the Nuggets, was apparently not moving from Denver, and Alexander was moving too slowly. Plus there was a rumor that Potamkin and Joe Robbie were meeting. A reporter from the *Miami News* called for a comment. I said I didn't know about any new alliance. But I thought, that's all we need—Joe Robbie back in the process.

Buffman came out with guns blazing. He held a press conference in which he ripped Potamkin, saying he was either a team player or he wasn't, and we'd better be in this together for a downtown arena or it wasn't going to happen. It was some performance. They were competitors for a franchise, but Buffman gave the impression that he was looking out for the public welfare. Then he and Cunningham had a press conference with three of the city commissioners, including Mayor Suarez, emphasizing the need for teamwork. So in a very short time, Buffman had monopolized the headlines and also succeeded in turning the public conversation away from his competitors. Buffman had less money than any of them, but he never gave that impression. He was unfailingly optimistic, a trait that I admired.

Our optimism was soon tested, however, by what I had feared all along—a confrontation at City Hall over final permits to build in Overtown. After Buffman announced his intentions, Potamkin and his allies lobbied the City Commission and Mayor Suarez to reconsider the situation, arguing there was not enough parking in Overtown, and that they should consider another site. He pledged to bring in capital, and to make an NBA franchise happen, if the five-member commission played along. Astonishingly, or perhaps not so astonishingly considering the reservations about Overtown, this campaign picked up momentum.

I showed up at City Hall at the crack of dawn to see Mayor Suarez. He had said he'd be there. But he wasn't. Nor did he show up the rest of the day. Or the next morning, or the rest of the second day, either. But I never left the place, worried that I'd miss my chance. Since then I've learned it's a trick of politicians: "Come by," they say, "we'll talk." But they have no such intention to do so. Suarez was being lobbied hard by Potamkin, who'd found an ally in Plummer. Potamkin argued that the NBA would never approve a franchise for a depressed part of the city; the commission instead should approve his ideas for west Dade or north Dade. Plummer was egging him on because he stood to gain plenty. He already had the promise of his $10 million for Coconut Grove, and if he could eventually kill the rest of the deal, he could get more for his district. He had one vote, and he could count on the vote of one other commissioner. If Suarez went with him, the Overtown arena—as fast as you can count to three—would be dead, and so would sports in Miami. I had to persuade Suarez otherwise.

Xavier Suarez, the first Cuban-born Miami mayor, was hard to read. At 36 and a political novice, Suarez was still exploring alliances. Now, looking back on that time, he says, "I acted as if I was the ruler of a small nation." He emphasizes the word "acted," because in those days Miami had a weak mayor system. The salary was a paltry $5,000 a year, and the only real control was having one of five votes on the City Commission. Everything else was persuasion. Yet the mayoral chair was something of a bully pulpit. "In Latin America," he observes, "they don't know who the governor of Florida is, but they know the mayor of Miami. But for me, there was a sort of built-in naïveté. Once I was elected, I said the kinds of things politicians say. I was critical of people." He was critical of me, calling me a "nonathlete" who was "making a lot of money." But he admits he was saying things he needed to say to establish himself. Now, he reflects, "Miami was the worst place in the world to be in government. We had mountains to climb."

I certainly did. When I finally cornered Suarez before the vote, I knew that everything rode on the next few minutes, so I pulled out all the stops. I got Billy Cunningham on the speaker phone, because I knew the mayor would be impressed by star quality. I knew Cunningham would spout the same self-promotional crap he always spouted, but it wouldn't hurt in this case. He did his best, but in the end Suarez was not convinced. I could see that he was weighing his own political future. He was thinking he didn't want to make an enemy of Plummer on a deal that might not bring results anyway.

He confided, "I don't know if I want to take the risk. How can you be certain that we'd get an NBA franchise? I'm told by those who know that it's not possible if we stay in Overtown. Are you sure it's the right place for us?"

I said, "We spent nearly 100 hours of research and getting testimony—it's the best chance to do the most social good, not just locate an arena. Because this is not just about sports, but the rebirth of the city. I know the pressure you're under. But you've got to look at it this way. If you're trying to avoid criticism, you can't do it. A vote either way will provide whatever impetus critics need. Think of the larger picture. This is a defining moment in the city's future. We spent 20 years of failure getting to the point we're at today. And though we can't guarantee a franchise if you approve the arena, we can guarantee we'll have no other major league sports franchises if you kill it. Parched earth for a decade. Think of the power you have today. Think of your legacy."

And in Miami City Hall, a place I had come to dread for all of its obstacles, the mayor later voted "aye." Plummer said, "I vote no, but I know it doesn't make a difference." My plan for Overtown carried, 3–2. The undertaker smiled his rueful smile at me, and winked. And I thought, there's gotta be a better place to make a living.

The next day Potamkin dropped his bid for a team. When asked for a comment by the press, I said nothing. It was not a time to gloat publicly, but to continue to demonstrate our serious sense of purpose. Privately, I called Potamkin and said, "I'm most curious about why you dropped out." He said, "It was fun while it lasted," and that he probably wound up selling a few more cars. He also said, "It's cheaper to buy season tickets to a franchise than to buy the franchise itself." I thought, with more than a little exasperation, "Well, thanks for all you did to screw up the works. And I won't be buying a Cadillac from you any time soon."

After I got back from a trip to New York, Buffman and Cunningham each put in $50,000 for the franchise, and everyone else withdrew. Now, it was time to educate Buffman on basketball and the NBA. And it was time for a full-court press. Pat Williams, a former general manager of the Philadelphia 76ers, said he had talked to NBA owners, and the conclusion was that "Miami won't happen." His research, however, was suspect. He was leading a campaign at the time to bring a team to Orlando—clear competition for us.

Buffman started selling season tickets, competing with Orlando in something of a hypothetical (but perhaps highly persuasive) exercise. We all called business executives, community leaders, friends, and everyone we knew to ask for commitments. We had 5,000 seats sold before long. But it didn't appear to be enough. People were sitting on their money, because, with all of the rancor and the long history of failure, they still didn't believe the arena was going to get built, or that we had a legitimate shot at a franchise. It was time, once again, for some public demonstration of our progress.

Bulldozing: Or Making Something Out of Very Little

But what could we demonstrate? The only thing scheduled in the next few days was a minor event: We had hired a bulldozer to knock down a small utility hut on the site of the arena. But I had an idea on how to make it a news event. On the appointed day, by the time I got finished describing the prospect of a simple act of leveling a modest utility shed, it seemed to the press as if the cranes and the skyboxes had already arrived. Reporters came en masse, though none of the city officials I invited showed, claiming "previous engagements," but assuming, I'm sure, that nothing would come of this. Wearing a hard hat, I announced this as a "major development in the history of South Florida, because we're finally building the arena." I turned to the bulldozer operator and gave a nod. He promptly knocked over the shed. It took all of 30 seconds, or less. The "event" made big headlines the next day. But, of course, I paid a price.

City politicians, by their own choice, didn't get to share the limelight, and receive their allotted (deserved or otherwise) share of the credit. City Manager Cesar Odio, in particular, was critical of the whole thing. The commissioners called an emergency meeting to "review" the arena plan. This was euphemism for beating the shit out of me.

To preempt this, I put in a call to Gary Bettman. He gave me what I needed, a statement that "the process in Miami was impressive," and went on the record saying I had done a "wonderful job" and "We look forward to your new arena." After I read the letter, the city commissioners remained silent. But I got out of there quickly. I wasn't sure what was coming next.

Odio and I never got along. He referred to me as a pioneer in the *Miami News,* which was nice, but I knew that when push came to shove, he was Plummer's guy, and I knew I could never trust him. (In fact, Odio was later investigated during a crackdown on Miami corruption. In 1996, an FBI videotape showed Odio counting $3,000 in alleged kickback money. Following conviction, Odio served a year in federal prison.)

The arena contract and the land lease were scheduled for approval on July 30, 1986. On the twenty-ninth, I got a notice from the legal counsel to the Sports Authority that the "current executive director would, under the law, be prohibited in serving in any capacity with a sports franchise." It appeared, on the face of it, to be a commentary on conflict of interest. Instead, it was a Plummer-orchestrated move. Parker Thomson, whom I consulted on the matter, advised me that this new measure was clearly illegal, and we could win in court. He asked me if I was planning to be involved in the NBA franchise. I said I hoped to. But now it appeared that I was out. Buffman, Cunningham, and Schaffel would all get equity if a franchise were awarded to Ted Arison. I would get, maybe, a certificate of appreciation for my wall.

On August 4, 1986, the official groundbreaking (as opposed to merely knocking down a utility hut) was held for the Miami Arena. Terri was there, along with our infant daughter, Katie. Buffman brought in singer Julio Iglesias to entertain and there were 15 speeches. I delivered one of them. Other speakers included Odio, Suarez, and Plummer, each of whom presented themselves as the single fathers of the arena. Ferre wasn't there. Nor was Raul Masvidal. Steve Muss and fat Steve Ross were nowhere near it.

It was all something of an anticlimax, anyway. Opening ceremonies are signals to close the chapter. I reminded myself of the obligation I took on the day I decided to quit Paul and Thomson—to go only where instinct advised. Instinct, in this case, clearly advised that I not stay around for construction and that I devise an exit strategy. I could take what I had learned in Miami to more accommodating places. A few days after the groundbreaking, Buffman asked me, "Do you want to do something that's not NBA related?" I said I'd think about it.

A week later, a 650-page contract with Decoma was signed, and then, three days after that, Terri and I went off to Jamaica. When I checked messages this time, there was nothing from Plummer. We had a wonderful vacation.

How We Sold the NBA on Miami (and Israel)

Now, all we had to do was sell the NBA—in October, it would make its decision on what cities out of the nine that had applied would receive expansion franchises. Our group was doing all the right things. But we had to be sure we had all the money we needed. For that we turned to Buffman's deep pockets, Ted Arison.

Arison's entrepreneurial abilities were inherited. His father had run M. Dizengoff and Co., in Israel, ship owners and general agents for several lines. After serving in the country's War of Independence in 1948, the younger Arison took control of the business. When he moved to the United States in the 1950s, he undertook a series of commercial enterprises that eventually led to ownership of Norwegian Caribbean Lines and then Carnival Cruise Lines. If Miami's ship was to come in, this was the man to steer it.

Arison, like Buffman before him, didn't know much about basketball, but he knew how to ask hard questions. Over lunch at Grand Bay in Coconut Grove, he traded seafaring metaphors for this one: "You're not leading us down a one-way tunnel to an oncoming train, are you?"

My answer: "Billy Cunningham and Zev feel good about the franchise. Schaffel is the right executive. The city is under control. The arena is funded." A few days later, Buffman announced Arison as his principal partner in the proposed new franchise. Everything was in place.

Terri and I were living in Miami Lakes at the time. I drove from there to DiLido Island. My mother wasn't home that Sunday. But I went out onto the dock in the back, and from that old perch inspected downtown Miami. I reached the inevitable conclusion. The next day, I called Larry Turner at 9 A.M. and announced firmly, "I'm resigning. I've teed this up. Now we need a construction guy to take us through the next phases." I would still, of course, be part of arranging the final pitch to the NBA, but officially I'd be gone.

Of course the NBA did not consider my timetable in its deliberations. The league delivered good news and bad news: Three expansion franchises out of the nine candidates would start play as early as 1988—more than we expected, and sooner, too; but the decision on the cities themselves would be delayed for six months, until April 1987.

In the meantime, word was getting out about what we had accomplished in getting this arena project off the ground (or rather *into* the ground). After I delivered a speech in New York at the International City Managers Association, I was asked if I had ever thought of building a national practice. The timing seemed right. Clearly, there was a need out there. Established teams in all major league sports were playing in outdated facilities, so their franchises were at risk. Baseball and football games in many cities were played in compromised stadiums that suited neither sport. And, on instinct, I understood that what I had learned about the presumption of failure in Miami was not limited to any particular geographic region. The more I read, the more it seemed that the opportunity for an adventurous career was, in a sense, back in the place where I started—with sports obsession and dreams for new stadiums and franchises. I was sure that many major cities that were underrepresented by pro sports would see in the Miami story—the forerunner of modern public and private partnership—inspiration for their own efforts. I thought, if this could be done in a banana republic, it could be done anywhere.

I needed a segue, a plan to introduce myself nationally. As I had a few years before, when I cobbled together a living by convincing Joe Robbie and Nick Buoniconti to pay me $9,000 each, I put together a proposal that would allow this. Buffman was at the heart of the plan. As a basketball novice, he still needed me to solidify his position with the NBA. He would help me in this transition. I also met with Jeb Bush, the Florida secretary of commerce, and persuaded him to appoint me special counsel to the Florida Sports Foundation, a $1-a-year job but one that allowed access to the top. From there I could push my vision of sports facilities as "economic revitalization" and "industrial expansion." But first, of course, I needed a strong finish to the crucial matter at hand.

Our Miami contingent—Buffman, Arison, Cunningham, Schaffel, and I—met with David Stern in New York in January 1987. We wanted, of course, to make a solid impression, and give a clear indication that, of all the candidates for teams, Miami had the soundest leadership. And I, of course, hoped to expand my reputation as someone who could play on any turf. The meeting, it turned out, was all about money. Stern was a tough bargainer. Through the years, as a lawyer and marketing expert, who started out as a helper in his family's New York delicatessen, he had overseen unprecedented growth—growth that was no accident, but carefully plotted. Stern said, "The expansion price is $32.5 million." We had expected something considerably less, in the neighborhood of $24 million. But with so many cities bidding, Stern obviously had leverage, and was using it. We all turned toward Arison, our money guy. I feared he would feel manipulated, and would say he had indeed been led down a garden path. But Arison was no stranger to leverage. He knew that Stern wasn't going to toss out a specific figure unless he was serious about Miami. Arison said, "I'll think about it."

Three weeks later, Stern announced there were now seven cities (down from nine) in the running for a franchise. The others were St. Louis, Pittsburgh, Orlando, Charlotte, Kansas City, and Minneapolis.

In the spring, we hosted the NBA's expansion committee, intent on showing the advantages of Overtown. This required, obviously, some work. Here's how Xavier Suarez now describes it: "This was a magical moment, and we had to prepare. We were doing it in an area that had signs that said this was an urban renewal project." The words urban renewal would scare off the NBA. "So we had people removing these signs. We also moved the homeless that morning by paying them to leave." So when we took the NBA officials around, the area was spotless, and person-less.

Meanwhile, we almost lost Ted Arison, who was already balking at the $32.5 million price, and didn't like being bullied by Stern. Then Hank Goldberg, commenting on television, reported that the NBA was "concerned" about charges connecting Arison with gambling figures. Without any proof, he was hinting at connections with organized crime. An exasperated Arison told Buffman he wanted out. "I don't need this." Buffman and I met with Arison and argued that we were very close to an NBA deal, and urged him to stick with us.

On April 21, 1987, the day before the planned franchise announcement, Buffman, Schaffel, Arison, and I went to Stern's office again to make one last pitch. I told the commissioner that investing in Overtown was "the right thing to do." Arison, meanwhile, was hoping for a reduction in the franchise price. Stern stuck to his $32.5 million. Arison got up from his chair and went to the door, and opened it, as if to leave. Arison said, "Well, I suppose I'll have to go across the street and see if I can get a better deal from the other people who are selling NBA franchises." Then he shut the door and sat back down. "But, then, there isn't anyone else selling NBA franchises, is there?"

The next day, at the Parker Meridien Hotel, Ted Arison met us in the lobby with a big smile on his face. Instead of three franchises, four were awarded, because the NBA couldn't choose from among Orlando, Minneapolis, Charlotte, and Miami. All had made persuasive and irresistible cases. We had our franchise.

There was still baseball and hockey to do. And for me, there was a whole new territory to explore. But for now, there were hugs all around.

CHAPTER 4

How to Buy a
Baseball Team (or Not)

*In the jungle of the marketplace, the intelligent buyer must
be alert to every commercial sound, to every snapping of a
selling twig, to every rustle that may signal the uprising
arm holding the knife pointed toward the jugular vein.*

DEXTER MASTERS,
author of The Intelligent Buyer *and* The Telltale Seller

I had a new and impressive-sounding title: President of Buffman
Sports Entertainment and Facility Development Group. And I had a license to travel anywhere to make any good deal.

The first stop was the city of Paul Revere, Brahmins, beans,
Kennedys, Red Sox, Celtics, and Bruins. Boston is just across the
Charles River from where I spent three years pursuing a law degree and
talking reluctant professors into letting me depart from the orthodox
path and follow my penchant for sports. Still, as I prepared for my first
pitch for something beyond the needs of my home state, I felt more
than a hint of anxiety.

Where would my new title and the Miami experience get me in a city
known for its political inbreeding? I knew I had the intelligence to take my
ideas national, but intelligence would not be enough. Credibility and persuasion were equally important. I was well versed in Boston's sports

venues but was not an expert on its colorful history of politics. Many native Bostonians could recite chapter and verse—or, more pertinently, court documents—that implicated prominent politicians such as James Michael Curley, a longtime mayor in the first half of the last century. Curley, the "Irish Mussolini," was sent to prison twice for political corruption.

My familiarity with local politics was limited to the period of my Harvard years. During the blizzard of 1978, I watched Michael Dukakis, who was running for governor, toss bread off a truck. Now, returning to Boston many years later, I was still an outsider. But, at 32 years old, my message had changed. I didn't have to know all the answers. Pleading ignorance could be helpful. At other times, I could rely on my experience and confidence about the process.

Instinct and research had brought me back to Beantown. I had read in *Amusement Business,* a trade magazine, that there was a group interested in building a new Boston Garden downtown. The old arena was a storied place, where the Celtics of Red Auerbach racked up championship after championship, and where on a compact surface of ice Bobby Orr led the Bruins to the Stanley Cup. But the Garden, built in 1928, was very much out of date.

I didn't get there until my Harvard Law School days. I remember the Garden as dingy, with narrow, splinter-filled seats. Still, I loved the place. At the time Miami had no team or arena, and I was in awe of the history of Boston's sports mecca—the championship banners hanging from the rafters and the distinctive parquet floor in which, it was said, the legendary Bob Cousy knew every dead spot.

As historic as the old arena was (not only as a temple of basketball and hockey, but where Franklin Delano Roosevelt and Winston Churchill once spoke), a new building was clearly needed. But who would build it, how would it be done, and could public money be raised?

I made a cold call to Jason Kravitz, one of the development partners mentioned in the trade magazine piece. "Mr. Kravitz, you don't know me, but . . ." And then went on to give a brief version of building the Miami Arena and bringing the Heat to town. I told Kravitz I could help him get a new arena built in Boston.

He replied, "There are a lot of feasibility consultants who can do numbers and conduct studies. What makes you special?"

I said, "Studies are useless, except as doorstops. But if you really want someone who can put together a deal, we need to meet." I was determined to turn my lack of national experience into advantage. I argued that success in Boston was important to Buffman Sports Entertainment because it would become the cornerstone of our national business. I promised Kravitz our undivided attention and every ounce of intensity we could offer. I said that the lack of immersion in Boston politics would actually be helpful because I came with no political baggage and no preconceived notions except those that might naturally occur to a Harvard Law guy who saw developments, or in this case lack of developments, from something of a distance.

In the end, Kravitz said, "We'll get back to you." It's something you hear all the time when you make proposals. But it's an expression I never allow myself to accommodate. Even back then, I knew enough not to leave the other guy in charge of the next move. It is always my intention to control the process. I said, "Great. I'll have a proposal to you within 24 hours." Of course, Kravitz hadn't asked for one. That night, I stayed at the Charles Hotel in Cambridge and drafted a 10-page plan to perform "facility development services." Signing it, I awarded myself a new Buffman title: Facility Development Consultant. I asked for $20,000, which is the amount Kravitz said his group had for a feasibility study. In the cover letter, I argued, "Don't do a study. Get this going." When I hand-delivered the proposal the next day, I told Kravitz, "This is the sort of attention you'll get if you go with us." I also said we had seven or eight other imminent deals (this was a stretch), and that if they sign with us quickly we would make Boston our number one priority. Frankly, $20,000 was a small number for the whole job. It isn't much above what I now get monthly from clients. But at that point it was important to land our first national client.

Just a few days later we had a deal, and then over the next year, we probably performed $50,000 worth of work, and laid all the groundwork for a new arena. We offered site and finance expertise, an innovative plan for tax-increment financing, and an outline of 20 action steps that were eventually used by part of a different development group. (When I became a consultant to the Boston Bruins, I was in town often and watched with fascination the contentious negotiations concerning the air rights over the old arena, to be used for office towers, as part of the way to pay for the new one.) When the Fleet Center (naming rights contributed $30 million to the cause) opened next to the old Boston Garden in 1995, it had 19,600 seats, 104 skyboxes, more than 2,500 club seats, a multimillion dollar video scoreboard, and parquet lifted from the old Boston Garden floor.

Amusement Business, the trade magazine that had tipped me off about Boston, turned out to be a gold mine for me and for Buffman's enterprise. Every time I read of a city's intention to invest in infrastructure, I made a cold call, and explained what we had to offer. Buffman, who had built indoor theaters, was attracted to the amphitheatre business. He figured whatever entertainment could be produced under a roof could be brought outside to larger audiences. And so, in the next months and years, I became something of a developer of large stages in lush settings. At first, I knew nothing about them, but figured that they had to be just like arenas—they were part of a city's infrastructure and, as such, could be built with public and private partnerships.

Buffman sent me all over the country to identify other amphitheatre possibilities—St. Petersburg, Orlando, Chambersburg, Harrisburg, Phoenix, Charlotte, and Columbus. At the same time, I was keeping a hand in the baseball process in Florida, moving tennis center negotiations along in Miami, and working with the mayor of Homestead on a baseball spring training facility.

The Name Game

"Are you going?" "Are you part of the pregame festivities?" If I heard these questions from friends and colleagues once I heard them a dozen times in the days before the official opening of Joe Robbie Stadium at Lake Lucerne in August 1987. "Yes" and "no" were my responses. I would be there, but not as part of the dedication ceremonies. First, I hadn't been invited to be on the field. Also, it was Joe's night. So, when the Dolphins took on the Bears (and lost to them 10–3), I would be a spectator, and probably one in need of a set of powerful binoculars.

I was certain that our new perch would be in the vicinity of the end zone. Edwin Pope, the *Herald* columnist, told me that Joe was personally reviewing the season ticket list to reward his friends and punish his enemies. We'd always had four season tickets at the Orange Bowl on the 50-yard line. When we applied for seat assignments at the new stadium, I kept the tickets in my mother's name. Not much camouflage there. There is but one Horrow family in South Florida telephone directories. Joe would know.

But I was surprised by the constantly manipulative way Joe's mind works. Our new seats, against all expectation, were ideal—on the 50-yard line. Later, I talked to Hank Meyer, a friend and longtime public relations wizard (he brought Jackie Gleason's television show to Miami). I said, "Joe must have been drunk by the time he got to the Hs." Hank replied, "I actually talked to Joe about you." Hank stressed the loyalty we Horrows had shown to the Dolphins since their inception, holding on to season tickets during good times and bad. "Joe's a son of a bitch, but he comes from a loyal family. And I said we need to reward loyalty."

The name of the stadium was something of an issue. And it became the final straw in the relationship between Robbie and Edwin Pope. In the days before the opening of the new facility at Lake Lucerne, *Herald* business reporter Marty Merzer researched a piece about how it all happened. He asked the columnist several questions, among them, "What do you think the name ought to be?" Pope replied sarcastically, "Joe Robbie Memorial Stadium—and the sooner the better." The next day, Merzer said he wanted to put the quote in his story. Pope objected, saying that it wasn't right to say in print that you wished somebody dead—even if that someone was Joe Robbie. He argued that it had been a private joke. Merzer told Pope that it was the best line in his piece. It ran as written, and Robbie was finally finished with the *Her-*

ald's most influential sports writer. And the new facility became Joe Robbie Stadium, without the Memorial. At least that was the name of it for the first few years.

Small Jackpots Don't Stay Small

Joe was still important to me, of course. There were baseball negotiations ahead, and I was still committed to bringing a major league team home. In the meantime, I balanced several things at once. The amphitheatre projects were all at various stages. Some were mired in political processes, as Miami's arena had been for so long, and some were showing real progress. And some suggested other opportunities—because every deal is a building block to something else.

In Phoenix, the project we developed to build an amphitheatre for large shows and concert productions introduced us to the most influential citizens of the city. When discussions among these people turned to the possibility of building a new baseball stadium that could attract Major League Baseball, I saw clear opportunity. Arizona, at the time, was thought of by baseball in the same way as Florida—a fine springtime destination but little more than that. But why couldn't Phoenix be home to a major league team? I learned from my Miami experience that you don't have to have a deal ready in your briefcase; you just have to believe that a deal is possible. I thought Phoenix had as much of a chance in 1987 for baseball as Miami had in the years before to lure the NBA. Though I spent most of my time on the amphitheatre project, I also negotiated a retainer with the Arizona Department of Tourism and Development for six months. My task was to help them save the Cactus League, which was the spring training league that had been in existence for decades, and explore opportunities for a major league franchise.

I didn't worry at all that I would be helping a Miami competitor because you can't anticipate the number of franchises to be awarded. We had just seen this in Miami when the NBA chose four cities instead of the expected three. Baseball would be better off if it got involved in two new promising markets instead of one. Nor would it have been a conflict of interest for me to advise Phoenix while helping Miami, as long as everyone knew about it and understood my dual role.

As it turned out, the Phoenix and Miami efforts had something in common—an idea that I helped devise in which, for the first time that I know of in professional sports, cities found a way to create leverage to use against major leagues. That is, in Phoenix (and subsequently Miami), we proposed a state sales tax that would become the primary funding source for a stadium if Major League Baseball met the deadline. That is, this was a sunsetted tax. The city agreed to levy it, but the tax would expire and nothing would be spent on bricks and mortar if baseball couldn't deliver an expansion team by the specified date. The new strategy worked. MLB wanted the Arizona marketplace, and saw the new tax as the only way to get it. It had to meet our demands for a franchise. And when it did, Banc One Stadium was built. It opened in 1997, and four years later, the Arizona Diamondbacks became World Series Champs—the quickest to ascend from sad-sack expansion team to the top of the baseball world.

Though it had its moments of rancor, the Phoenix amphitheatre deal was nothing like the struggle to get an arena built in Miami. I argued to public officials that the theater should be treated like infrastructure, and that it was appropriate to seek public money, somewhere between $15 and $20 million, as part of a public/private partnership. The city council held a public hearing on the matter, and many people spoke, most of them against it. They complained that the noise would ruin their neighborhood, and that traffic would increase to a point where it would be unbearable—run of the mill, if passionate, objections. I, on the other hand, argued that the overall quality of life in the city would improve. For my effort, I was awarded a chorus of boos. But the city council, aware that objections were largely limited to the immediate neighborhood, voted 7–0 in favor of the measure. All was well—except for Zev Buffman's ears. When Buffman came to visit the proposed location for the stage there was a pained look on his face. He said, "We have to change the site."

I said, "I have no idea what you're talking about."

He said, "Listen? Do you hear that?"

I said, "Do I hear what?"

He replied, "The sound of an airplane." He was referring to the Phoenix airport several miles away.

I said, "I don't hear anything."

He said, "Think of an opera in the evening while a 727 is taking off—the audience hearing that noise."

I said, "What noise?"

He said, "You're an expert on basketball crowd noise. I'm the expert on opera noise. We're moving the site." So the new amphitheatre was built in the west valley, many miles from the location originally chosen.

Fehr, Nicklaus, and a Twins Killing?

Yes, I was learning about amphitheatres. But my fascination with large outdoor stages had its limits. I had to find a way to direct the conversation, and the business, back to Miami baseball. To that end, Buffman and I answered a call.

Donald Fehr, the executive director and general counsel of the Major League Baseball Players Association, provided that opportunity when he announced plans to produce a feasibility study on which communities could support baseball. This could be one study that wouldn't be for chumps. It could be very useful for Miami.

He, of course, wanted to push expansion, providing more jobs for his players. He hired us because he had read about me in national newspapers, and was impressed that I knew how to get public facilities built. When he came to Miami, I introduced him to Mayor Suarez, Raul Masvidal, Armando Codina (a prominent developer), and Buffman. It was a secret meeting. No press. We would leak information when it was convenient, but it wasn't yet convenient or smart to do so. Fehr, who calculates every move, also intended to release information at his own pace. At the meeting, he argued intensely and directly (with no time for small talk) about the need for expansion, and by its end, he had everyone talking and thinking baseball, and that it could happen in Miami. We were actually even thinking that Joe Robbie's new stadium—though built primarily as a football venue—could be our answer.

A few months later, Fehr publicly identified eight cities as expansion candidates: Miami, Tampa, Denver, Phoenix, Indianapolis, Buffalo, Charlotte, and Portland. Though Fehr was not representing Major League Baseball management or owners, momentum was building, and a buzz was created. And a buzz is sometimes a signal that you'll travel to unexpected places—in this case, eventually to the headquarters of a golf hero of mine (and millions of others).

I got a call out of the blue from a member of the American Bar Association sports panel, who had heard me speak about baseball. Larry Greenberg told me about his client, Carl Pohlad, owner of the Minnesota Twins. Pohlad had asked Greenberg to help find him a buyer for the team. Now that Greenberg knew of my interest in South Florida, he thought I was the place to start.

"If you find an interested party," he said, "Carl is willing to do a deal, and relocation would not be an obstacle." It seemed more than a little odd. The Minnesota Twins were, at the time, a solid franchise. They had been around since 1961, the year Calvin Griffith moved his Washington Senators to Minnesota. In 1965, they had gone to the World Series powered by the batting prowess of Harmon Killebrew, Tony Oliva, and Zoilo Versalles and the arms of Jim Kaat and Mudcat Grant. In 1984, Griffith ended 65 years of family ownership when he sold the team to Pohlad, an enormously successful local banker. That season, the team moved into its new indoor home, the Metrodome. Three years later, in 1987, led by manager Tom Kelly and all-stars Kirby Puckett, Jeff Reardon, Kent Hrbek, Gary Gaetti, and Frank Viola, the Twins beat the St. Louis Cardinals for the World Series Championship. Greenberg's call came only a few months after the seventh and deciding game. Why was Pohlad interested in selling? It wasn't a question so much as a riddle. And, as I write this, it seems clear that he was playing games, just as he has been since Major League Baseball announced its intentions to undergo "contraction" by eliminating teams. Pohlad, apparently, instantly offered up his franchise, hoping for a hefty buyout. But back then, Pohlad seemed like just another self-interested owner looking for a willing buyer, and I was only too flattered to get involved.

I wondered what I'd do with the information and the opportunity until I read an in-flight magazine article about superstar golfer Jack Nicklaus. The Golden Bear had won his last Masters title, at the age of 46, the day after my daughter Katie was born. I knew that he had gone into business in Palm Beach—Jack Nicklaus/Golden Bear International, designing golf courses and pursuing other development opportunities. But the article also mentioned he was a baseball fan, something I didn't know. Was he enough of a fan to become the owner of a major league team?

I made my usual "You don't know me, but" call to his offices, and spoke to Dick Bellinger, Nicklaus's business chief of staff. I said I had some information to present to Jack, and that I would like to come to see him. Bellinger said, "You can't see him now, but you can see me."

At our meeting I told him, in confidence, that the Minnesota Twins were for sale, and that I thought Jack would be a perfect buyer. Bellinger said that Jack had never been involved in anything that large before, but seemed intrigued. I couldn't guarantee that Pohlad would sell the team to him, but I could assure a meeting. When I left Golden Bear that day, it was with a good feeling. I was certain I'd get a call soon from Jack.

The call came from Bellinger. "Jack is interested," he said. "This is the right time for him to branch out." I told Buffman this could be the right match. Even more than Billy Cunningham in the case of the new Miami Heat, Nicklaus brought household name recognition and credibility. He ranked far above Arnold Palmer, Ben Hogan, and Sam Snead in number of major golf titles, and exuded a Midwestern wholesomeness.

Even though we had not yet met Jack, I led a delegation on his behalf to Minneapolis in the spring of 1988. Pohlad, who was even then elderly and frail-looking, hobbled into the conference room with a cane and sat down with us. He shook hands with Buffman and the others, and then said, "My number is $62.5 million. You guys seem like the right guys. I've always been a fan of Jack Nicklaus. And I'm a good golfer." Pohlad could hardly move. But his ego was in no way handicapped. I asked him if the franchise was portable. He explained that he still had a few years left on lease at the Metrodome, and this could be an impediment to moving the team elsewhere, "but you never know."

He said, "Before I make a commitment to you, I of course need to meet with Jack, too." Pohlad then got up from his chair, thanked us for coming, and limped out of the room. When we returned on the plane from Minnesota that night, I said to our group, "This was the best meeting we could have anticipated. You can't expect a prominent Minnesota banker to advocate moving the franchise, but the fact that he didn't shut the door is a good thing. Perhaps the only way to get in the game now, and Jack has to know this, is to buy an existing franchise like this one, sit on it, and wait for the opportunity to move it." Franchises have historically been mobile. The Dodgers and Giants, of course, are classic cases, but the phenomenon was around long before the migrations from New York to California—ever since the invention of professional games, when owners first conceived the idea of seeking greener markets. Had you been a National League fan, for example, in 1876 you might have rooted for the Hartford Dark Blues or the Louisville Grays. And of course in the century that followed there were moves aplenty: Philadelphia Athletics to Kansas City Athletics to Oakland Athletics. St. Louis Browns to Baltimore Orioles. Boston Braves to Milwaukee Braves to Atlanta Braves. Washington Senators to Minnesota Twins. And now, in our case, the Twins looked to be again ready to load the van. The scenario reflected that of a hit film of that year, *Major League,* in which the Indians' owner stripped her club of talent in order to lose regularly, discourage fans, and ultimately move to Miami. It doesn't work that way; but then almost nothing in baseball franchises works in predictable fashion. Clearly, we all needed to think we would be happy in Minnesota, just in case the franchise wasn't portable, or that no suitable stadium plan emerged in Miami.

The wall around Nicklaus was still up. One of Golden Bear's executives, Tom Peterson, said, "Jack wants this done secretly. If it ever got out he would have to deny it. Jack doesn't get involved in failures—he wants this thing to be a sure thing before he would attach his name to it." When we dropped Peterson off, I told Buffman that we needed to all meet and to talk this out.

On June 22, 1988, we sat down with Jack for the first time. All of his people were sitting around the table by the time he made a late appearance, dressed in shorts—he had just come in off of his own practice tee. He was pleasant, and I was excited. I started to explain the history of South Florida sports to date. But he interrupted me.

"We don't have time to hear about your accomplishments. Let's assume we'll work together. Just tell me about the deal." I explained that Jack would have to put down only a portion of the purchase price because hefty credit lines from banks would be available. Franchises are worth a lot—historically, they haven't gone down in value. A major loan was a certainty. He would only need $10 million of his own funds. Buffman would come up with several million more, and the banks would do the rest. Jack said, "I don't like to get into investments where my limited partners are not substantially committed." This was code for the idea that he'd be lending his name only to the project, and he wouldn't be putting out any cash. Why would the Golden Bear have to risk anything, after all? His very name would assure success. Let others take the risk.

Jack was different from what I had seen of him on television. He was cordial, but matter of fact. He said all the right things from a business point of view, and he spoke in a supremely confident, off the cuff way. He said at the end, looking at me, "I want to get to know you better. Please feel free to spend more time with me." He didn't say that to Buffman.

I made my first visit to Jack's house in North Palm Beach, in a development called "Lost Tree Village," where there is a practice putting green and three impeccably manicured grass tennis courts, a practice sand trap—all of it in the care of a full-time agronomist. Steve Nick-

laus, Jack's son, and I played tennis, and he killed me, 6–2, 6–1, although there were some questionable calls. It was one of the first times
in my life I accepted line calls that were way out. We also played nine
holes of golf. Steve shot 37 and was upset. I shot 48, displaying my
usual (at the time) penchant for getting my money's worth on the
course, swinging more often than my opponent. He said, "My dad likes
you very much. His business is very important to him. And you guys
should spend more time together. So come whenever you want. But
come by yourself." The message clearly was: We don't want to deal directly with Buffman, who, it was implied, was not to be trusted because
he was a theater producer and promoter.

In a Case of Ethics, Support the Boss—Sort of

In July, we got word from the Twins that our offer to purchase was in
order, and Carl Pohlad was comfortable with it, pending a meeting
with Jack. A week later, I brokered a conference call between Nicklaus
and Pohlad. I warned Nicklaus that Pohlad liked to talk, and to "be prepared for that."

Nicklaus said, "Hi, this is Jack." Then Pohlad spent ten minutes talking golf. He said, "I've been taking lessons. But I need a new driver. I hit
the ball into the woods too much. Hopefully you'll give me a few point-
ers." Jack's eyes rolled.

He scribbled a note to me: "Can I stop listening and start talking?"

I shook my head, and whispered, "No—just set up a meeting." The
two went back and forth ten times, talking about their respective
schedules and how important they each were. They were already into
October in their calendars. I butted in on the conference call. "Can we
move this deal forward? Can we meet on a weekend?" I thought Jack
would kill me. He thought a weekend was an invitation to Pohlad to
say, "Let's play golf." Jack wanted a strictly business meeting. Pohlad
suggested getting together the following Saturday in Chicago. "I've got
to give a speech there. Thankfully, my hip is acting up, or I'd give you a
good game."

I said to myself, "Thankfully indeed."

Jack brought a new, customized driver with him to Chicago—an offer of good faith. Pohlad said, "Thanks very much. I'll call you when I'm well enough to use it." Then Jack said, "I want to own a baseball team, and I want to own it in South Florida, but Rick told me I can't buy this team conditioned on that, and he's advised me to take the risk." Pohlad said, "We should have a deal shortly."

Afterward, Jack put his arm around me. "You did a great job, whether or not we buy the Twins. I'll be talking to you soon about another idea I have."

By August I could see my relationship with Buffman deteriorating at an increased pace. I was in the office one day and heard him say to one of his bankers that he personally had found Jack Nicklaus, and that Jack was going to put in all the money for a baseball franchise. At the time, this was not our understanding, and Jack, I knew, didn't want the news out. I also understood that Buffman was going to try to find other money sources, since he didn't have as much as he gave the impression he had. Now, I saw how he was going to come up with his piece—by promoting the Nicklaus angle. This, it turned out, put me squarely into an ethical quandary.

Nicklaus called and asked if I was "comfortable" with Buffman's capital, and wanted to know how much he came up with for the Heat. I was clearly not at all comfortable. I had begun to suspect that Buffman was much more talk than bank account. That surely was the case in the matter of the Heat. Ted Arison had provided the bulk of the cash. Still, Buffman was paying my salary. On the other hand, I knew that these quandaries happen for a reason, and I had to think this through. The Buffman/Horrow era was ending. Jack was my bridge to other things. How could I take that bridge without burning what was behind me? I said to Jack, "Do your own due diligence and come up with your own conclusions."

I met with my old mentor, Parker Thomson. He could provide some clarity, and, now that many of the amphitheatre projects were on autopilot, perhaps he could negotiate a way to get me out of Buffman's enterprise gracefully. Working with a promoter without capital made no sense—I might as well go out on my own and raise capital myself. I had no idea if I could do it, but now was the time to try. Parker negotiated a "step down package," meaning I would still do some consulting with Buffman and if the baseball deal happened we would share in it, but that I was basically on my own. For the severance package, Buffman, despite earlier assurances, refused to acknowledge any interest for me in the Miami Heat. After some tough negotiation, I ended up with one-third of one percent of the purchase price—a symbolic $30,000. (The Heat now is worth an estimated $180 million.) Clearly, I would never make this mistake again.

One of my first independent moves was to capitalize on old law school connections. I met with the dean of Harvard, who approved a new sports law class that would start the next year. I had been badgering Jim Vorenberg (my former professor) to start the class. It would be taught by Paul Weiler, a full-time faculty member, but I would appear a few times each fall semester and be called the "Visiting Expert." We never talked compensation. I still teach the class each fall and the pay doesn't come close to covering travel expenses. But it gives me a chance to sharpen my arguments in front of bright and skeptical students.

Though I was nearly out of Buffman's door, we were together, or almost together, on a few occasions. Zev, his wife Vilma, Terri, and I went to the first exhibition game of the Miami Heat in the fall of 1988, played in Broward County. It was, of course, a celebratory night, even if the Heat lost to Seattle 116–97. The game was something of a backdrop to the full-court credit-taking. Zev did not sit in the seats very long. He constantly gave interviews, and passionately accepted all congratulations without going out of his way to point out that he had not been alone in the process. I was there as a fan, and somehow wanted to be more than that, but I understood I couldn't be.

When the first game was played at the Miami Arena, Cleveland beat the Heat 96–71, and Zev and his gang were in their own special courtside seats. Edwin Pope wrote a nice article for the next day's paper, basically calling it my arena, and saying the citizens of South Florida shouldn't forget what I had done (even if Zev did).

The rift was clear now. And then the *Herald* ran a story about the holes in Buffman's finances. Jack Nicklaus called and said, "You handled this professionally. I knew you couldn't say much when I asked you about him."

Not long after, his man Bellinger called, and we made a golf date. I met him at Admirals Cove in Jupiter, a Golden Bear Enterprises course. He shot a 75, and I shot a 94. I like to think I was playing client golf—making myself look foolish for the greater good. But in 1989 I was simply terrible at the game. I didn't practice. My swing was too quick, even though I had a horrendous pause at the top of my backswing. I wasn't a believer in taking lessons to get better. I had never taken lessons in business, so why take them in this game? (In time, I changed my mind about this, and am glad I did—now I bury my clients. They've got to know how confident I am in everything, even on the links.)

In the dining room at Admirals Cove, Bellinger said, "Jack is interested in diversifying his business—can you do any more than just build arenas?"

I said, "I'm going to teach a Harvard Law course. We've obviously been trying to get the Twins together. I can do whatever you're thinking of asking me to do. I think I'm a supreme generalist." I had no idea what I was talking about.

He nodded in all the right places. "I can't tell you what we're up to, but I'll call you later."

The Name on the Line

It was a route I'd taken many times before over many summers. I flew to Boston, rented a car, drove up Interstate 95 through Portsmouth, New Hampshire, and Portland, Maine, through little towns called Naples and Harrison, and then through the place that we as children called Four Corners, to Island Pond. I stopped at the end of the pavement, took down the chain that blocked the path to the dirt road, and then drove a hundred yards more to the center of old Camp Chickawah. "Old" because it was no longer a camp, no longer a summer getaway for boys from Manhattan and Miami. Now, it was just the suggestion of a magical place. The cabins that housed a dozen campers each were still there. So was the soccer field, though overgrown, and the meeting house, where we chose up sides and plotted strategies.

Camp Chickawah had been a place where I saw things clearly for the first time. Through the years, as I moved along in my career, I came back to it again and again to review the past and decide on the future.

I was 12 years old the first time I made the trip, and had been away from home only once—a disastrous week the previous summer at a camp near Chicago, my mother's hometown. I was homesick and miserable. This would be just as bad, I was certain. The Maine countryside was foreign—all those hills, woods, and lakes. Nothing like Miami, where any incline above 10 feet can be referred to as a mountain, and is invariably man-made.

The first face I saw was that of the senior counselor, Mickey Saltman, who made it a special point to meet me at the bus, to sense the wariness in my eyes, and to say, "We'll take good care of you here." It was as if he knew that I was a loner, somebody much more comfortable with my boxes of souvenirs and box scores than with 150 rowdies. It was as if Mickey knew the answer to the question I hadn't even yet formulated: What's the point of doing something worthwhile if my father wasn't there to see it? "We'll take good care of you"—it's a phrase I remember distinctly. He kept his promise. I wasn't forced to go out every minute with the boys and play every game. I could receive my daily subscription of the *Miami Herald* and spend an hour or two alone in the cabin transferring published box scores to my own forms.

I thought about Mickey as I returned to the old place. About how he became a surrogate father to me, how he celebrated my eventual emergence as the baseball team's hard-hitting catcher. I remembered playing fiercely competitive Scrabble games with him over the many years I worked as a counselor there, and after that, when I returned as just a friend and an alumnus in search of peace. I was on a visit to camp when he told me my mother was on the telephone; she had the news that I had just been accepted to Harvard Law School. Mickey was as excited as I was. Years later, he served as my best man when Terri and I were married.

He and Camp Chickawah always represented sanity and calm in a frantic life. By the summer after my Miami triumph, the camp was in transition (it eventually became an escape for girls), and Mickey was on his way to a new job in Texas. But for me it remained a place of clarity. Now, I could see that all the decisions I had made in the last few years were leading to one obvious conclusion: that I could do this on my own if I put aside conventional expectations and the idea of public adulation. Yes, I wanted credit. Any person with a healthy ego does. But I understood that credit was not the right goal. And that there is something else that drives pioneers.

I walked the bases at the old baseball field. When I finished the tour of the infield, I crouched in the way I had crouched behind the batter's box a thousand times at Camp Chickawah. But instead of a baseball I took a pen out of my pocket. I drew the first logo for a new company. Home plate now read "Horrow Sports Ventures."

CHAPTER 5

The House That
Jack Nicklaus Built

Success is a consequence and must not be a goal.

GUSTAVE FLAUBERT

Bears hibernate, even golden bears. I didn't hear from Nicklaus for a while, which was fine. There were other opportunities to seek, other lessons to learn in the meantime. One of them was that self-imposed poverty can lead to a viable business and to an income far exceeding anything I had imagined. All objective measures indicate that I shouldn't have accepted Al Rosen's paltry offer to consult for the San Francisco Giants.

Rosen, who grew up in a neighborhood near the Orange Bowl and graduated from Miami High, went on to a brief but brilliant Major League Baseball career with the Cleveland Indians. In 1953, he came within a base hit of winning the Triple Crown, and was named the American League's Most Valuable Player. When his career on the field ended, he found fruitful work in front offices, and now was the Giants general manager.

The team trained in Arizona, where Rosen read in the newspaper about the new amphitheatre and how it came to be built. He called to ask if I wanted to do "modest" consulting for the Giants, to help the team get public funding for a new spring training facility in Scottsdale.

When we met, Rosen seemed enthusiastic in every way but one. He offered payment of $5,000. This was not for each month, but for everything, no matter how long the process took. And no expenses paid. I knew that if I were to take this deal, I would actually lose money. So I took it.

In my case, I had a backup. Jobs that I had begun for Buffman had to be finished—and I would be paid for those. But I knew that if word ever got out about the Giants deal my new business would be compromised. So I inserted a clause in the contract that under no circumstances were the Giants—or I—to divulge the payment arrangement. Down the line, when asking another client for real money, this clause would prove useful. For now, we settled on payment far below my market value. It was an investment I had no choice but to make.

I knew I had to make good on the Giants project, no matter what they were paying me. It would lead to other opportunities that would enhance the fledgling Horrow Sports Ventures. I went off to Scottsdale, where the city council approved putting the Giants spring training stadium on the ballot. I was then, and am now, very particular on how to present a referendum to voters. I insist that the wording be precise, and the presentation positive. In this case, we were pushing a resort tax, with the idea (as in Miami) of having the tourists carry most of the financial burden. I pitched the Giants on providing the rest—making a commitment to developing the area around the ballpark to encourage baseball-related retail. That way, voters would clearly see that the team was taking a risk, and that all parties were in this together, sharing the burden. Moreover, I argued that with a new ballpark, retail development was inevitable. Why shouldn't the Giants benefit from it?

The referendum passed—as usual, in a squeeze. And three years later, Scottsdale Stadium, in the heart of the historic district, opened to great fanfare and favorable reviews. It fit the landscape and cityscape— adorned as it is with turn-of-the-century lamps, framed antique baseball gloves, and sidewalk bricks in the shape of home plate. Fans particularly like the earthen berm seating. They can spread blankets on the lawn and enjoy a picnic as they watch the rites of spring unfold.

Whenever I argue on behalf of economic development, blankets on the lawn and an air of community celebration can get lost amid the numbers. Critics will point out—they never fail to—that there are many ways to calculate and interpret numbers, and that, in their view, these infrastructure projects aren't as economically viable and valuable as portrayed. But, even if their arithmetic is accurate—which it isn't—they leave out the intangibles. They don't grasp the value of community spirit like that in Scottsdale, or in dozens of cities across the country where a sense of camaraderie and optimism is pervasive.

And, if you can't always calculate a project in dollars and cents, it is also true that you can't calculate the value of your effort that way when you make an investment. For me, the Scottsdale Stadium effort was the key to my future path. Once more I was behind the scenes. But insiders noticed. And within a year, my "contribution" to the San Francisco Giants began to reap its rewards.

Payoff of the "No Tell" Clause

The first dividend from the investment I made in the Giants was instant. I got a call at my Phoenix hotel from Hank Peters, then the general manager of the Cleveland Indians. He said Rosen had spoken in reverent terms about what I had done for the Giants in arranging new spring training facilities. Peters had the same problem. The Indians, who had traditionally trained at the old and dusty Hi Corbett Field in Tucson, needed a better place. The new owner, Dick Jacobs, hoped to move from Arizona to Florida. Peters asked, "Do you have time to help us, too?"

I was coming in prequalified, thanks to Rosen's glowing recommendation. So I said, "I'm extremely busy." I was being coy, playing hard to get. Jacobs, from what I had read, had deep pockets.

Three weeks later, I went to Hank Peters's office at the old Municipal Stadium on the shore of Lake Erie. The lobby featured photographs of Tribe stars of the past—the distant past, including Bob Feller, Early Wynn, Earl Averill, Tris Speaker, Bob Lemon, Larry Doby, Lou Boudreau, Leroy "Satchel" Paige, and, not incidentally, Al "Flip" Rosen.

Peters and I spent about three hours talking about goals and objectives. He was high on Dick Jacobs, and on the future of the team. He offered details of the plans for a new stadium about a mile away on East Ninth Street, a state-of-the-art facility, designed by HOK, the same firm used by the Orioles at Camden Yards, the downtown stadium that would open for the 1992 season. Jacobs Field, as the facility would eventually be called, would represent Cleveland's return after several humiliating decades to baseball eminence, and once and for all banish the term "cavernous" and "empty" from stadium references. The problem now, he said, was the team needed, and needed soon, a suitable companion facility in Florida for its spring work.

I told Peters about the sales tax–rebate legislation I had gotten Jeb Bush, then Florida's secretary of commerce, to approve legislatively for new facilities in Florida. This was while serving in my $1-a-year job as special counsel to the Florida Sports Foundation. I could propose the tax-rebate model for funding a spring training stadium. Why not? Baseball is industrial relocation, isn't it? A new Chevrolet plant has bricks and mortar and it holds the promise of new jobs, and so does a ballpark.

We talked about some of the sites that could be available. Traditionally, Florida towns sought Major League teams as tourism and image boosts. Some, including Daytona Beach, were in the market for a team.

Peters asked, "How much are the Giants paying you?" I had expected the question, of course, and was ready with a firm reply: "I am bound by a confidentiality agreement with them not to divulge the fee." Peters didn't press me further, and he took me to see Dick Jacobs at his office in the Terminal Tower. This was the headquarters of the Richard E. Jacobs Group, owner and manager of 38 regional shopping malls in 15 states, making it the largest such firm in the country. But when I got to the penthouse, I found anything but a penthouse attitude. Jacobs was no stuffed shirt.

He conducted one of the shortest and most congenial business meetings I'd ever had. When I started my presentation, Dick interrupted me. "Hank tells me we need to get this done, and you're the guy. How much does it take to buy half of your time?" I said, "My business plan calls for a $200,000 yearly base, so half my time is $100,000." I was hoping and praying now that Rosen had kept his mouth shut about my measly $5,000 for his whole deal. But I had nothing to lose at the time. I was high-balling. Besides, Rosen never asked me for half of my time. I didn't think the number was outrageous. Had Rosen revealed the secret, I would be laughed out of the room.

Jacobs said, "That's a great number. We'll pay you $5,000." He paused. And then said, "per month."

Time Isn't for Sale—Vision Is

As the phone rang, and as I signed up more clients, I began to understand that I couldn't use traditional math anymore. It wasn't time I was selling. It was vision, and expertise. That is, it would make no sense to turn in time sheets as a lawyer would. People were hiring me to make a large promise that no one else could make, and then to deliver on that promise. Period. I didn't have to justify my time. I just had to work miracles, and (perhaps almost as important to some) to show up for meetings.

I also learned a variation on the old axiom, "When you need something to be done, ask a busy person." The more you do, the more in demand you'll be, the higher the price you can ask. In my case, there was another benefit. I still had two overarching goals. One, of course, was to build my business. But equally important, at least from a spiritual point of view, was the necessity of bringing Major League Baseball to Miami. It just so happened that these two notions were entirely compatible. Everything I was doing in my new business contributed toward the second goal. For example, the Caribbean World Series, which I produced in 1990 and 1991, gave the United States a chance to see how supportive Miami could be to baseball that wasn't quite up to Major League standards. That is, we had to play the games in the Orange Bowl—a football field, which made it impossible to have sensible outfield fences (if you could poke a fastball 280 feet to left, you had a homer). Still, we drew huge crowds.

Moreover, my new role as "part-time" president of the nascent Senior Baseball League gave me access to the most powerful man in the sport. I wanted Major League Baseball to be a backer of the Senior League, and for that I needed the support of then Commissioner Fay Vincent.

Vincent, a former movie executive, had been brought into the league's headquarters by his predecessor, Bart Giamatti, who himself had left the presidency of Yale. Both Giamatti and Vincent were smart, but there was a difference. Giamatti was a risk taker and a person who fought hard for what he believed. His hard stand against Pete Rose, banishing him from the game for apparent gambling violations, proved very stressful. Giamatti died of a heart attack not long afterward.

Vincent lacked Giamatti's vision. I could see this in his reaction to my proposal. The Senior Baseball League had been an inspired idea (not mine), because it brought together big-name ballplayers who could still play the game, even if they'd lost a step or two (and 20 or 30 feet on their fly balls). Many were eager to spend the cold months in the sunshine of Florida, to pick up a few bucks and some adulation, and (for some) pick up again with their former spring training mistresses.

The proposal I made to Vincent would clearly have been in the interest of Major League Baseball. I argued that it would promote the game in general and spring training in particular. It would be a way for Major League teams to connect with their history. In the case of the Gold Coast Suns of Pompano Beach, for example, the team was composed almost entirely of former Baltimore Orioles. Bradenton had the Pittsburgh Pirates. The Winter Haven Sun Sox were the old Red Sox. And there would be intangible benefits, too. But Vincent declined the opportunity with the fatal response, "That's interesting." Interesting is what people say when they want no part of it. Even so, the effort had kept alive the buzz about Florida as a baseball destination. I now had access to baseball's upper echelon. I felt the momentum was leading to an inevitable conclusion.

We still had, of course, Minnesota's Carl Pohlad on the hook, and he had an existing franchise that could be bought. But Pohlad was not returning my phone calls. I began to suspect that he wasn't sincere in these negotiations, that his real motive had been to become friends with Jack Nicklaus, and for Jack to teach him how to hit the ball into the fairway once in a while. But if Nicklaus's bid was dead, there were others in the works.

In May 1988, I gave a speech to the Sports Lawyers Association in Phoenix. I got a call from an accountant representing Morty Davis, an investment banker who founded the D. H. Blair Company and was worth about $500 million at the time. Davis, I was told, wanted to be involved in the baseball expansion process; he might be interested in creating a franchise for Miami. Indeed, he was. My dream was moving closer to reality. Not only did I feel that it was inevitable that my hometown would at last be classified among Major League cities, but it seemed, from the circumstances, that the name Rick Horrow would appear among the list of owners. Surely I could get an equity stake, if Morty Davis were successful.

At the time, however, it was in my interest to keep an actual team owner happy, and so I scouted several communities in Florida on behalf of Dick Jacobs and the Indians, and came up with seven possibilities, looking all the time for a place that would meet Jacobs's expectations for public money. "Get as much as you can," he had instructed me. The short list included Winter Haven, which was about to lose the Boston Red Sox (to Fort Myers), Ocala, Homestead (where I had been working on a public facility), and Citrus County, north of Tampa.

On a trip to Florida to scout around, Jacobs was intrigued by the two most remote locations. In Citrus County, he figured the Indians could be a big fish in a small pond. In Homestead, he was near Miami. But most of the Major League training sites were clumped in the middle of the state. As much as Jacobs liked Homestead, he worried about the minimum of two hours in a bus it would take to travel to a road game, or whether it would make sense to take the city up on its offer to let the team use some old DC-3s.

Our other option was also fraught with difficulty. The Citrus County Commission insisted on a 30-year lease if it was going to come up with public money to build a stadium. There would be no easy answer to spring training.

The Well-Placed (and Painful) Apology

It would be misleading to say that I wasn't on occasion in some trouble. Sometimes I could see the trouble coming, and sometimes I was blindsided. My work producing La Serie De Caribe (The Caribbean World Series) was an example.

In the opening game at the Orange Bowl, the Dominican Republic beat Venezuela, 9–7. Before the game, a *USA Today* reporter walked the field with me and asked, "How can you play here? This is a football field. How do you think people will feel about baseball here?"

I said, "We've gone to great lengths to prepare the field. Besides, these guys play in pretty humble circumstances back home, and they don't mind." The next morning I flew to Boston to teach my first Harvard class. When I got to Cambridge, I picked up a copy of *USA Today*. It detailed the Dominican Republic's triumph, and it also had a piece pointing out that the director of the series called Caribbean stadiums "cow pastures." My Harvard professorial debut was shot to shit. I worried about what awaited me back in Miami. In fact, there was a call on my answering machine from the head of Latin American baseball, inviting me to an "inquisition" at the Shawnee Hotel in Sunny Isles the next morning at 10. "You come or else," he said. I had intended to have dinner with my co-instructor, Paul Weiler, celebrating the birth of a new course at Harvard. Instead, I caught the night flight.

The next morning, I walked into the lobby of the hotel and noticed dozens of men, smoking cigars and talking in animated fashion. When they saw me, they stopped, and seemed to back away. The meeting room seemed cold and humorless. Before we began, I was asked if I wanted an interpreter. I thought they would offer a blindfold, too. The program called for me to be introduced by the chairman. Ordinarily that would be fine. But not in this case, where after a heated Spanish conversation (which I wouldn't understand) I'd have to dig myself out of a deep hole.

I knew my only chance was to take control. So I grabbed the microphone. "I have nothing but the highest respect for my Latin comrades. It would be silly of me to disparage this organization and all who are connected to it. I didn't mean to show any disrespect. Ours is a wonderful event." I apologized for even getting myself in such a position, but I also placed responsibility on the "overzealous, lazy, disrespectful" American media for inaccurate reporting. It was an easy argument to make to this crowd. One of the things Latins agreed on was the bias they saw in the media. Media from all over Latin America had descended on Miami to cover the baseball series, but the *Herald* treated it as something of a second-rate event, paying little attention. At the end of persuasive speeches, I usually look for someone to say, "Attaboy, Rick." But here, no one spoke. On the other hand, no one lynched me. I was happy to get out alive.

Even with all this, the series had been useful. It was something of a financial and sporting success. It had provided a public demonstration that baseball, even in such extreme circumstances, could draw in Miami. I could now use this tournament as a promotional tool. And I would continue to learn that every triumph—even one in which you eat humble pie—can lead to a victory somewhere else.

Fair Warning

In May 1989, Dick Bellinger called from Jack Nicklaus/Golden Bear International. He suggested a "fundamental change in what you do with your life." I wasn't interested in a fundamental change, and was not eager to have someone like Bellinger dictate it. Still, I was willing to meet, and remained intrigued by Jack. A few days later, I was at the Golden Bear offices.

Bellinger said, "Jack would like to get into the sports agency business." He wanted to represent many of the biggest stars in sports. It seemed to me a crazy idea, driven entirely by the motivation of making a fortune. Sports agents were beginning to become stars of the sports pages. Players were commanding millions in contracts, and agents were getting a hefty percentage just to sign the deal. Jack could see the dollar signs. But it is a hard, competitive business. This offer felt funny, and I asked Bellinger for a few days to think it over. I'd be adding another half-time job—my seventh or eighth. And it wouldn't be doing what I knew how to do.

Two weeks later, I met Bellinger at Le Bistro, in North Palm Beach, in the uncharacteristic position of trying to talk someone out of spending money. I presented a memo that listed the following five warnings:

1. Jack would be dealing with kids half his age, who make twice as much money, and who don't respect him.

2. You may have to use Jack more than he wants to get targeted athletes. Play golf, be on his boat.

3. Agents don't have long-term contracts. They're subject to the fickle attitudes of punk millionaires.

4. It's not as lucrative as golf course design—where Jack gets a million and a half just by showing up, using his name, making a few keen observations about the landscape, and then handing over the real work to a technical team that would finalize the design. (Nicklaus, Gary Player, Davis Love, and Arnold Palmer have become experts at this.)

5. I'm not prepared to register as an agent, or run this business as an agent. We could hire people who do this. I could manage it, as well as manage other things. But I'd never be full-time. I'd roll this into my company. I would consider Jack and Golden Bear a client, and we could work out a fee.

Bellinger took this all in, admitted he hadn't thought about some of these things, and said he'd present it all to Jack, and I'd hear from them. Quite apart from my usual procedure—pressing for answers and providing arguments for signing a deal—it was all right with me if Bellinger took his time. Maybe it all would go away.

Fruits of Exposure

Sometimes you wonder why you put yourself out for what seems like no reason. Maybe you know that someone out there is reading or watching. My new business's beginnings were the direct result of publicity I got in Arizona, and of Al Rosen reading that publicity. Now, I was appearing on many local television shows, pushing baseball for Miami, without always getting the kind of solid response I'd hoped for. But I knew—and I still believe this—that every effort contributes to momentum and eventually yields fruit.

It wasn't long after I made one of my routine bring-baseball-to-Miami appearances when I got a call out of the blue from Mike Schmidt, the Hall of Fame third baseman of the Phillies, who asked, "Could I be useful to your baseball group?" I told Schmidt about Morty Davis, and it seemed to me that the former baseball great could play the Billy Cunningham role—the well-known sports hero—in our effort. Schmidt was aware that Cunningham, without risking his own fortune, had been made prosperous by the Heat deal. Davis, on the other hand, could use star quality.

Davis agreed to pay me to help with a formal application to Major League Baseball, to introduce him to baseball people, and to lend my name to the effort. I also worked out a protection clause—I wouldn't be burned this time. If a franchise were awarded to the Davis group, I would get an equity share. I also lined up others who I thought should be part of the group, and could lend credibility, such as Maurice Ferre, who, though he was no longer in public office, had strong name recognition and a large following.

Amid all of this Dick Bellinger called, but not with a reaction from Nicklaus about my concerns on entering the agency business. He asked me instead to fly to Cincinnati to meet with Jack's old friend and advisor, Charlie Mechem. This, apparently, was part of an approval exercise. If Mechem thought I was qualified, Jack would think so, too. I didn't relish this application process but following through was important. Mechem would be a good contact.

He was cordial, old world, charming. He had been counsel to the Taft law firm in Cincinnati, and had an extensive record of local activism. For one thing, he had helped Paul Brown found the Cincinnati Bengals. I told Mechem my thoughts about Jack getting involved in the agency business. I knew it wasn't what he wanted to hear, but he seemed grateful. At the end of our conversation, he said, "You and I will have conversations down the road." As it eventually turned out, we had a lot more than conversations.

When I got back from Cincinnati, Bellinger called and said, "It's time for you to meet Jack." I thought, "I've already met Jack." This was almost a summons. Bellinger wanted me to present my perceptions about the agency business. I had outlined the terms already, and Bellinger said that Jack had seen them. But the meeting was perfunctory, and Jack didn't seem informed at all. He extended his hand and said, "Welcome to our family." I was pleased, but perplexed that we didn't discuss business terms.

With Bellinger, I worked out an interim consulting agreement for six months, at $8,000 per month, to help develop the structure of Golden Bear Sports Management. It was my biggest retainer, but I wouldn't give up Horrow Sports Ventures. I couldn't. My business was working well, and the agency business was not in my long-term strategy.

Unsportsmanlike Conduct

By this time, however, it was clear that I couldn't do all this work myself. So I opened an office in Miami, renting space from the law firm of Fine and Jacobson, and hired a young lawyer as an assistant. He was the first in a string of people I recruited over the years who showed promise but, in the end, couldn't get the deals done.

It would have been useful to have an assistant to deal with the Nicklaus agency business, but I was stuck with it, and began to introduce Jack and his people to members of the sports hierarchy, including Fay Vincent and Donald Fehr. Dick Bellinger pressured me to move my base of operations from Miami to North Palm Beach. I said that I would in time, but reminded him that I had other work to do. This annoyed him. And, for the first time, it occurred to me that he had sold me to Jack as a full-time employee rather than a consultant.

Moving was not convenient. Our baseball group was working on a tight deadline. We had about 45 days to make a presentation to Major League Baseball's expansion committee. Hardly a lot of time when everything rides on how well you do it. Nicklaus himself seemed to be dropping out as a franchise buyer because the Twins' Pohlad had been unresponsive. Suddenly, however, real competition for a Miami franchise cropped up.

Most significantly, Wayne Huizenga, co-founder of Waste Management and then founder of Blockbuster Video, got into the act. He already had an equity stake in the Dolphins, the result of a cash loan to Joe Robbie, who was strapped for money after he built his stadium. Huizenga's idea was to bring baseball to the home of the Dolphins. Robbie, for all of his folderol, had at least had the foresight to build a football stadium in a square form—a model that would work better for baseball than the old donut-shaped facilities because most of the seats would be closer to the action. It still was far from ideal and, in the long run, a real baseball stadium would have to be built to ensure franchise stability (something that has not happened). Still, Huizenga's idea to bring a team to Joe Robbie Stadium set off new competition and infighting about how to make South Florida's best case for baseball.

Our Davis group introduced Mike Schmidt with great fanfare, and made hay out of the inclusion of Maurice Ferre and then Garth Reeves, publisher of *The Miami Times,* the city's African-American newspaper. But then Abel Holtz, a businessman who had his own ideas about owning a franchise, appeared before the Sports Authority and asked for that group's single endorsement. I showed up and argued that the body shouldn't endorse anybody. "You should get a stadium built for whoever gets the bid." In the end, the authority held off on saying anything.

My idea was to coordinate the presentation for South Florida baseball. That is, instead of presenting it mainly as a competition between groups, to pool our resources to be sure we impressed league executives generally, and then worry about how to award the franchise. This was right out of the playbook when we were going after a basketball franchise for Miami. I called Joe Robbie to see if he was interested in the concept, but he wouldn't take the call. He asked the interested parties to meet with him the next day—that way, he could control the outcome.

In the end, there was little in the way of agreement. The Holtz group said it would play in Miami, and only in Miami. Huizenga and Robbie, of course, were committed to north Dade. Our group didn't care, as long as we got baseball.

The Miami contingent met at the Parker Meridien in New York. Our hope was that the three groups would each make a presentation, but talk only about themselves and the value of Miami, and minimize any negative portrayal of the other competitors. Fat chance. Still, we held up our part of the bargain. The Davis contingent went first. We made an hour's presentation to the Major League Baseball owners, talking about how well capitalized we were, about Mike Schmidt's involvement, Morty Davis's money, and my record as a franchise builder. We also stressed ethnic diversity—our group was the only one of the three that included minorities. But we were respectful and didn't trash anybody.

We left the proceedings confident we had made a strong presentation, and would await word.

The Bear Market

It seemed to me that I had enough positive developments elsewhere that I could still be candid with Nicklaus about the sports agency. When the subsequent meeting with him and Bellinger finally happened, I made a formal two-hour presentation on the ups and downs of the agency business, cautioning him as I had in the memo to Bellinger about the demands it would make on him. He said he would commit to the business for four or five years, and that I could count on him. When Jack left the room, Bellinger hugged me, and said, "We got what we wanted." I wasn't sure what he meant. Then he wanted to sit down and negotiate a long-term deal with me. This seemed odd, too. We could simply extend what we had. Clearly, something was up.

Jack asked me to come to his house and play tennis with his little group of Sunday players, business associates and friends, including Dick Bellinger. I stayed afterward, and watched the Dolphins beat the Jets 17–3, while Jack talked about the game and drank beer. I thought, "I've arrived. I'm sitting in Jack Nicklaus's living room." And what a living room—more like a Hall of Fame, with all of its dozens of trophies from tournaments all around the world. So what if I missed my first Dolphins home game ever? Here I was with one of the world's biggest sports heroes talking about plans to announce Golden Bear Sports Management. It would be, for me, an almost four-year association, much of which would be fruitful, but much of which would be foreign to all I had previously worked on and prepared for. That afternoon in the Nicklaus den I didn't know—though my experience and instincts might have suggested this—that I would soon be torpedoed again and again by one of the men watching the game.

A few days later, I called Mike Schmidt, and asked him to throw out the first ball at the second Caribbean baseball championship series. He asked me for an appearance fee. I said, "Your appearance fee is you get to go out to dinner with me afterward, because I want to talk to you about something." We went to a Cuban restaurant in Little Havana. I explained about Jack Nicklaus's new agency business, and asked him if he would be interested in joining the team. Mike said, "I'd almost do it for nothing. It'll get me back to baseball. And I'd love to play golf with Jack." I figured I had my first major triumph for Jack, and a triumph that would cost very little. But what I didn't know was that it wasn't my prerogative to make excellent deals at Golden Bear.

I arranged a breakfast meeting at the City Club, and I told Dick Bellinger this was an opportunity to have Mike as an advisor, and that he might not have to pay anything to get him. But at the meeting Bellinger asked him, "How much do we need to pay you?" Schmidt said, "I need $150,000 a year." Dick said, "OK, you're on." I was stunned. This was the first indication of where the real authority rested. Afterward, I said to Bellinger, "Do we have a budget here? If we do, don't penalize me because you just spent $150,000 out of my pocket." He said, "You're insubordinate." I had no idea, until that time, that I had been working for Dick, not for Jack. I had brought Schmidt into the deal, and my payment was grief.

A Baseball Payoff

But soon, I had excellent, if bittersweet, news. I was a loser and, in the same breath, a winner. John McMullen, owner of the Astros, called from Houston. He said, "Tomorrow, the baseball owners are going to pare down the short list and choose the Huizenga group to represent Miami. Your group was brilliant, and your strategy of flexibility was brilliant, and you should be flattered, because Joe Robbie spent five minutes of his presentation before the board talking about how we shouldn't do any business with Rick Horrow. In the end, we paid no attention to that, but we had too many questions about [Morty Davis's] capital." This was McMullen's way of saying that Wayne Huizenga was worth a billion dollars, and nobody else applying for a Miami franchise had anywhere close to that. Still, the silver lining was clear enough. Big-league baseball was seeing my hometown as a logical place for expansion. It would happen after all those years of dreaming and arguing that such a thing was possible. Presumption of failure? Who even remembered it? No, I wouldn't be sitting in the owner's box at Pro Players Stadium (former Joe Robbie Stadium) when Huizenga's Florida Marlins made their debut in 1993, but I could soon buy a ticket to a game any month of the summer, and wasn't that all I had ever wished for?

For a while, things also seemed to be going well in the effort to find a new spring home for the Indians. The team's entourage received a tremendous welcome from 3,000 residents of Citrus County. A high school band played under a sign that said, "Thank you, Dick Jacobs." After I spent 48 hours negotiating a letter of intent for the move, *USA Today* ran a big story about the Indians' plans in Florida. It appeared as if the deal was done.

I went to the Citrus County armory for a public hearing on whether the county should enact a tourist tax. The meeting started at noon and ended at 4 A.M. The business leaders spoke first. There were 10 of them, all in favor of the tax, all arguing that a new Cleveland Indians spring training facility would bring jobs and big tourist dollars for the community. Then came 740 naysayers, or thereabouts, arguing into the evening and the next morning. One old man accused me of being Satan. He wadded up a dollar bill and threw it at me, and said, "That's what I think of you baseball owners." Another old man said, "Go back to Cleveland where you came from." At 3:50 in the morning, I gave a speech to the commission, arguing "You have an opportunity to bring in out-of-town money to hotels—a golden opportunity." And I fell back on an old argument. "Sometimes courageous leaders take courageous stands."

In the next weeks, however, I could see this was all for naught. Though the County Commission had backed us and approved the idea, the numbers weren't there. Financial advisors did a study that showed a 2 percent hotel tax wouldn't raise enough money to build the kind of stadium Dick Jacobs needed. The idea of being a big fish in a small pond had really appealed to him. But the owner took the news well. "See if you can cut a deal in Homestead," he said.

"Diversity" at Golden Bear

Golden Bear, meanwhile, was getting more troublesome. I attended a managers meeting that included Nicklaus at Grand Cypress in Orlando. Bellinger introduced me as someone who will register as an agent, run the new company full-time, and make the company money in the next two years. The next day, I confronted Bellinger. All three things he said, one after another, were incorrect. I wouldn't be an agent myself, surely wouldn't be full-time, and there was no way I could guarantee a profit within 24 months. I said I needed to see Jack to talk about it. Bellinger said that wasn't necessary. He said Jack knows the real deal. "This was just a show for other managers."

I said nothing about this when Jack held a golf outing and had dinner at his house for a select group of executives. What I did say was that to expand the agency business we had to be more diverse. I had just signed Cal Ripken as part of the business, so now there were two superstars connected with Golden Bear, but it was still an all-white operation. Out of 100 employees, the number of ethnic workers was zero. If the company was going to attract young black superstars it was going to have to look black and act black. Jack told me to go find a basketball guy.

I called an old friend, Ed Snider, who runs the Philadelphia Flyers, and asked for Julius Erving's home number. I called the legend known as "Dr. J," and said, "You don't know me, but I've started a sports management business for Jack Nicklaus and we'd like to talk to you about getting involved." Erving could surely give advice on how to cater to black athletes. He was interested, and we set up a time for a meeting. I was selling Erving as high-class marketing.

I brought the happy news of Erving's recruitment to Augusta, where Jack was playing the Masters. After he shot a 68, good for second place on the first day, I expected him to be in an ebullient mood, pleased with his game and with the progress of our new enterprise, and that I had finished the Ripken signing and was about to corral Dr. J. Instead, he glared at me and said, "Dick tells me you cost us a lot of money with Mike Schmidt. Are we sure you're not going to negotiate that kind of deal again?" The easy thing to say would have been, "Why don't we ask Mike what he was willing to take when I talked to him?" But that would have thrown Bellinger under the bus in Jack's presence. I liked the organization and the things I was doing. So I said, "[Bellinger and I] collaborated, and we all felt that you're going to get more return out of a motivated Mike Schmidt. But I do think it's important that Dick do the negotiation."

And so he did. He reached an agreement with Julius Erving. I later met Julius when he was doing something in Tampa, and asked him whether he thought the deal that Bellinger had negotiated with him was fair, and he said, "I'm delighted. I get $100,000 to make a call once in a while." I said to myself, "It sounds like Dick just gave away the store again."

I was befuddled by all of this, and needed some perspective. Charlie Mechem could give it to me, but it was tricky to seek it from him. Mechem, the lawyer who had originally checked me out for Golden Bear, had left Cincinnati to become commissioner of the LPGA in Daytona, and his organization was now one of my clients. (I had convinced the state of Florida to help fund a new headquarters and two golf courses through a tax-rebate plan.) When Charlie and I had dinner, I told him about Bellinger. He said, "Jack has always been a good friend but, as to his staff, you'd better watch your back." As the months went on, I could see why. And I could also see that at Golden Bear integrity had an unusual definition.

I met with Julius Erving in Palm Beach and got him into a plush office at Golden Bear. He said, "We need to do a brochure. Why don't you take some of your black staff members and be sure to include them in the pictures." He figured he could use the brochure when he visited potential black clients. But of course there were no black staff members. I said to Julius, "Part of your job is to make the organization more ethnically responsible." He said, "I got you. But I don't know if they're paying me enough." I said, "You told me they were paying you $100,000 for a few phone calls. I think we're adding one item to your scope of services."

I told Bellinger we needed the brochure quickly. When it was time for the picture session, all the executives showed up. They were all white, of course. With one exception. Here was one black guy in the middle of the group, dressed in a tie, whom I'd never met before. When I inquired about him, I was told he'd been asked to put on a tie and to pose for a photograph, and that the company had paid for an hour of his time to do this. Otherwise, his only connection with Golden Bear International was that he came by once a month to wash the windows.

To Homestead, at Last

We finally resolved the Cleveland Indians spring training dilemma. When we investigated Homestead, and saw the plans for new facilities there to be funded largely by the proceeds from a convention tax, Dick

Jacobs fell in love with the idea immediately. His baseball executives were skeptical. They still didn't like the distance the team would have to travel while on the road. But Jacobs was happy to be 20 minutes north by highway from his Ocean Reef condo. He said, "Let's do a deal here." I asked, "But how do we get around the two-hour bus ride to the closest road game?" He said, "The players shouldn't mind a couple of hours on the bus—they're making millions."

When I wrote the terms for the Homestead deal, however, I was careful to be sure I fully protected the Indians' interest. A clause near the bottom—a standard one that I was careful to be sure was included—said that the team could break its lease if the facilities were severely damaged by "an act of God." I had no idea, of course, that such a clause would have to be invoked. I am a better lawyer than meteorologist.

The Indians, as it turned out, never played in Homestead. On August 24, 1992, the most devastating natural disaster in American history—Hurricane Andrew—with winds registering up to 169 miles per hour, ripped directly through the city. Before it finished its destructive path from the Bahamas to Florida to Louisiana, Andrew destroyed 126,000 homes, 10,000 businesses, and was responsible for 23 U.S. deaths. It also demolished Homestead's beautiful new stadium. It now looked like a war zone. The bleachers were half down, the fields under water, the fences collapsed and scattered. The next spring, the Indians were obliged to break the lease and move instead to Winter Haven, which had formerly been the home of the Red Sox.

No one, of course, could have anticipated such a turn of events at the time of the signing. Quite the opposite. I had been thrilled by every prospect of Homestead as the Indians solution. In fact after the signing I went to Golden Bear headquarters and told Jack about how excited I was to finally solve the Cleveland dilemma. I could see that the news did not interest him in the slightest. In fact, he must have wondered why I had been involved at all. The next day, Jack asked Bellinger what I was doing working on other stuff. Bellinger told him that he had no idea. As far as he knew, I was supposed to be a full-time Golden Bear employee.

It got worse. At an executive committee meeting, Bellinger said to me, "You are $250,000 over budget." I said, "Well, Dick, $150,000 was Schmidt and $100,000 Erving, and we didn't have to pay either that much, and you did both deals." This was the first time I confronted him publicly.

Afterward, he was outraged. I said, "I assumed you wanted an executive committee that was free to challenge your opinions." He said, "We'll see about that."

At the next executive committee meeting, with Jack again present, I figured it was my chance to set matters straight and to present a realistic picture of the business. I said we're at a point of definition in the business because every client, as I had predicted, wants to meet the person whose name is on the sign out front. I turned to Jack. "You have to be prepared to spend more time recruiting or at least being part of these visits as you said you would." Jack was stony cold. He said, "Dick will be getting back to you." This was a horrendous way to run a meeting.

An hour later, Bellinger called me into his office and said, "How dare you confront Jack with such information without running it by me first." I said, "It was only an extension of a memo that I wrote to you and Jack over a year ago, that said the business would take some time, and that Jack would have to be personally involved. You all bought into that. I thought Jack was happy with what we've done so far. If there's a problem we'd better talk about it." He said, "I'll call you when I'm ready to talk to you. You're dismissed for now."

Another executive committee meeting was scheduled for December 1992. The day before, I got a one-sentence memo that said I wasn't invited. A few days later I went to Jack's house for tennis, and for dinner, but something had clearly changed. I hung back with him and tried to raise pressing issues. He said, "We really can't talk now. Anything about business we need you to go through Dick at the office." I wanted to say that I believed in what we were doing, and that we could make this a success. I did tell him that we had just signed Dorothy Hamill, the 1976 Olympic gold medal figure skater. I had visited her at her Palm Springs home, and found her just as charming as I had anticipated. She was eager to do our bidding—to appear at skating exhibitions for hefty fees and make endorsements (all of which would give Golden Bear a hefty cut). With her signing, Jack's enterprise would engage an audience almost as big as the one Jack had built—but in a different sport.

Sadly, Golden Bear and Jack didn't see the possibilities in the icon to icon branding. "Sounds nice," Jack said, as if figure skaters don't matter, nor all the effort it took (considerable) to recruit her.

I was summoned the next day by Bellinger. He said, "Don't you ever talk to Jack again about new clients. He's under enough pressure. He doesn't need to hear it. Any communication you do needs to be done through me."

The Last Shot

The handwriting on the wall was tall and in bold colors. I could see that this enterprise was wrong for me. For all of the prestige of being connected with Jack Nicklaus, there was a great downside: I was undermining my own personal reputation.

It had all been a ruse. That memo I wrote 14 months earlier, which I was assured he read, he had never seen. He never knew that I predicted it would take five years to make the business profitable. Never heard about how expensive it would be, or that I wouldn't be working full-time.

On February 12, 1992, I was fired. Not by Bellinger, but by Tom Peterson, one of his lieutenants. "We're restructuring Golden Bear," he said. "You're terminated. You'll be given two boxes and an hour to clean out your stuff." I said, "I'm not cleaning out anything until I can talk to Bellinger." Peterson said, "Bellinger doesn't want to talk to you. But you can talk to Jack."

I went to the house. Jack said, "I think you're a wonderful person, and lucky for us to have you here, but I can't keep you around and preserve my existing organization."

I was rumbling inside, but I responded calmly, as I always do. People expect you to be emotional and angry. I needed to convey to Jack that it might hurt him more than it hurt me. I said, "If that's the way you feel, you might want to think about not preserving your existing organization. You'd be better served to challenge your staff to answer tough questions, rather than surrounding yourself with people who tell you what you want to hear." (In fact, in the years that followed, Golden Bear ran into a good deal of trouble with the Securities and Exchange Commission. Eventually, three officers, including Bellinger, settled with the SEC after an investigation into a variety of alleged violations.)

As I left Jack's house, I felt as if I had been struck down by an old hero. Betrayal in a case like that is almost unbearable. It's one thing to face disappointment with the likes of Joe Robbie—I had no illusions about him. But Jack Nicklaus had always been a hero to me, maybe even a father figure. I was crushed. Though I made it a point never to burden Terri with any professional difficulties, I made an exception in this case, and confessed more than a few doubts. As always, she was supportive. She said this all would soon be forgotten. Well, of course, she was wrong about that—I haven't forgotten it. But she meant that I would move on, which I quickly did.

I called Charlie Mechem and said, "I hope my firing by Nicklaus doesn't affect our relationship with the LPGA." He said, "Between you and me, I don't know how you lasted as long as you did. But you'll always have a home with me." Also, I dropped the Cleveland Indians and picked up the Baltimore Orioles organization, which decided at last that it couldn't find a new spring training facility on its own. (This gig has lasted a decade, though it would have been far shorter if the anticipated move to Disney World had happened. That fell through largely because the team insisted that it control all baseball marketing efforts. Had Disney agreed to this it conceivably would have had to change the name of its hit movie *Angels in the Outfield* to *Orioles in the Outfield*.)

In the fall of 1992, I gave my last speech on sports violence at the University of Oklahoma. Something told me to go through with it, though the time for such speeches was over. Instinct again. And instinct is a great teacher. That night, one of the members in the audience was Ron Norick, the mayor of Oklahoma City. That he was there in the wake of the Nicklaus disappointment changed everything.

CHAPTER 6

Pas de Deux at Second Base

With an eye made quiet by the power of harmony,
and deep power of joy, we see into the life of things.

WILLIAM WORDSWORTH

Looking back on my Oklahoma City experience, it seems only natural that an outpost in the prairie would be the ideal place to pioneer new ideas about sports deal-making. But in 1993, I couldn't imagine this. All I knew about Oklahoma was that it's where the Sooners play football, and that Mickey Mantle and Johnny Bench were born there. The capital city was merely a new client, one I was glad to have after the Nicklaus debacle. In short order, it become much more than that. At the time I was involved in a variety of projects, including an attempt to buy the Miami Dolphins. But Oklahoma City became something of a rival to my hometown as a symbol of what could be done in desperate circumstances when people are loathe to work together. It also showed me how sports could flourish if I paid more attention, among other things, to the world of art.

My first visit had been almost precisely two years before Oklahoma City became known internationally as the target of a terrible act of terrorism, a crime that I viewed in a way that most outsiders couldn't have. I arrived at a time when the city faced a difficult, if more traditional, threat. It had always been a place of boom and bust, from the

1889 land rush when, almost overnight, 10,000 hardy souls settled on former Indian land to establish a capital city. A little more than a hundred years after its discovery, it was now in the midst of its longest bust ever. When First National, its biggest and most respected financial institution, went under, public confidence dwindled to zero. Long before that the downtown had been abandoned by major retailers. The old and luxurious Skirvin Hotel, with its grand ballroom, sat empty. As a place to reside the city was no longer attractive. Court-ordered busing, which forced the integration of schools, was one of the factors that encouraged a general migration of middle-class white families to the suburbs, leaving the center city primarily to families without children, and poor minorities, including Native Americans and African Americans.

In the wake of the oil bust, city services and facilities were at risk. A school bond issue failed, and so did a measure to build a new library. A domed stadium proposal and several other ballot initiatives were defeated. To be sure, Oklahoma City had remnants of wealth—many citizens had salted away their money from the boom days, and suburbs such as Nichols Hills were populated by *Town and Country* types. But the general populace had suffered from a declining job market and from an atmosphere of gloom and a communitywide loss of confidence.

Mayor Ron Norick's efforts to lure jobs had been unsuccessful. United Airlines and American Airlines had considered Oklahoma City among their potential sites to build large maintenance facilities. American backed out first, and then United chose Indianapolis over Oklahoma's capital. The airlines' executives explained they were concerned over "quality of life" issues. They didn't see the necessary public facilities that would make the city attractive to employees.

Norick was at his wit's end by the time he came to the University of Oklahoma to listen to what I had to say about sports violence. I touched on my involvement in Miami sports, and this gave him an idea. When he finally called me a few months after my appearance, he told me some of the history of the city, and what he was up against. He said he had called local leaders together to explore and solicit ideas to restore confidence, jobs, and prosperity. There was almost unanimous agreement that new publicly financed infrastructure projects would help get the city back on its feet economically, and give it a sense of pride. But there the agreement stopped.

Although all identified similar feelings of loss and need, it was clear that each was protective of his or her own turf, or what was left of it. The sports people wanted better sports facilities. Tourism officials wanted public money to make the city a more attractive destination. Culture mavens argued that museums, theaters, and the like should be the key to revitalization. All competed for attention and ballot initiatives, and everyone understood that the public tolerance for new taxes was limited—Oklahomans as a whole have traditionally been a frugal bunch. Norick yearned for a way to get people to work together for the common good. He had ideas for projects—there were so many needs—but the situation was chaotic, full of egos and jealousies. In short, it was my kind of situation.

Playing the Room at Slow Speed

Before I could do anything, though, I had to pass through the interview process. I was just one of three candidates for the job of consultant (and mastermind of the rebirth). Of the three, I was perhaps the one who would raise the most eyebrows. Ron Norick was a savvy politician, and the son of a former Oklahoma City mayor. His father had been legendary as a public figure, having addressed successfully the city's critical water supply issues and annexed a good deal of land. The legacy then, was to formulate ambitious plans, no matter how improbable they seemed. But to do this Norick knew that he needed help. He also knew that he'd have to entice the private sector to come up with the money. To that end, he put together an ad hoc committee that represented a variety of constituents, and then called in three candidates for the consulting job.

I arrived at Will Rogers World Airport prepared, I thought, for my interview. I carried with me a briefcase full of accomplishments, research on the community and its leaders, and an argument ready on how my relationship with the commissioner of the National Hockey League might give Oklahoma City an edge in getting a franchise if an arena were built. I also was prepared to haul out details for nonsports projects I'd been involved with. But I didn't anticipate having to talk much about them.

I took a cab past small oil wells only a few hundred yards from the runways to a nearby strip of hotels. The location of our meeting, at one of those hotels, was significant. Downtown was so irrelevant and unaccommodating that discussions about its future wouldn't even take place there.

I met several new faces at the interview. Norick introduced me to Rick Moore, his assistant, as well as leaders of local organizations. Everyone there, including the mayor, harbored biases about favored projects.

Norick spoke slowly and carefully. He talked about the significant challenges facing the city, and paused when he did for emphasis. Reflectively, gently, he said, "I believe in this town. We are on the verge of something great. And I believe that the people of this town will live up to their generational obligation." He paused and looked out of the window. He said, "We are committed to improving the quality of life here."

When Ron asked me for my presentation, I began more slowly than I otherwise would have. I didn't want to sound like an arrogant outsider, or, as Rick Moore later put it, "the city slicker who would tell the poor, dumb Okies what to do." But before I could get far into my credentials or demonstrate my knowledge of the community, a woman named Jackie Carey, who represented the local arts groups, issued a challenge.

"This is not a sports project," she said, with a smile that was meant not to comfort but to make a statement. She was clearly referring to my background. Sure, I'd moved the Cleveland Indians spring training site from Arizona to Florida, and the LPGA headquarters from Texas to my home state, and lobbied on the steps of Miami City Hall for politicians to change their minds and to agree to build an arena in a blighted neighborhood, but none of that would mean a thing to Jackie Carey.

If I had come to town with the idea of selling myself as an arena builder who occasionally dabbled in other venue projects, I was not thinking broadly enough. The Oklahoma City opportunity had intrigued me because it went well beyond sports to transportation systems and libraries and other facilities, but it left me with something of a hole in my résumé. Still, I was prepared to acknowledge this shortcoming and to argue that it wasn't a fatal flaw.

One of the other candidates for the consulting job was someone connected with San Antonio's Riverwalk, which had focused attention on the city and helped turn it into a tourist attraction. Jackie asked about the particulars of undertaking a similar project in Oklahoma City. "I haven't built anything like Riverwalk," I acknowledged. "But it takes the same skills, and the same techniques as selling an arena." I explained that it required devising a practical process, sticking to the process, articulating a vision, and selling that vision.

And I got the job.

Find the Insider

Ron Norick was keenly aware of the limits of his power and influence. It was unusual for a mayor to make the call to a consultant in the first place. Simply to arrange for it he knew he'd have to go outside of normal civic circles so that the funding could be handled privately (in this case, it was the Chamber of Commerce). He was wary of extending himself beyond that, or he would alienate parties that might perceive sinister motives. I would have to rely on someone else for inside information, and for the real word about the forces we were facing.

Instinctively I knew it would be Rick Moore. He was a gregarious figure, and like me a sports fan. He knew how persistently one constituency had lobbied against another, and of the subtleties of the relationships. Over the next year, we went (according to my log) to 330 meetings—an average of 10 a day when I was in town, being sure to pay close attention to each party, whether seemingly favored or not.

Rick helped sort out the priorities and realities. People there trusted him. When they saw me with him, they trusted me, too. He was bearded and, at the time, I was too, so we became known as the twins named Rick. Together we met with all of the hopeful candidates for public largesse—people who represented institutions that clearly required help. The mayor's specific idea had been to select a few of them and to figure out a way to present each to the voters for approval. In the final process, nine projects were favored—an ambitious program, unprecedented in scope.

A new baseball stadium in Bricktown, the largely abandoned warehouse district, would replace the facility out at the Fairgrounds. As the home of the city's Triple A team, the old stadium was something of a joke, but not a very funny joke. It had electrical problems and code violations galore, and was, according to Rick Moore, "a lawsuit waiting to happen." The Myriad Convention Center required expansion so that it would become much more attractive to major gatherings. The state Fairgrounds needed a major overhaul. The Civic Center Music Hall had to be brought into the present—almost gutted and rebuilt in order to make an improved home for Ballet Oklahoma and the Oklahoma City Philharmonic, as well as retain its capacity to attract large Broadway road shows. A new sports arena, with skyboxes and other features, would announce the city's capacity to lure big-league basketball and hockey. A new library to replace cramped and outdated facilities was clearly in order. The riverfront along the North Canadian River could be developed, and a canal, San Antonio-style, would run through the city and attract tourists. All of this would be connected by light rail. The latter was a particular dream of Ron Norick's, who pictured visitors and residents alike taking advantage of a quaint and reliable system. But for that to happen, all the other things had to be completed, or the light rail system, he observed, would "take whom to where?"

Rick Moore and I talked about several issues that the list raised. How would these be presented to the voters? How would we create sustainable momentum? How would we get some of the institutions that didn't make the list, such as the State Historical Society and the Oklahoma City Art Museum, to get behind the effort? We had an enormous obstacle—the track record of dismal public support for infrastructure projects. Individually, none of these needs had significant support, or appeared that it would succeed in a referendum. Just as important as all this, we had to raise the money for a campaign to sell the public on the need for these improvements.

The more I thought about this, the more it seemed clear that we couldn't sell each project individually. In Miami, I had seen how hard it was to get approval just for an arena. We decided to "bundle" nine projects into one—have one marketing campaign, one presentation to voters, one ballot initiative upon which everything would ride. A comprehensive package. A grand plan for the city. On the face of it, it may have seemed absurd. In a city where nothing seemed to be approved, we were about to ask citizens to support a $237 million package, much more costly than anything they—or any city residents in the United States to that point—had heard of. But I saw it as an idea whose time had come. Instead of competition between civic groups, I could, in theory anyway, get them to work together toward a common goal of something for everybody.

Up to that point, Mayor Norick had been playing his cards close to the vest. I knew he wanted all of these projects, but that he also was considering the conventional approach. But I was convinced we should go after the bundle. I told Rick Moore that we could reduce the shock value of the enormous sum by convincing voters that, with our approach, they'd actually save a good deal of money while finding the ultimate solution to their urban problems. Ron said, "Sure. But how?" In frugal Oklahoma City, an outsider could easily be hogtied to the next departing Greyhound bus for urging taxpayers to fork over $10,000 let alone $237 million.

The Natural Setting to Suggest the Impossible

Ron Norick and I teed off at 6 A.M. at Oak Tree Country Club, where Ron is a member. I could see right off that for him golf is a release. He is an excellent player, a four handicap. I am, as I have indicated, less excellent. But for me golf is an opportunity to accomplish nine or ten things by the eighteenth hole. By the thirteenth, Ron had beaten me into the ground, all but assuring he would win our small wager. But I didn't care. I seemed to be succeeding in my modified kitchen cabinet session.

I talked to Ron about the frugality of Oklahomans, and said that if we could show them a way to pay for these improvements in an economical fashion, they would be persuaded. One of the options to pay for major public works, though it was never used by cities, is a temporary sales tax increase, a sort of pay-as-you-go plan. It is a bigger burden in the short term but in the end saves a mountain of interest payments. Also, adding a penny to each dollar of purchases doesn't sound like much—it doesn't sound like a $237 million comprehensive project. And not a dollar would go to interest. Looking up from the rough that day (one of the few times he played from the rough), Ron smiled and said, "I hoped you'd come up with a painless approach like this."

City Hall's lawyers were not sure of the idea's legality at first, but I could find in the statutes or case law no specific prohibition against raising the sales tax by one cent over five years for a specific purpose. And so we settled on the plan. With the help of key city leaders, we would refine a plan called MAPS, an acronym for Metropolitan Area Projects Strategies, an idea that would serve me well in the years to come.

The legal issues, and the problem of selling the voters on the plan, were far from the only obstacles. Before the package could even be presented, we were obliged to address the issues raised by all of the competing constituencies. Individually, their dreams had been doomed. Together they could succeed—join forces to sell the public on a revolutionary and inspiring plan for the city. But it wasn't customary, or convenient, for them to work together. A marriage between arts groups and sports groups seems bound to fail. Arts leaders were lukewarm, at best, to the bundle, which included only one arts project, and which ignored the art museum. I clearly had a challenge ahead as a consultant whose reputation up to that point had been almost exclusively connected to sports projects. How could I get the arts groups to kick in the money we needed for our marketing campaign if I couldn't convince them of the worth of the project as a whole? These people were the most well-heeled in the community, the people who had a long record of making things happen. Without them, our scheme had no chance to succeed. Everything rode on a meeting in a grand and beautiful Tudor-style house in plush Nichols Hills. I had to convince Sandy Meyers, by acclamation the head of the cultural community, to play ball. She had access to every big giver, and I needed every single one of them.

Strangers at the Table

I knew we were in for an unsettling hour; it would be my job to argue on behalf of ideas that Sandy Meyers would despise. Nothing she championed was in our bundle of nine projects. As the most promi-nent leader in the arts community, she was a preeminent supporter of the Oklahoma City Philharmonic and Ballet Oklahoma, but she was against refurbishing their home, the Civic Center Music Hall.

She and her husband Stuart spent their winters in Naples, Florida, where she had been impressed by the new music hall there, a state-of-the-art facility. This is the model Oklahoma City should use, she would argue, not a plan to fix the old place. She would also be bitter, certainly, that my bundle had no provisions for the art museum, which required substantial expansion and improvement. Still, I hoped that I could convince her that our plan was the only workable one, and would act as a kick-start for the arts community.

Over coffee, I asked her questions designed to put her at ease, en-couraging her to talk about herself. Softball questions. But Sandy is not a person easily manipulated, and she found a way to get right to the point. She told me about her father, a congressman who represented Oklahoma. He had dreamed of a great performing arts hall in Wash-ington. Sandy thinks of the Kennedy Center as "My father's dream made real." Her own dream was the new performing arts hall for her hometown.

I explained that the decision of what to include in MAPS had more to do with what we could get the voters to accept. MAPS had to be diverse in its ambitions. It was true that it included two new sports venues—an arena and a new baseball stadium—but it was a hard reality of doing public business. A comprehensive plan slightly weighted toward sports would be more attractive among the general public than one weighted toward the arts. This wasn't a condemnation of the arts, or a statement that the arts weren't important—only a political reality, supported by public polls. There was an attitude in many parts of town that the arts are patronized exclusively by people of means, and they shouldn't be asking for subsidy from the working poor.

I argued that going after public money, as we would in MAPS, would generate civic pride and boost a campaign for private money—that there would be a momentum upon which she could build for museum funding. I could see from her body language that I might as well have been selling swampland in my home state.

"You don't like me," I offered.

"Should I?" she asked.

"Well, maybe if you just hear me out," I replied, having no idea what I was about to say. I knew that if I didn't change that body language, if I didn't manage to see a sincere smile, our project was doomed. So out of instinct, and perhaps desperation, I took a risk, one that I knew I'd have to explain later to Mayor Norick.

The Ad Lib Clause

One of the things that any negotiator must do is demonstrate flexibility. Be willing to face the consequences of going outside authorized boundaries. In short, put your contract on the line. I knew I wasn't only sitting across the table from Sandy but from her friends and from the whole arts community as well. I had to think of a way for her to be able to report back to her friends, "Well, for a sports guy, he's not entirely a philistine. And he's charming, if in his own way. We should support this plan." I had to offer Sandy a new idea.

The arguments I was making about the momentum of our plan, and about the projected economic expansion of downtown, led to a natural conclusion. What if MAPS turned out to be more successful than we imagined? What if the economic impact was much greater, and therefore the tax yield higher? In short, we'd have a bigger pot to distribute. What would happen to that extra money?

"All right, Sandy," I said. "We'll establish a supplemental list of projects that will become eligible for a hypothetical pot of public funding if enough can be found." This seemed logical to me. And, when she thought about it, to her, too. The problem, of course, was that I was not authorized by the people I was working for to make such a deal.

By the end of our first private meeting, Sandy seemed satisfied that she could work with me. Which I figured was enough, until I got the total buy-in.

Later that day, I had to break the news to Mayor Norick that I had unilaterally expanded MAPS, and told him why. I did this with trepidation. And yet one of the services I was offering Oklahoma City was the art of improvisation: of reinterpreting the civic landscape according to circumstance, of thinking creatively on my feet. If I could come up with ways to enhance the project—to gather support from previously reluctant, or even hostile, quarters—without jeopardizing the central idea, the client should be all for it.

Norick, in fact, was elated. The idea didn't take a penny away from the $237 million. There was no risk there. If the project was more successful than expected, well then, they could have their money. Norick smiled the smile of a man who had his cake and was about to eat it.

Rally Round the "Bad News"

There are, however, many kinds of opposition. One of them is low expectations. Not long before MAPS was devised, a production of Oklahoma City's Lyric Theater seemed to issue a warning, a hint of the community's inferiority complex. The Lyric Theater produces a variety of summer stock shows every year. One of the shows in the pre-MAPS era was *42nd Street*. The company, which usually builds its own sets, was able to rent the complicated and beautifully constructed sets of the Broadway touring company for the week's run. The day after opening night, one of the key members of the production staff saw a familiar face outside the theater, an elderly man who was part of the old arts guard. The man revealed that he had seen the show the night before. When he was asked how he enjoyed it, he replied, "I didn't." He explained that he didn't approve of the sets. The member of the staff asked why not—after all, they were awfully good sets. The old man said, "That's right. They're too good. We don't need people around here to get used to that."

Whether the old man was speaking for everyone or not, it was clear we faced difficult odds. A preliminary poll of voters showed that only 32 percent favored a sales tax for the purpose of building and renovating city structures. And the mayor couldn't count on support from the city's newspaper. Edward Gaylord, publisher of the *Daily Oklahoman* and one of the most influential figures in the community, told Ron Norick, "You must be crazy. You'll never get it passed. And besides, that canal is the dumbest thing I ever heard of." Fueled by the powerful newspaper, there was grumbling all over town: *Another boondoggle. Another criminal use of taxpayer money.*

This was my cue. This is where I do my best work—when discouragement seems to rule, and when the odds seem long. I pointed out to the mayor and to our supporters that we were already ahead of the game. Having the support of 32 percent of voters six months before the election was a positive sign, not a negative one. All we needed to do was win over 19 percent, and we had the deal done.

One of the key strategies was to present a united front—a team of key players from every constituency. That meant that I had to convince arts, sports, tourism, heritage, and community leaders not only to work together but to sing each other's praises. I had to persuade Joel Levine, the music director of the Oklahoma City Philharmonic, to go out in public and make speeches about the value of having a handsome new facility to watch Triple A baseball, and I had to get supporters of basketball and hockey to understand the value of bringing musicals about the French Revolution and opera phantoms to town.

Many of the meetings that Rick Moore and I attended over the months were what might be referred to as internal ones. The message was that there was only one route to success, the route that everyone took together. Our investment of time and effort was a great factor in winning support.

The mayor had given me an idea I could expand upon. He had mentioned at the interview meeting the idea of "generational obligation." By this, he meant that ordinary citizens who had long benefited by the sacrifices of their parents and grandparents now faced an obligation to contribute to the common good. This argument could be used to persuade community leaders to work together, to raise campaign money, to get people to write letters to the editor supporting the concept, to put out yard signs saying "This Is For Our Kids and Grandkids," and to be precinct captains in the effort to get the vote out. In my role as full-time consensus builder, I also had to be part historian, part information analyst, part cheerleader, part lightning rod. I could say things that politicians couldn't say. Ron Norick, for example, couldn't tell Sandy Meyers she represents a small portion of the city, and that even though her ideas are important to the quality of life, they don't bring votes. So, I was able to take the heat off of the mayor and others who were involved so heavily in the project. I could do this because I knew not to take criticism personally. There are bound to be objections. It was my job to convince those who could be convinced of the validity of our cause.

As time went on, I became entirely immersed in this project, making it easier for me to sell it with great enthusiasm. In walks through old Bricktown, I could easily imagine the district as a heart of tourism and commerce. In so many cities, old and stately buildings such as these had been torn down, considered beyond saving or passé. If Bricktown had been destroyed, there would never be enough money or craft or will to build such a neighborhood again. We were just in time—if only we could get the voters to see the possibilities. I could imagine, too, a

baseball stadium made of the same kind of red bricks as the old ware-
houses, a jewel of a place that would offer vistas of downtown. All of
the other improvements—transportation and arts and the library—
took on special significance. I could easily conjure an image of the rebuilt Oklahoma City, and thriving downtown, and a citizenry alive
with prospects and with hope.

It was an odd confluence of people and time. The city needed me,
and I needed the city. When I set out from Miami to establish a nationwide business, I assumed one thing, at least, would be different—
that I wouldn't develop the emotional connection to projects I had developed at home. But, to me, this was every bit as important, perhaps
even more so. I was now not only a sports facility guy. I had developed
a way to address urban issues that was new and innovative.

Later, I was profiled in the *Daily Oklahoman,* and referred to as "The
Music Man." It is of course a label that is not entirely positive—except
that in the end it works out, when there are trombones and proper in-
struction enough for all, and when the community is reborn. The profile began with a quote from "Professor" Harold Hill: "You pile up
enough tomorrows and you'll find you are left with nothing but a lot of
empty yesterdays. I don't know about you, but I'd like to make today
worth remembering." It also quoted me in my message to the voters:
"You are on the cutting edge. Make the right decision."

I pushed the power of numbers. People can understand 3,600 new
jobs and a $230 million total economic impact during the five-year
construction period. I stressed the retention of existing jobs, and that
the city would continue to receive millions of dollars from convention,
tourism, sports, and cultural activities as the construction was going
on. I suggested strongly that the NBA or the NHL or both could become interested in Oklahoma City; after all, what franchise wouldn't
consider a community where a new facility—a paid-for facility—was
ready to welcome them?

This was all very positive—and I believe that positive messages are
the most persuasive. But I also used leverage. And, in this case, there
were obvious negative messages. To those who support baseball, for ex-

ample, I made the point that the Triple A team was in jeopardy—there were many cities lining up to lure the locals away. But generally I used a much broader argument. This was clearly a high-stakes game because we chose to approve or disapprove nine facilities at once. Although the upside was great, the downside was that failure, in an area renowned for once being the heart of the Dust Bowl, would once again leave parched earth. I also argued that all eyes that were positively fixed on Oklahoma City would be negatively fixed for a long time to come if the referendum failed.

"What's in It for Me?"

We met often with the various constituent groups, and had convinced them to buy into the MAPS project. Now I had to apply similar techniques to engage the public in the debate through any number of community forums and groups. Many of these meetings were not comfortable. The African-American community wondered how it might benefit them. Questions from the working-class south side showed their suspicions of the elite north side. Workers in the lower socioeconomic categories were skeptical, with an attitude of "since I don't go to fancy concerts, what's in it for me?"

A part of my response to each of these concerns embraced everyone. That is, I made use of statistics that showed the low average rate of pay in the city. I argued that new business would be attracted to the area because of the new opportunities, and that better-paying jobs would be created. But I also had to devise arguments, and new ideas, that would attract very different groups of voters.

When it comes to senior citizens, no taxes are low enough. Many live on fixed income. And yet I still wanted to find a way to get them to vote for our project—because they come out in very large numbers. So we devised a rebate plan (it became a tool in other cities for me) that would allow them to both support our efforts and spread the word, and each year receive something in the area of $30 as a rebate for the sales tax they would likely pay.

In talks in the black community, I stressed the value of MAPS to the near east side, long a center of a vital black neighborhood and what would be the home of the new baseball stadium. I used examples from other cities of the urban revitalization that occurred around such stadiums.

In the case of the blue-collar workers in the city's south side, the baseball stadium was also a draw. But it was the idea for the canal that would, in the end, engage them.

The canal was no mere cosmetic trick; it was a metaphor for the whole project, and was a physical manifestation of the idea of communitywide consensus building. The canal would be built using the existing system of waterways. The city's highways had cut off the south side from the downtown—made it seem remote, its citizens an afterthought. The new canal, which would run underneath the Interstate, would tie the south side with downtown once again. It was an important symbolic connection, and one that I stressed. Of course, when talking to south side groups, I talked more about the baseball stadium and the canal than I did about a major renovation for the hall in which the Philharmonic plays. And, in conversations with arts groups, I was less likely to engage them in fantasies about Triple A baseball championships than I was about the chance to lure world-class performers to town. Still, there were arguments that worked across the board.

Let's Mess with Texas

I had to seize intangibles, had to rally the community on something that, for all of their differences, drew them together. I knew about the rivalry on the football field between the two large state universities, but I quickly figured out that it extends far beyond the goalposts. Texas is seen as a place of swaggering success, a place that warns, "Don't Mess With Texas." The state has big-league teams and cultural icons and even exports its lore. But more important, Texas always seemed to lure good-paying jobs from Oklahoma. This went beyond interstate competition and annoyance to a serious economic dilemma. Something had to be done, and one of the things I did was try to turn the momentum around, arguing that Oklahoma was just as fine a place, or finer, than Texas.

Community leaders were working together, singing each other's praises. Maestro Joel Levine talked to his audiences before concerts, pushing MAPS. He acknowledged that they might not be baseball fans, and that baseball fans may not be flocking to the Philharmonic, but that everyone had to support each other to make this work. We like to think of this as a metro area, he said. "Well, what makes a metro area? It's facilities such as a great concert hall, and a baseball stadium, and a great library, and a convention center, and a sports arena."

As we moved toward election day, I drew on a certain sense of resilience in the citizens of the city and the state. Oklahoma is home to extremes—tornados, blizzards, droughts, floods. Rick Moore's wife, Vicky, told me, "This is a hard place to live in many ways. Even the plants have to be tough. We don't have the most majestic or beautiful of natural resources—no mountains or major rivers, or oceans. We just have the plains. And wonderful people of pioneer stock."

It seemed to us that as the December 14 vote drew closer, we were gaining momentum and closing the gap. Was it enough? We couldn't rest. For a long time now, I had bought into the Oklahoma City vision. I became a believer. I wanted this to happen for them, and for me. I could see that this city, located as it was in the heartland, could be a model city in the effort to revitalize urban America, and that I had found a key, through the strategy of bundling projects, to achieve it. But this referendum had to succeed, and from all the evidence we still faced long odds. We had to keep working the public, and to that end, we organized an old-fashioned pep rally at the Myriad and set it for a couple of nights before the vote.

But real life intruded. For one thing I had my final Harvard class of the semester to teach, which I didn't teach. My log for the week reveals this entry: "Last Harvard class. R.H. absent." A more important event was the birth of our second child, Caroline. The Gaylord publishing family (of the *Daily Oklahoman*) offered the use of their private jet for the trip to Miami. I got home just in time to see that Terri had made dinner, packed for the hospital, and was ready to go off to deliver. I stayed home for five days, celebrating Caroline's birth the same way I had celebrated Katie's seven years earlier: I wore nothing but pink.

I got back to Oklahoma City in time to see thousands of people come to the Myriad. Bands played. Vince Gill, the country singer, performed. The Oklahoma City Philharmonic, led by Joel Levine, played Christmas music. Barry Switzer, the legendary football coach at the University of Oklahoma, proclaimed, "I'm tired of going other places and seeing wonderful things that other people have. It's time we had wonderful things here."

I, too, gave a speech. "I am an outsider," I said, "but I have come to believe in the spirit of Oklahoma, and its destiny. . . . In years past, your parents and grandparents sacrificed to make this a wonderful home. You benefited from that sacrifice. It's time now to live up to the responsibility you inherited. It's time to grab, too, the headlines. People around the country will be watching. People who always read about Texas this and Texas that. Well, in the next few days, the eyes of the nation won't be on Texas. They will be on the good citizens of Oklahoma. Let's steal business that was going down I-35, across the Red River, and into Dallas. Let's believe in OUR future. Let's mess with Texas!"

On the night before the MAPS vote, I sat in my room at the Medallion Hotel, just across the street from the Myriad. I ordered two Bloody Marys and a cheeseburger from room service, but wound up eating and drinking very little. My stomach wouldn't allow it. It struck me that I was onto something—a new way of thinking about how to build sports facilities. The bundle could work in dozens of cities around the land. But only if it worked in Oklahoma City. If we were to lose, I'd have to start over, and think of a new approach.

On December 14, we assembled at the Bricktown Ballroom, the evening's campaign headquarters, and we prepared for a late night. The absentee ballots had us behind, as did the early returns. We had commissioned an exit poll, and the pollster assured us that no matter how bad things looked at midnight, we'd win, 54 percent to 46 percent. We all looked at the guy as if he were crazy. At 1 A.M., I looked over at Ron Norick, who was on the phone. He frowned, but only for a moment. He put down the phone, the frown turned into a great smile, and he gave me the thumbs-up sign. The final tally was precisely as predicted by the pollster. Norick and Oklahoma City would soon have their $237 million. And for me, "the bundle" would become a nationwide signature.

"Okies Love Hockey"

In March 1995, I met with Gary Bettman to discuss for the first time the prospect of Oklahoma City as an NHL franchise. Bettman, in the years following the Miami Heat deal, had moved from the number three position in the NBA to the commissioner's office of the National Hockey League. We talked of old times, and had a few laughs about Miami. Then we turned to the subject of expansion. Like the NBA and Major League Baseball, the NHL was in a period of growth, and had advanced far from its original formation of only six teams, all of them traditional hockey cities.

I said, "Oklahoma City has all the right elements for a franchise." I clicked through the traditions of the place, its indomitable spirit, the numbers showing that the metropolitan area was growing quickly, the community support for a new 20,000-seat arena that wouldn't cost a franchise a thin dime. I said, "It's good for the NHL to look at a market it wouldn't otherwise have known because it wasn't on anyone's radar screen. It leads the Central Hockey League in attendance, so it has a hockey legacy, and built-in interest."

Bettman offered an honest reply. "None of us know Oklahoma City. You have a tremendous uphill climb." That's a euphemism, of course, for not a chance. He said, "We've got to be sure the TV market is big enough." As he reminded me, though I didn't need reminding, gate sales are but a small part of revenues. And, besides, there's a big difference between Central Hockey League and National Hockey League realities. He said, "Having fans come at nine bucks a ticket is not the same as a $30 ticket. But," he concluded, "if anybody can carry this off, it's you. Let's get together with some key people."

I made a few calls in the following days, but I never expected—nobody ever expected—that the momentum we had built in the city's recovery would be lost in the instant it took a terrorist to detonate 4,800 pounds of ammonium nitrate.

The Terrible News and Its Aftermath

I was at a meeting in Daytona Beach, discussing strategies with executives of the LPGA. I had been rehearsing a speech I would deliver that evening to the city council to urge approval of a new hotel lease deal. Just after 10 o'clock I took a break and went into the lunchroom and I saw people watching CNN. I sat down for an hour and couldn't move. Live coverage showed that the Alfred P. Murrah Federal Building had been blown to bits, its nine floors collapsing on the first, which had just welcomed 21 children to the day-care center. It was not known at the time how many people had died, but it was feared to be in the hundreds. I didn't think I knew anybody who worked at the Murrah, but I certainly knew the community, and its spirit. Suddenly, I felt as if this was a double loss—the loss of life and a city's soul. I called Ron Norick's office but couldn't get him. I couldn't find Rick Moore, either.

In fact, Ron and Rick had just emerged from the mayor's monthly prayer breakfast at the Myriad Center at 9 A.M., Oklahoma City time. Two minutes later they heard the deafening blast that not only destroyed the Murrah but damaged dozens of buildings near it. Rick Moore ran a few blocks to the explosion site to aid in the rescue efforts. What he saw in the next few minutes affected him for years to come. He suffered a depression and guilt over not doing more to help. He couldn't shake his condition until, years later, a psychiatrist was able to recover Rick's buried memory. He was able to recall that a policewoman pulled him away from the wreckage and carnage. She said professional rescue workers would take over, and that all civilians had to leave the area.

Just 11 days after the bombing, I got a call from Gary Bettman. He asked how the city was responding to the tragedy. By then I had spoken to the mayor and knew particulars of immediate recovery efforts. As the days went by, rescue workers found survivors among the rubble, the last survivors. In all, 168 people had died, including 17 children. It was hard to say where the city was, except still in shock. But Bettman wasn't calling simply out of sympathy and curiosity—he had an idea. "There's a chance," he said, "that we could move the Quebec Nordiques to Oklahoma City."

This was amazing. It isn't often that a commissioner calls to suggest transfer to a city. In fact, in my experience, it was unprecedented. The world had come to know the capital of the Sooner State from the instant of the bombing. Bettman, certainly, had seen the stunning photograph of one-year-old Baylee Almon, fatally injured, carried from the rubble by a fireman. Thousands of newspapers around the world had published it—a photo taken by a bank employee who was fired for his effort (he hadn't been excused from his post). Bettman, it seemed to me, wanted to do something to help heal the spirit of the city. He asked, "Can you get your people into our office and meet some of our people?"

I warned, "Gary, this had better be serious. I'm not sure I can get folks in Oklahoma City to focus on hockey two weeks after such an enormous tragedy." He assured me that he would have the owner of the Nordiques in the room. At the end of the conversation, Bettman said, "I'm not expecting the mayor." He apparently assumed the mayor would be engaged in the recovery efforts.

I called Ron at his house, and told him about the opportunity. The NHL was serious about finding a new home for the Nordiques, and the team's owner, from all accounts, was enthusiastic about Oklahoma City. Quebec, though steeped in hockey tradition, was too small a market to support a major league team, and there were any number of cities that wanted to court a franchise. Ron said that if the owner of the Nordiques would be there, he would be there, too. We brought an entourage from Oklahoma City to meet Marcel Aubut in Bettman's office. But when Bettman saw Norick, he appeared to be uneasy, even annoyed. He said he hadn't expected Norick to come in light of the tragedy. I said to Bettman, "You asked me to bring Oklahoma City people. There's no more important Oklahoma City person than Ron Norick." Gary looked uncharacteristically angry.

Ron and I presented the Oklahoma City case to Aubut and Bettman—the spirit of the city, the MAPS project, and, not incidentally, the about-to-be-constructed 20,000-seat arena, a free gift to the Nordiques. Aubut nodded his head, smiled, but never stood to shout, "*Formidable!*" He was cordial and seemed impressed, and thanked Bettman for telling him about Oklahoma City, of which he had known very little, but I could see his heart wasn't in it. He told us he would be in touch after he met with a contingent from Denver.

We were aware, of course, that we wouldn't be the only candidate, but still, it seemed as if something untoward was up. At the end of the meeting, Bettman didn't look me in the eye. Clearly he understood that he had crossed a line. Norick and our contingent sensed a difference between what I had represented as the seller's enthusiasm level before the meeting and what he actually displayed. Ron was not, however, upset with me. We had worked together for two years, and he assumed that I would go after this deal as hard as I could. And I did. I told Bettman that Oklahoma City was prepared to offer $80 million for the Nordiques in an exclusive bidding project. But when Aubut returned from Denver I knew that he had no intention of ever coming to the plains. We were being used for leverage. That's why Bettman hadn't expected, or wanted, the mayor to come to the meeting.

I understood the concept of leverage completely—I had employed it, and would employ it, wherever I could, particularly in deals I would undertake after Oklahoma City. But this one was particularly unfortunate—it even seemed malevolent—in the wake of the Murrah bombing. Though not at all on the same level, it was something else to mourn. I found it necessary to haul out tales from my Miami experience—the patience it took, and the number of years, and the setbacks. I reminded Ron and the others of the need for persistence. No, you don't get it the first time you try, or even the second. But eventually it will happen. (And today, Oklahoma City is on the NHL's short list for expansion or as a location to move a franchise.) Norick and his colleagues took this all in stride. Besides, they had a lot to do.

I didn't return to Oklahoma City until the spring of 1998, three years after Timothy McVeigh committed his unspeakable crime. The community was still raw from the tragedy, as it would be for some time to come. And there was much unfinished business, including the question of how to build a proper and sensitive memorial to the victims. (The memorial that was finally built is astonishing in its detail and its spirit. It is well worth the trip to Oklahoma City to see, particularly the less publicized inside display, a part of which seats you in a replica of a building across the street from Murrah as you listen to a tape recording of a Water Commission meeting—and wait for an explosion that shakes the earth.)

By the spring of 1998, many of the nine projects in MAPS were under way or completed. Mayor Norick told me how valuable the process had been to the bombing recovery effort because by then community leaders and citizens were old hands at working together. The bombing had not caused any cutback in MAPS plans. Quite the opposite, citizens approved several million more dollars to pay for unforeseen construction problems. Dr. Bob L. Blackburn, the Oklahoma state historian, said that the MAPS project was "instrumental" in recovery efforts. "There is a rebirth of that old boom spirit that built Oklahoma City, the spirit of 1889, that sense of confidence that tomorrow will be better than today if we invest and work together."

On opening night of the 1998 Triple A baseball season, I stood on the infield of the handsome new Southwestern Bell Ballpark in Bricktown with others who had participated in the MAPS process, as former New York Yankees teammates of Mickey Mantle (Tony Kubek, Bobby Richardson, Yogi Berra, and Whitey Ford among them) helped inaugurate the beautiful stadium in the heart of the new tourist district. Historian Blackburn said, "The night was an affirmation. Legendary baseball players came down from Mount Olympus to our place. And we were connected with greatness."

It has been a decade since Ron Norick first called me. He is now out of public office, a partner in an investment firm. His accomplishments are well remembered. There is a street downtown named after him. And he was acknowledged at the opening of the new Ford Center sports arena (Ford Motor Company bought naming rights) in the late summer of 2002. Rick Moore was also a part of the festivities. (He is now executive director of the Oklahoma Municipal Contractors Association.) At the Ford opening, there was a buzz about the packed schedule, including NBA and NHL exhibition games.

The new library is about to open. In the spring, summer, and fall months, Bricktown, through which the new canal runs, is alive with tourists and students. It is the latter group that frequents the bars and nightspots until 3 A.M., though I am not certain any of them use the public transportation—the new trolley system—to bring them safely home.

The Civic Center Music Hall has been refurbished to the tune of $52 million, complete with a hook in the ceiling to connect the chandelier for perpetual returns of *The Phantom of the Opera*. Its gala opening week included a concert of the Oklahoma City Philharmonic with trumpeter Wynton Marsalis as soloist.

Sandy Meyers, the arts leader who eventually became very supportive of the refurbishing effort, loved it when Marsalis took a moment out from the music and told the packed house, "This is a place you can all be proud of." Sandy was satisfied that the compromise had been worth it. Her only criticism on this night was that—from her perch in the best seat in the house—she noticed too much dust on the stage.

CHAPTER 7

Leverage at 150 Miles per Hour

*A billion here and a billion there, and
pretty soon you're talking real money.*

SENATOR EVERETT DIRKSEN

As you know by now, to me sports is something akin to religion. I pray over box scores. I inspect every statistic. I own a voluminous repository of professional sports information that, in a bizarre set of circumstances, could prove useful. If you want to spout off at a cocktail party, for example, about how many home runs second baseman Duane Kuiper hit for the Indians and the Giants in his 12-year Major League career, you need only consult my garage beforehand. (The answer: one.)

An exception to this box score devotion is stock car racing. Or was. I never looked at the results from Daytona or Talladega. Race car drivers, in my view, weren't even athletes. They were guys driving around in circles, exercising the balls of their right feet. Real athletes swung 2-irons or Louisville Sluggers, or played smash-mouth defense for the Bears. I had no interest in the origins of stock car racing, or how it evolved from dirt-track county fairs in the South. I had no idea who might be leading the annual Winston Cup standings. Though I knew of the sport's general popularity, I was unaware of the level of intensity true NASCAR fans bring to the oval; or that many can recite the height and weight of the right front tire changer in a middle-level driver's second-string pit crew.

I surely had no concept about the structure of the sport—that it is divided into the famous racing organization, NASCAR, and the lesser known ISC (International Speedway Corporation), which holds the power in terms of the placement of races and tracks, though there is a very thin line between them, crossed by family members. So when the racing brass at Daytona called to inquire about my interest in helping them, it surely may have seemed as if they called the wrong person.

Still, my track record, so to speak, led me once again to Daytona. Charlie Mechem, of the LPGA, had recommended me, and the racing official who called me got right to the point. Rather than ask when it was convenient to travel to ISC headquarters, Hardy Smith dictated the date. I had about 96 hours notice for a meeting with Lesa France Kennedy, the organization's executive vice president. This would mean rearranging commitments and losing control over my schedule, something I am loathe to do. Also, Smith refused to reveal any details about the meeting or ISC plans over the phone. "But," he said, "it will be worth your while." I was skeptical, and yet Charlie Mechem hadn't led me astray before, and I owed him. I said to Smith, "I'll be there." As it turned out, the ISC and NASCAR project turned out to be the most intense leverage exercise of my career.

Always Do Things a Certain Way—Unless You Don't

"Do you know why you're here?" It was the first question from Lesa France Kennedy, who sat at the head of the table, with attentive members of her staff on each side. Lesa was dressed in an understated suit, and was clearly in charge. And if I had any ideas that the head of the ISC would talk like a good old boy they were instantly dispelled. A good old boy doesn't hold a Master's degree from Duke.

My first instinct upon hearing Lesa's question was to launch into my seven-minute spiel, but in this case that would have made no sense. So, following my rule of Always Do Things a Certain Way—Unless You Don't, I said, "I have no earthly idea why I'm here beyond the fact that it obviously has to do with the business of the industry." I was, of course, validating Hardy Smith's need for secrecy. And so he and Lesa were happy with the answer.

Lesa's second question: "How much do you know about the racing business?" I figured the meeting was over before it began. It occurred to me that I may have been sold as a racing expert by one of her staff members. How was I to respond? "How's old Cale Yarborough doing these days? Or is he dead?" It was one of those moments where you can't fake your way through a conversation.

So I said, "At the risk of making this a very short meeting, I know nothing about the business. I've never been to a race, I don't watch it on TV, I don't read about it, and I don't talk about it. I'm not a fan. If that's what you're looking for, you've got the wrong guy. But thank you for your time."

I can only imagine now what Lesa must have been thinking. She grew up with the sport. Her grandfather, "Big Bill" France, was the founder of NASCAR, guiding it from back-country dirt racing to big business. Her father, Bill France, was still president of NASCAR, and as an executive who presided over racing's proliferation, had become one of the most powerful figures in sports. Lesa herself had been around the business all of her life. During high school, she worked in the Daytona ticket office and the mail room, and eventually worked her way up in the industry to the point where she was now, as I came to view her, heir apparent to her father at NASCAR.

Of my total ignorance of and lack of interest in stock car racing, Lesa said, "That's refreshing for us. We usually work with people who are immersed in the business, and we need a fresh perspective from time to time." It was a crucial 30 seconds of interchange, in which she played my weakness as a strength, and showed strong leadership. Even now, we laugh at that first meeting, and I reveal what I could have said. "Explain this to me—do all the cars go in the same direction, or do they hit each other halfway through the race like in demolition derby?"

Lesa is one of those who responds to my playful ignorance—using it to business advantage.

The Soundness of Silence

In that first meeting, I got through a critical point without controlling the agenda. But as I have said, flexibility and adaptation are crucial. Silence can be useful. And as hard as it is for me to be silent, I made it a point to keep my mouth shut during the next unbearable 15 minutes when Hardy Smith dutifully provided background.

He said, "The evolution of NASCAR as a southern sport with southern roots and the economics of racing have required the organization to look at urban areas. ISC is taking the lead in thinking about developing tracks." Smith provided descriptions of ISC's major facilities in Daytona, Talladega (Alabama), Darlington (South Carolina), Watkins Glen (New York), and Phoenix (Arizona). The existing tracks, he explained, were built basically as bleachers and concessions stands around a circle; they did not anticipate what has been happening in every other sport, where skyboxes and other money-making ideas were introduced. Nor were these facilities particularly adaptable to non-NASCAR events that could provide new revenues for ISC. He said it would likely cost something more than $200 million to build a state-of-the-art facility, and that ISC would likely need help financing it. He described the role of NASCAR in this as the racing organization and ISC as the facility and sanctioning body. I didn't know enough about the two organizations, or their respective missions, to ask an intelligent question.

Smith said, "We'd like to take this sport national. We'd like to build huge facilities that have never been built before. We'd like to create a process that we haven't done before, and do something we know nothing about." All the challenges that inspire me.

I could sense that Lesa was mindful of internal politics. There were clearly those in ISC and NASCAR who were skeptical of going after public money. It hadn't been done before. All tracks to that point were built privately. Racing officials thought that going after public money was sheer folly—a waste of time and resources. Paying me $9,000 a month would be throwing good money down a rat hole.

When Smith finished, I started a 10-minute speech in which I said my real expertise was not stadiums or arena building but public/private partnerships and facility building. I said that creating a new track for NASCAR racing was a natural, and that I was certain the public sector could be courted. I argued that ISC should not be wary of approaching public officials because they need new ways to enhance local economies, and ISC had an answer to their prayers. What the organization needed was the expertise to put the project together, and generate the best possible offer in the best possible location for expansion. I made it all up as I went along, but I made it up out of experience and instinct and with the kind of self-assurance that I bring to every table. I could verify that a race track process was a stadium process was an amphitheatre process. I argued that we could create a situation in which a variety of communities would bid for a track and the NASCAR racing and other lucrative events it would bring with it.

By the time I met with the ISC people, I had extensive experience in the NFL process for Super Bowl bidding. In each case, the question of economic impact on a city came up. In each case, cities competed intensely for the Super Bowl because it is recognized as a powerful economic generator—bringing many thousands of people to town, and hundreds of millions in revenues. I argued that the economic benefit provided to a city for a one-time Super Bowl could be matched each year at a new ISC race track with a single annual NASCAR race. I didn't have the formula worked out, but was confident that it could be proven. I further argued that the events, racing and otherwise, held other weeks of the year would just be gravy.

Picking up on Lesa's observation that ignorance in my case could be an advantage, I said, "I'm in a better position to do this than you are. I've done it before and can be objective about arguments concerning a sport you're very close to. Though I'm not a race fan, I am a fan of big business, and this is big business. Very big business."

There were nods all around, including the most important nod in the room. In a few days, the deal was done. The stock car industry was officially counting on a man who, up to then, had been ignorant, or perhaps even dismissive, of its accomplishments.

Playing the Infield

During my first year with ISC, 1996, I went to a NASCAR race every third week. The first race was in Daytona, the Pepsi 400.

The parking lot was my first clue about the possibilities. I looked at as many license plates as possible in one hour—and counted 35 states. I talked to as many visitors as I could, including a couple from Minnesota who told me they attend 20 races each year, and that their family schedule was geared around NASCAR. In the infield, there was a tent city with 50,000 residents, most of whom had arrived at the beginning of the week. There were food concessions, medical facilities, and even a makeshift jail for rowdies. The fans themselves represented every profession: doctors, teachers, lawyers, dental hygienists, retail employees, plumbers, and salesmen. They were men and women. They were young and old, ranging from the casual fan to the visibly obsessed. Some told me of family traditions going back many years. They had loyalties to particular drivers. It wasn't like the sports I had known where there was a home team. To NASCAR fans, everywhere is home. It's a singular cultural sports phenomenon.

I was impressed with the access to the inner sanctum offered to the public. Fans are free to walk around the garage area where cars are getting ready for battle, and where the drivers are preparing in their trailers. Should they choose, spectators can participate in the prerace prayer service. All of this had been unthinkable to me; it would have been like inviting season ticket holders into the locker room to watch the Miami Dolphins put on their jock straps.

I watched drivers in prerace meetings, talking over where to pass and when to pass. I saw expressions of concern and confidence. I began to understand the high stakes and the tremendous pressure of people whose job it is to make the right decisions—if they want to win and if they want to stay free of profound injury—at speeds that exceed 150 miles per hour in very tight quarters.

I watched Bill France draw a crowd while going from trailer to trailer, place to place, looking at last-minute conditions, talking to sponsors and drivers. There was absolute reverence and respect from everybody, as people reacted to the son of the father of the sport.

On his daughter Lesa's advice, I climbed a small spiral staircase to the top of the tower, a bird's nest that provided a spectacular view of the proceedings. I watched the fighter jets go over, fireworks exploding after the National Anthem, and I noticed a sea of corporate colors connected to hospitality tents. I knew that skeptical public officials who would have to ask the voters for a lot of money would become believers if they saw this unabashed and brilliantly conceived display of patriotism, and that we would end up comparing goose bumps.

The races themselves are noisy and dirty and—well—fast. Cars travel at breakneck speed with only inches between them, and the drivers get to rest only about 16 seconds every couple of hours, when their pit crews take over. I had been wrong, obviously, in my view that drivers are not athletes. Experiencing it in person, as always, helped. I saw for myself the enormous economic and psychological impact of a major sporting event on a city. I was psyched, and ready to sell the great race nationally.

A Possible Double Play

We drew circles. The idea was to inspect arcs of 250 miles around major cities to identify facilities and events that might compete with stock car racing. Among the cities that survived the first pass: Seattle, Houston, Sacramento, Denver, Portland, Chicago, and Kansas City. We wanted to identify as many credible possibilities as we could, which would lead to the creation, in theory anyway, of a bidding war. Even so, the short list got shorter.

Chicago, an enormous market, took itself out of the running when it developed its own track plan that would be outside of ISC's purview. There are, it turns out, competing racing circuits. Seattle was a problem for a couple of reasons. The Kingdome was a relic. The Seahawks wanted a new stadium, and the Mariners had just finished the controversial campaign to raise public funds for what is now Safeco Field. At more than $400 million, this was the most ambitious and costly stadium yet, made so largely by the retractable-roof design. It made no sense to seek public funding for a new race track in this competitive atmosphere. In addition, the city's rainy reputation didn't help matters. This is so even though Bill France observed, "Hell, we can race on the days it doesn't rain." It was an interesting comment in light of the fact that his father, Big Bill France, NASCAR'S originator, was famous for many miracles—one of them successfully commanding a torrential downpour to stop before it washed out a Daytona 500 race.

Kansas City appealed to the ISC. This was the heartland. It was one of the only places on the map where a 250-mile concentric circle didn't intersect with lots of other competing attractions. There was a lot of racing history in the area—small tracks all over Kansas and Missouri, a kind of minor league system that fueled fan interest. There was something else that attracted me: the idea of double leveraging.

Of all the communities we considered, Kansas City was the only one in such a singular geographic position. That is, there was Kansas City, Missouri, and, just across the border, Kansas City, Kansas. There may not be much of a distinction physically, but economically the circumstance was a potential gold mine. One city could be played off against another, and better yet, two state governments would get involved in promoting their competing cities.

There was another promising factor: a history of regionalism and mutual support. Just three years before, voters in five counties (including both states) passed a referendum to fund a new entertainment district in downtown Kansas City, Missouri. It was the first infrastructure referendum that I could find that crossed state lines. The Kansas City area was generally on a roll. It had hosted World Cup soccer matches, boasted a new international airport and a good deal of new construction for business, and even had the distinction of swiping a corporate headquarters from sunny California. When Transamerica Insurance moved from downtown L.A., it was so concerned that its employees would balk at having to leave the Promised Land for Nowheresville that it made an astounding offer. If any employee turned out to be unhappy with the relocation, the company would move him or her back home, all expenses paid. Only one person took Transamerica up on the offer. Despite the general opinion of Californians, everything was, indeed, up to date in Kansas City (and the traffic moved during rush hour).

Of course, as always I wanted to keep the general competition as keen as possible. Even though Kansas City was clearly the first choice, we weren't shy about mentioning other options. In fact, we inspected each possibility, and I worked with key people in these cities. I didn't go first to mayors, or other public officials. I went to the people who had the most at stake—economic development directors, for example. In each case, I made arguments about race tracks as engines of economic development. In each, not surprisingly, there were skeptics. Some may have been influenced by an array of academics who question the real economic value of sports infrastructure. Still, even people who are sports fans can present obstacles.

In Kansas City, officials were uncertain about the prospects of NASCAR racing. Kevin Gray, head of the Kansas City Sports Commission, was taken aback when I first called. "Great," he said, "but we already have Lakeside Speedway and Heartland Park." Gray now admits he didn't understand the difference between the minor league parks and those that host NASCAR. "I figured it was '55 Chevies with gun racks on the back."

For Bob Marcusse, head of the Kansas City Area Development Council, it was a different problem. "Our typical project was a major manufacturing plant, not a race track." So we had to introduce them, and others, to the appeal of NASCAR, and to its financial charms.

Purple Book, Direct Prose

In the advertising business, they used to call it a visual aid. Everybody loves to have something to look at and refer to—to be wowed by. An idea appears validated and quite real simply because it exists in a book, particularly if the book is beautifully printed and is full of stunning photographs, imaginative architectural drawings, and, in this case, compelling reasons to follow up on ISC's invitation to entertain the idea of NASCAR racing. It was called informally the Purple Book, and it went to every city that was a candidate for the new track. I supervised its production, and wrote many of the key portions, particularly those intended to lure potential cities and explain to them what they had to do to succeed.

This was a tricky business. I wanted the first part of the process to be under the radar; it shouldn't look like a leverage process, even though it was. Some people, and some newspapers, might claim that the big, bad race organization was trying to play one city against the other—which is precisely what we were doing. Still, most people inherently understand the nature of competitive bidding, and are all right with it as long as it's done fairly. We had to be careful to preserve the integrity of the process. This wasn't going to be a bid for the Olympic Games, where personal payoffs seemed to be the rule. Our process would be an honest one, and the Purple Book would express precisely what was needed to play. It was a way to put something on the table that told our story, and to convince the guardians of the pots of public money that we were serious and professional.

The Introduction of the Purple Book explained ISC's mission, the location of its tracks, information on its national radio network, and an array of other related companies. It was important in this section to create an expectation among the target audiences that they had already won something—they were on the short list, and they hadn't even known it. The Industry Overview described the proliferation of racing. "From 1990–94, the sport grew 47 percent—more than the NHL, NFL and Major League Baseball combined. According to many sources, including *Forbes* magazine, NASCAR continues to grow 9 percent a year, far surpassing any other professional sport."

For the Economic Impact section, we hired an economic research firm to calculate and verify numbers. It determined how many days people stay at races, how many meals they buy, how many column inches are written in national newspapers about the events, and the impact on secondary businesses (gas stations, restaurants, and even maid services that clean the hotel rooms).

The Economic Impact section featured the argument I used at our first meeting, but now verified by fact: "While the Super Bowl delivers nearly 100,000 visitors to a host city for a one-time event, creating substantial economic benefit to the community, auto racing's two premier series—NASCAR and CART/IRL—draw a weekly average of more than 170,000 fans, creating annual economic benefits to communities exceeding $200 million (roughly equivalent to a Super Bowl).... Known for traveling long distances, typical race fans spend multiple nights in local hotels and patronize area businesses, spending millions of dollars locally. These habits make race fans unlike NBA, NFL, NHL and Major League Baseball fans, who live within relatively short distances from events and therefore do not require food or lodging."

I also wanted to be sure that we showed photographs that revealed a lot of activity: vans and tourists and trailer parks—a city in the infield. I wanted pictures of corporate hospitality, so that business leaders would see this as a place to entertain clients. I could also lure these corporations into a public/private partnership in the building of the track, because they would see, in vivid images, the goodwill they'd get out of it.

When I wrote the Facility Overview section, the people at ISC thought I was crazy. The idea of applying the stadium and arena concepts of stick and ball sports to race track development was something no one ever thought of. Why couldn't it be done? And why wouldn't the lucky community we chose be just thrilled to help us pay for it? Politicians and tourism officials would be attracted by the promise of the civic pride and the economic development that would result. Corporate communities would be attracted by luxurious suites and the specially designed hospitality village.

More than half of the book was devoted to selling the idea; it was designed to attract the immediate attention of candidate cities. Only near the end came the price that would have to be paid. And even then, I was concerned about sticker shock. I wrote it as delicately as possible, and employed language that was vague, giving everybody plenty of wiggle room. The Criteria section provided a general notion of what a community needed to do: "First, the host city must have the ability to develop a premier state-of-the-art motor sports facility in a reasonably short period of time. The second consideration, but equally important, will be the location's ability to annually support multiple motor sports events with attendance of up to 80,000 spectators per event day in the inaugural year, progressing up to 150,000 spectators per event in the fifth year of operation. . . . To accommodate the anticipated influx of visitors into the area for the event weekend, a substantial base of hotel rooms, a high traffic airport and a comprehensive road network will be essential."

The Purple Book, once conceived, was not difficult to produce, but on occasion I incurred unexpected obstacles. One of the obstacles I created myself. To make the book truly persuasive, I knew that we had to spend money on preliminary architectural designs. That is, we needed a concept design that might, in the end, not be anything close to what we'd use but would at least provide an idea of what a revolutionary new track would look like. For this task, I immediately thought of Ron Labinski, a principal of HOK Architects, which had designed Camden Yards, Jacobs Field, the baseball and football stadiums in Kansas City, and many other new facilities. Labinski was viewed as the father of the new architecture for stick and ball sports.

For me to bring him into a NASCAR and ISC meeting would have very little risk, or so I thought. I briefed him on what to expect, and told him something of what I had learned since I had gotten NASCAR religion. This, I said, was one of the most successful sports groups in the modern era, even if this fact was not particularly known in mainstream circles.

In the large, elegant, formal boardroom, all 30 seats around the table were filled. I said, "I have the unique privilege of introducing the best to the best." Then Ron started talking. "I've built stadiums all over the world, and done more than anyone else alive. Today, I've taken time out of my busy schedule, because Rick said I should." I could see, from everything he was saying, and from his body language, that we were heading for disaster. I looked down, not knowing what to do next. It was probably not a good idea for me to ask Ron softball questions. Even though he was my guy, I had to begin to distance myself. I said, "As I told you previously, Ron (so they didn't think I didn't prepare him), ISC wants to be a pioneer in building multipurpose entertainment centers, just as you've pioneered in baseball and football stadiums." This, I hoped, would get him in the right direction.

He said, "I'm not sure you can do that with the crowds that attend NASCAR races." The tone was arrogant and condescending, as if to say race fans are not big spenders, or sophisticated. I couldn't believe what I was hearing, and neither could the Frances. Lesa and her father looked at each other with expressions of astonishment. I looked down again at the conference table, trying to find in its polished grain some suggestion about what to say and do. I didn't want to make eye contact with the Frances. I made sure that when they looked at me they saw someone shifting in the chair, as if the warden's assistants were attaching the last straps before execution.

I evoked a principle I use sparingly. I stayed very quiet. I used my own body language. I shook my head, avoided eye contact with Labinski. I didn't want it to appear as if I were coaching him. In the next few minutes, everyone was able to save a little face by discussing the retail opportunities of a multipurpose facility. We shifted the focus, and Bill France's graciousness ended the meeting on a pleasant note.

Still, in the hallway, I felt the obligation to speak to Lesa about what had happened. I said, "Ron is a good example of an industry king gone wrong, not giving you the respect you deserve." I showed my loyalty to her, my willingness to be a team player. I could be objective enough to criticize my own action, and this was damage control. She said, "You're right. Stick to deal-making. Avoid architecture." It didn't make me feel very good, but I had it coming.

Bid Business, or the Case of the Fairy Shrimp

How much public money could we reasonably expect to get? This was the question that Lesa Kennedy had for me at each juncture. I had no idea. I said, "Anywhere from zero to 100 percent of what we need." She didn't like that. But I certainly didn't want to be in the prediction business. I said we might be able to get $50 million, or about one quarter of the cost of a new track. If we could get that, my monthly stipend would seem like peanuts. If not, I would have some explaining to do. Still, I was confident it would happen. I could see ahead to an effective money-raising campaign in which I would follow the three primary techniques of leveraging: ratchet the stakes, ratchet the stakes, ratchet the stakes.

And so I visited cities outside of the Kansas City region to drum up interest, and to enhance the bidding process. Houston had a vision of a large site developed into two tracks: one for horse racing and one for car racing. Sacramento wanted to build a track in an abandoned airfield. On our tours of these cities and others, I took Lesa Kennedy with me, for several reasons. For one thing, she had to ultimately approve the chosen market. For another, we would give the appearance of keeping every city in the hunt for the purposes of increasing leverage. Just by going to each, it heightened their interest, and these visits reflected positively on our process. One of the things I stressed to Lesa was that the process didn't just leverage one city against another but allowed us to be in control of the effort. It also allowed us to learn the nuances of local situations, and to play their strengths and their weaknesses against other possible sites.

To be sure, all the candidates had strengths and weaknesses, so it was important to show real interest in each case. We had no guarantee that Kansas City would work out, and if it didn't, we didn't want other candidates to feel as if they had been slighted, and that we were turning to them out of desperation.

Houston was obviously a burgeoning market, particularly in the years when the name Enron meant prosperity and could be displayed on a baseball field and there was no shame, or sense of great failure or rampant fraud, attached to it. But Houston, for all of its wealth, did not promise very much in the way of immediate public support. The city would provide some land, and some funding for roads. Cash for a new race track itself would have to wait—for a little while, or perhaps a long while. The Sacramento situation was more promising from an immediate financial point of view, but it also carried with it daunting environmental and practical problems. The site the city was pushing contained an active church that couldn't be moved; it would have to be accommodated somehow in a track design. I could just imagine parishioners singing hymns that were drowned out by race cars zooming around them. Other buildings on the acreage contained asbestos. And then there was the case of the fairy shrimp. I'd heard of many kinds of shrimp, but these had escaped my notice. Fairy shrimp, it turns out, are an endangered species. They live in vernal pools that form in the cool, wet months of the year—vernal pools that happened to be in the midst of the Sacramento site.

This is more than you may want to know about these crustaceans, but they swim upside-down with their 11 pairs of legs. Fairy shrimp are not known to inhabit permanent bodies of water, and are dependent on seasonal fluctuations in their habitat, such as absence or presence of water during specific times of the year. Nothing in the literature of endangered species indicates it would be a good idea for them to swim at race car tracks. Still, it was my intent to keep the fairy shrimp problem local. No need to talk about it in Houston or Kansas City, where folks would suspect that Sacramento wasn't really a viable candidate.

In each case, at every meeting, I gave people at the table something to do: specific follow-up tasks. In Sacramento, I urged officials to find out what it takes to deal with toxic waste, fairy shrimp, and the church problem. In Houston, where they didn't have an answer about public money despite their best intentions, I could see that I might have to go after state or federal help. I asked people to identify those sources. In Kansas City, there were many sites to be explored, and each obstacle evaluated.

In each case, we brought key local officials to NASCAR races to see for themselves the impact of the sport at its highest level. Bob Marcusse remembers that when he saw all the activity and the crowd, "A light went on. This was big-time sports, and big-time economic impact."

Leverage is always in the eye of the beholder. And I always conveyed its particulars and essence as strongly as possible. Houston and Sacramento said they would have trouble making the deadline for the bid—and it was clear, in each case, there might be deal killers. But I kept them in the process, and helped them shape their presentations. I went to each city several times within a 30-day period to coach them, helping them provide persuasive answers to each of the criteria outlined in the Purple Book. Even though they couldn't meet all of the requirements, they could come close enough to represent legitimate competition and move the process forward.

This was, to me, a midpoint and not an endpoint. I knew there remained a lot of work ahead, and the most important thing was that bids, no matter how flawed, be submitted. There was still a presumption among public officials that there was a big difference between publicly funding a stadium and a race track. Meanwhile, we could always simply say that those cities present opportunities, if also a few "challenges." Even in the environs of Kansas City, fast becoming the preferred location, there were problems in each possible location for a track, though none as profound as in Sacramento and Houston. For the first time, I worried that I might not get anything from anybody—just a lot of birds in bushes and fairy shrimp in vernal pools.

The Credible Process

It's important to develop a credible competitive process, one that is free of misrepresentation. That is, although I considered Sacramento and

Houston to be valid candidates, I would never say that they were perfect candidates. In this case, I was able to say to the Kansas City folks that, for the good work they have done, I could put the other cities on the back burner. The message was clearly that Kansas City was on a priority track. Once the three bids were in, it had won the first part of our contest, which gave it the right to participate in the second part. If Kansas City continued to perform, we would work with them as our primary candidate, though not exclusively—we made this clear. The process, as always, had to remain forthright and objective. I told people in the other cities that we were still interested in them, but that we were going to focus presently on Kansas City. I reminded each runner-up that they had some major issues, many of which could be worked out, and that if we had some problem in Kansas City, we'd call. And, even if we chose Kansas City there was no reason we couldn't build a second track, an expression of optimism that satisfied them for the moment.

In the Kansas City area, including parts of the state of Kansas, I inspected eight or nine possible sites, and several of them became finalists. We had first arranged a national competition, and now we were intensifying the local competition.

On the Kansas side, the key questions involved the difficulties of acquiring property from two or three dozen landowners, and building the roads that needed to service the new facility. Could they employ eminent domain, getting the state to condemn property on behalf of the public interest? Would the state pay for the roads? Would it help finance the facility with bonds? In Missouri, we faced several of these same issues, particularly the question of whether the state was willing to help find a public source to help build the track. That is, in each case we asked for a transportation plan, a plan to acquire the full property, and an assurance that the neighbors wouldn't become enemies of a race track. These were not easy issues, and I worried that none of the candidates locally could deliver on all of them but, as always, I'd worry about the details later.

In each case, the people vying for the track were cordial and informational but competitive. They and their staffs tried to sway me. I wanted to keep my role as the designated asshole: Here are the things to do, and if I were you, I'd do these things. But if you don't deal with these things adequately there's another site in this region that will. And if none do, we'll go to another part of the country.

Instinctively, we knew this wouldn't be necessary. Local officials were champing at the bit. And one mayor in particular, Carol Marinovich of Wyandotte County, Kansas, campaigned furiously on behalf of her community. She produced a video with community members speaking on behalf of the place, and developed a personal relationship with Lesa France Kennedy, inviting her to lunch often, and talking woman to woman about how to make this business deal work.

We met with many Kansans. I coached Lesa on how she needed to look confident about the future of the sport, and about what Kansas had done so far. It was my job to express reservations about whether Kansas could finish the job. I argued that we could use the same economic model used in Florida to finance the move of the LPGA from Texas, by using the Kansas tradition of what was called "Star Bonds," a little utilized law in Kansas. The idea would be the same as it had been in Florida. We'd actually borrow money against anticipated tax revenues once the facility was built. But that had taken some time to sell back home, and I had no idea if Kansas would go for it.

Then Dennis Hays, the Wyandotte County administrator, said, "Maybe we could advance a few dollars to help build the track." Aha!

I didn't know what "a few dollars" meant and I wasn't about to ask. Afterward, Lesa couldn't understand my ebullient mood. We'd surely need more than a few dollars. I explained to her that this was the first mention of any public money for the track itself. I said that for someone like Dennis Hays to say what he said required just the sort of leap of faith we needed from public officials. He was willing to pay now and collect later. Never mind the number. The public/private partnership that we had been hoping for was beginning to emerge. The camel's nose was in the tent. Or, to mix metaphors, we had a minnow on the line as we went back to Missouri.

When we arrived for the meeting in Kansas City, we were welcomed by an overflow crowd. There were 45 bureaucrats, technocrats, site planners, lawyers, and financial experts. This was the meeting where we had to show the carrot and the stick. I introduced Lesa, and talked briefly of her vision for the sport, which was what got us to this point. In a few concise minutes, she explained the history and future of stock car racing, and her enthusiasm about Missouri, and the prospect of locating a track there. Then she turned it over to me. I could be the bad guy. I said, "All we have is talk."

Lesa still gives me grief over this meeting because of my unscheduled departure, which left her holding the bag. I went on about how the process had illuminated a promising possibility—how we clearly have a very important economic engine to bestow on a lucky region. I said that to get into the game we'll need a quick deal, some free land, all the roads necessary, and (I was making up the number) at least $40 million in public support. I didn't mention the word "Kansas," because I didn't need to. Everyone knew. Competition was assumed.

I had advised Lesa I would lay out a number and then she could back off on it if she needed to. She was prepared to do that. But she wasn't prepared to carry on the negotiations alone. I had just gotten a message that my scheduled flight to Washington had been cancelled, and I needed to get to the capital to testify before the Senate Judiciary Committee, which was deliberating on the value of public spending for new stadiums and arenas. I couldn't miss this, obviously. So I booked an earlier flight. I left Lesa to face the Kansas City group, including a number of scared politicians and bureaucrats who had just heard the number $40 million and were shaking in their chairs.

Here's how Lesa remembers it: "You gave a little speech, introduced me, and said, by the way, 'This is what she wants, and laid it all out. I'd like to stay and talk more about this, but I've got to catch a plane.'" She says she wanted to kill me. As it was, the meeting ended amicably. And my premature departure was one of the best things that could happen. She told the group, "We've turned it all over to Rick, for the right deal, and I won't get into whether $40 million is the right number or not."

The bureaucrats left with a clear sense of Lesa's enthusiasm, but with the reality that the deal wouldn't happen by itself—somebody in Missouri had to step up to the plate. Again, Lesa turned a potentially difficult situation into a winning one.

I got up the courage to call her that night from Washington and find out how the meeting went after I left. I heard restrained anger, and one-word answers, for two minutes. I said, "I'm sure they're scurrying around tonight trying to find the public money."

The Precisely Worded Challenge

I had done enough talking, enough promising, enough groundwork. It was time to play the leverage game to the hilt, time to climb aboard the ISC Gulfstream and head for Missouri and Kansas, and close the deal with one governor or the other. It was time to show the Frances that their investment was not in vain, and that we could get big money from either Missouri or Kansas, or both, much more than $40 million. We'd do it all on the same trip. I told Bill France we would get our deal done by the end of the day. It was D-Day.

My strategy was to go to Springfield, Missouri, first and get a commitment, even if it was a small one. That way we had something in the bank—a real threat to Kansas. I said to Bill, "Let's allow each state to sell themselves as much as they can. On any financial issues, I'll be the aggressor and you'll be the son of the founder of NASCAR. Lesa will be the visionary, and I'll be the bad guy. I'm good at that, and I'm used to it."

We met with Governor Mel Carnahan. I remember him as polite and gracious. (This was three years before he was killed in an airplane crash while running against John Ashcroft for a U.S. Senate seat.) The governor said he read the material we'd sent him, and that he was not a race fan, but he was impressed by how far the sport had come. Carnahan, I could see, was doing some selling, too. Perhaps we would settle for a lower number if the working arrangement were cordial and full of mutual respect. Bill France told the governor that he was "ready to make a commitment in the region," which is language I asked him to use. That is, he would invest ISC and NASCAR assets to show his faith and the risk he was willing to take, if the public would join him as a partner. "Ready to make a commitment in the region" is not a way of saying it's signed, sealed, and delivered for Missouri. It says, "I'll do this, if the conditions are right, somewhere—and it might be in nearby Kansas." We didn't want Missouri officials to think their offer was the right offer. The governor said he was impressed with the progress so far, and that his staff had briefed him. Neither comment cost him a dime. He wasn't going to lay his cards on the table.

We were aware that he was under his own political pressure to balance government largesse. The St. Louis area had received much help in recent years. Perhaps it was time to give something to the other side of the state. Perhaps he just wanted to play the leverage game himself, and see what he was up against with Kansas as an opponent.

My question to him wasn't "Are you ready to make a deal?" It was "Are you ready to use public funds in the building itself, knowing you'll get the money back over time based on our economic model."

He replied, "We have traditional incentives in place that you can use. Job credits, for example, which could produce about $5 million for you."

You hear these things all the time. "Use the system. It's already in place. Don't bother me with variations." For bureaucrats, even effective leaders such as Mel Carnahan was, it's a convenience. He doesn't have to turn us away. He can say, "Here's something. It's better than nothing. And you won't have trouble getting it." But it's hardly worth the effort. It was time to take a risk, and to represent Kansas's "few dollars" as something of a windfall.

I replied, "You could offer tax credits to anybody. What we're offering you ought to inspire the state to participate in a much more direct way. What I'm asking for is a special law that other states have enacted, and that Kansas is apparently willing to use, that will return tax revenues to taxpayers."

He relied on the desperate answer of the cornered decision-maker: "We've never done that." There was a very long pause. Bill and Lesa had instructions not to speak when the negotiations got tense. They did their job. It was up to me to take the next step, which was to save the governor's face, and our process along the way.

I said, "Maybe you can have your economic staff look at this more carefully." He nodded. This was good enough for me. I didn't want to close the door before our meeting in Topeka and leave us with but one viable candidate. Leverage had closed the gap, but I needed more than that. I needed a deal before the Frances dismissed me as just another big talker. They didn't say it that way, but I could feel the tension. What I had heard so far was promising—but promising means very little in the political world. It was my job to turn promise into commitment.

The trip to Topeka lasted 40 minutes and shook us up. The Gulfstream bounced around in a terrible thunderstorm. But the minute we landed, we knew the trip would be worthwhile. Governor Bill Graves sent a limo to meet us at the airport, and we clearly got the sense that we were big fish in a small pond—and that we could still reap the benefits of being near the large pond nearby, across the border. The Wyandotte County site was clearly the choice—Mayor Marinovich had made the difference there. The governor could see that, too. And I had seen his own enormously positive reaction to a race at Daytona, where he had led an entourage of state and local dignitaries. The press had called it a junket. It didn't understand the value of what NASCAR could offer, but Graves did.

Once we sat down with him in his office, I said, "This is the time to make the decision to create the biggest economic development project in your state. It will be your legacy. We think the economic model supports a Star Bond allocation of $150 million." I knew the number could be stretched to more than $200 million. But sometimes you have to back off on the side of caution. In this case, bonding institutions might object to the higher number because this was the first time this had been tried in the region.

The governor didn't flinch—a clear sign that we had a deal. He said, "I will assign my staff to work with you around the clock to get this done, based on what the numbers support." He wasn't saying yes to the $150 million, but he was saying yes to the idea of public support.

I looked at Bill and Lesa with a slight nod, and they nodded back, almost imperceptibly, beautifully hiding their delight. I said to the governor, "Let's work this out with your staff." We shook hands. It was a done, if not entirely completed, deal. On the plane back home, we popped a bottle of Dom Perignon.

Everybody, Start Your Engines

There was still lots of work to do. We put together a master checklist of 450 items before the deal could be finished, from who takes care of the construction overruns to how many seats are given away to the Kansas City Area Development Council. It took four months to nail the whole deal down because of the number of details to work out; this, after all, was the first new track to be built with public money.

We slowly evolved to the final number with the governor's staff. We settled for a total package of $140.2 million, which represented about two-thirds of what the track would ultimately cost. ISC put in the rest. The Frances were ecstatic. Their $9,000-a-month investment in me had ultimately represented a figure that was less than one-tenth of one percent of the Kansas payoff.

The track, as anticipated, took several years to build. The first NASCAR race was held at the new Kansas Speedway on September 30, 2001, drawing about 100,000 people to the grandstand and infield. Lesa France Kennedy arrived early in the week, saw the crowds already flocking there, and had a feeling that it was all something out of a fairy tale. She called a friend and said, "You won't believe it. People are actually coming to this." Her friend said, "Well, yeah. That's what they do at speedways."

Before the race, I took a personal tour of the facility to see for myself what a couple of hundred million dollars could buy. Many of the stats were published in press materials: 1.5-mile oval, 15 degrees in the turns, 10.4 degrees in the front stretch, 5 degrees in the back stretch, pavement width of 55 feet, and seating capacity of 75,000 and, when the second phase is finished, a capacity double that, which officials pointed out would easily accommodate the entire population of the Virgin Islands. Eleven million tons of dirt were used in track construction. This is equal to 1 million dump truck loads or enough earth to fill an NFL stadium five times. Also, to equal the length of storm sewer pipe used in the project, the Sears Tower in Chicago would have to be laid end to end 45 times.

For all of this and more, public officials and International Speedway Corporation dignitaries took their bows that day. I chose to stay behind the scenes, and out of the headlines. It was more important for the Frances and for the governor and his staff to be recognized for their intensity, and for their leaps of faith.

CHAPTER 8

Building the NFL

Don't sell firewood by a forest, nor fish beside a lake.

CHINESE PROVERB

In the beginning, there was pro football—the game that my father and I shared. It only seemed natural that I would come around to it again. And yet if my fantasy had played out, I never would have had the chance to become a consultant to the NFL. I would have been, instead, a franchise owner.

When Joe Robbie died in 1990, his nine children inherited the Dolphins and the stadium he built. The Robbie kids never developed a reputation for getting along. And now that they found themselves in a financial pickle, the prospects of working out of it seemed dim. Strapped by hefty inheritance taxes, they had no choice but to sell Joe Robbie Stadium and the team their father founded.

I paced around my house, fantasizing about my future in the owner's skybox. There wasn't very much out there that could make me give up Horrow Sports Ventures, but this opportunity would. It would bring me full circle, and I knew I had the sufficient wits and instincts, if not the deep pockets, to a run a pro football team. I would obviously need a money man who would understand the value I would offer. My role would be as managing partner, with an equity stake in exchange for franchise expertise and making the sale happen.

Of course, I had to find this enlightened baron. So one day I opened *Forbes* magazine.

George Lindemann, who lived near Palm Beach, was one of the pioneers of the cellular phone industry. From what I read about him, I didn't have the foggiest idea whether he was a sports fan. But I had nothing to lose by making a call and saying, "You don't know me, but . . ." Lindemann instantly bought the pitch. Yes, he had made a fortune in the telecommunications industry, but, as with all ambitious and egotistical men, he eventually learned that fortunes are not enough. These entrepreneurs want something more—adulation that widget manufacturing won't bring. At first, however, Lindemann seemed secretive, reluctant to have his name appear in the sports pages. This was all right with me. I could use the situation to my advantage in dealing with the Robbie family.

I hadn't been on anything like decent terms with the late patriarch. But now I had leverage with his offspring. As the front man, I kept Lindemann behind the scenes just as he had requested. I asked Tim Robbie, the eldest of the siblings and executor of his father's estate, if my participation in a deal would pose a problem. He said it wouldn't; after all, he was interested in getting the most he could for the Dolphins, and the more bidders the better. But I was taking no chances. I told him that I represented a serious buyer who wouldn't make an offer without my participation. Tim said, "We won't veto a deal because you're involved." Still, it was clear we had competition. Wayne Huizenga, the Blockbuster founder who prevailed in the Florida Marlins sweepstakes, had the right to match any bona fide offer within 30 days of the original. This was a result of a deal Huizenga had made with Joe Robbie eight years earlier, when the Dolphins owner, strapped for cash, gave up 15 percent of his franchise to Huizenga and the right of first refusal in the case of a sale.

The *Miami Herald*, of course, looked into the financial state of the Dolphins and its likely sale and found out about Lindemann's interest. It was now impossible to keep his name out of the press. He was particularly worried, I discovered, that the paper would learn about his son, a member of the polo set, who was under investigation for insurance fraud in a matter involving a dead horse. But the *Herald* never referred to it, and with only some trepidation, Lindemann stayed in the game.

We ended up offering $137.1 million. It came with a $1 million "break-up" fee. That is, I insisted that if Huizenga matched our figure and the Robbie family took his bid, we'd be reimbursed $1 million for our expenses and trouble. At critical times in the negotiation process, it's important to press as hard as possible. The seller certainly isn't going to suggest such a clause, but if he's smart, and there's enough at stake, he won't object either. Tim Robbie agreed to all this, and we shook hands. He said, "We have a deal, contingent on putting it on paper." Which should have worried me.

Our lawyers worked around the clock for a week, and we prepared press statements. The closing was set for Monday, January 24, 1994. This would be a great day for me, a dream fulfilled. On that morning, we were ready to go to downtown Miami to sign the papers when Tim Robbie called Lindemann's lawyer. We put him on speaker phone. Robbie said, "I have good news and bad news. The good news is we are selling the Dolphins and having the press conference in an hour. We are selling the team for $138 million. The bad news is it's not to you."

As it turned out, we were not only the runner-up in the Dolphins bidding, but I got outsmarted even in the quest to collect the break-up fee. The Robbie family was pretty close to Huizenga, and we figured that once we set the price, all Wayne had to do was decide if it was a fair deal, and if he'd make his offer. He did this over the weekend—before our closing date. He told the Robbies they didn't have to wait 30 days. Not only that, if they signed over the weekend, the sellers could get an extra $900,000 and, to boot, save $1 million. According to our agreement, no break-up fee had to be paid because the closing date hadn't yet been reached. Lindemann was out a million.

Our group was, of course, discouraged by this unforeseen turn of events. So I did what I always do. I came up with another idea. I said, "Let's buy the Tampa Bay Buccaneers." Lindemann was incredulous: "Are you serious?" I replied, "Sure." As it turned out, we came close, but didn't get them, either—lost out to Malcolm Glazer's $192 million. (We were outbid by a few million.)

Still, as I have said, one enterprise inevitably leads to another. In this case, the entrepreneurial efforts and my record of building sports facilities in those years caught the attention of National Football League officials. I had several conversations with Roger Goodell, then vice president of the NFL, about ways I could become involved in the league's efforts. The NFL was on the verge of a new and expansive era, but it found itself in need of help.

The Tipped Playing Field

The NFL had grown up, largely, in rented facilities. In the early years, teams played at a lot of baseball stadiums. In the '60s and '70s, that changed, but only marginally for the better. In cities such as Philadelphia, Cincinnati, Pittsburgh, Atlanta, and Oakland, among others, large donut-shaped stadiums were built as economical compromises to accommodate both baseball and football. But neither game could flourish in these circumstances. The donut accommodated many seats, but few were close enough to the action. Also, these facilities came along before the era of skyboxes, club seats, parking revenue for teams, and wide concourses to sell lots of goods. Many also suffered from profound structural or design problems. At Candlestick Park in San Francisco, temporary bleachers used for football rocked in the wind. The Silverdome in Pontiac suffered from lack of air conditioning, which made it stifling until October. Experts determined that the Kingdome in Seattle would not survive an earthquake of any significance. Denver's Mile High Stadium had severe engineering problems. In Cincinnati, there was such a shortage of bathrooms that women had to wait an average of 45 minutes in line.

At one point, of course, it had seemed to me that multipurpose stadiums were the answer. But now this worked against the new economic realities of the NFL. In short, an NFL owner who didn't have a state-of-the-art stadium would find himself at a great disadvantage.

The league's financial base relied on two significant revenue sources quite apart from ticket sales. The first—equally sharing television revenues—was forged in the early 1960s. It was an enlightened plan, something that baseball never embraced. The result was that there really were no poor franchises, even if there were small-market teams. As the years passed, television revenues increased dramatically, much more than in any other sport. Pro football, unlike baseball, seemed made for television. Network contracts for hundreds of thousands turned into contracts for millions and, recently, a seven-year deal (a combination of Fox, ABC/Disney, ESPN, and CBS) worth $18 billion. This windfall is shared equally. The trouble was that all of this is figured in the formula to pay players. In exchange for the right to impose a salary cap, owners developed a specified pool of funds that would include television money as part of the deal. This way, the salary cap could rise as time went on, and the players, in collective bargaining, would approve of the plan. But it wasn't an ideal arrangement for owners. By splitting all this income (called Designated Gross Revenues, or DGR) with players, their profits were diminished. The league was careful in negotiations, however, to retain certain revenues for owners outside of DGR considerations.

This second source included fees from skyboxes, club seats, related facilities, and stadium naming rights. Teams could keep that money. So some franchises began to show much more impressive bottom lines than others—and these, invariably, were teams with new stadiums. It was important to the league that new facilities get built so that revenue could be enhanced and, at the same time, that the franchise base remain stable. These seemed, on occasion, to be two incompatible ideas. It surely was not an easy objective in a landscape where so many cities had dreams of franchises, and seemed willing to do whatever it took to secure one.

A prominent example of the problem was the Cleveland situation. Owner Art Modell quietly entertained offers from other cities because of the dilapidated condition of old Municipal Stadium. The Browns— a franchise that boasted Hall of Famers Otto Graham, Lou Groza, Marion Motley, and Jim Brown, among others—traditionally sold out that huge stadium because of its loyal fan base. But even the NFL conceded that owners such as Modell would find themselves at a disadvantage without a modern facility. So the league needed a way to handle all of this—to balance stability with growth and change—something of an impossible task. That's why league official Roger Goodell called me.

The Cost of Credibility

Goodell said that Commissioner Paul Tagliabue had followed what I had done in other places, and wanted to know if I could work full-time as the league's stadium development expert. I was flattered, of course. Working for the NFL in New York would be prestigious and rewarding. But, for one thing, I didn't want to move my family. Katie and Caroline were in school. Terri's parents and my mother lived within a quick drive of our house. Moreover, I felt a sense of history and roots, and that I was destined to stay in South Florida. Despite dismissing the idea at one point, I still held on to the notion that one day I would run for political office there. If I moved out of town, I'd be taking a step backward. There was another thing. I am a multitasking kind of guy. I prefer that when I wake up in the morning I instantly think of several clients. Over the previous five years, I averaged 150 to 180 nights away from home, but we were all used to it. The kids actually didn't mind. Caroline and Katie preferred when I wasn't home for dinner during the week. Then Terri could make them French toast and pancakes instead of steak.

I told Roger that as much as I would like to, I couldn't move to New York, and couldn't give up Horrow Sports Ventures. Perhaps I could help as a consultant.

Roger said, "Why don't I introduce you to key owners who are about to get into the stadium issue, and you can work out independent deals with them?" Bingo. What a bonanza. I could have 10 or 12 clients from the NFL alone. I'd collect half a million dollars a year. So I said no.

There are times when you have to step back and ask yourself what you're about, what you really want, and what will be the most useful way for you to prosper in the long run. This was such a time. If I decided to be a door-to-door football stadium consultant, and even though it would be with the blessings of NFL officials, I would be perceived by owners as no different from hundreds of vendors, concessionaires, and facility developers who come calling. I wanted instead to solidify my brand. I wanted the highest level of credibility. And to get that, I felt as if I had to work from the inside. I wouldn't be an employee of the NFL but I'd carry a title, Facility Development Consultant (a term I made up). I would be the commissioner's right arm. I would use all of my experience and expertise to address the NFL's challenges. I would apply the technique of bundling, in all its variations, to each city. The commissioner's office would provide something of a wedge. A setup like this would bring a level of credibility that would be useful to me specifically in stadium deliberations and in other venues. But I would do it by having the league as a client. I could argue that they could achieve this more economically than if they put me on staff, because I still had my other clients. And by now I knew what to say if eyebrows were raised, or someone actually said (which they didn't), "Aren't you spreading yourself too thin?" Action and results counter such objection.

In a few days, I had a contract, and I set about to learn the institution from the inside.

The NFL is, in some ways, a tight-knit league. The public perception is that it is run by fat-cat owners who smoke the same brand of cigars and, with certain notable exceptions such as Al Davis, get along famously, and who, as one, contrive to always do what's best for the league. But it is in many ways just like any other institution—full of egos and conflict. It has its old guard and its new kids on the block. It comprises markets both huge and modest, where local sentiment varies, where ownership is viewed as either enlightened or incompetent. Moreover, political situations, values, and histories vary in each city.

My mission may have seemed fairly consistent in each location—try to get a stadium built and a franchise stabilized. But I knew that in every case I would have to emphasize certain franchise strengths and minimize weaknesses. Some of what I argued may seem, on its face, inconsistent. I prefer to think of these actions as demonstrating a necessary flexibility, in the way a quarterback would at the line of scrimmage when, seeing the defense stacked against the run, he calls an audible for a play-action pass.

If you think of the business strategies developed and applied so far as a football playbook, you can perhaps begin to see that, on the one hand, you follow a certain plan and structure, and, on the other, you must constantly adjust and improvise.

Go, Team, Go! (But Leave Your Colors Behind)

Of all the assignments I could have begun with, this was the most delicate, and it had enormous opportunity for failure. As it turned out, it was a demonstration of the risk necessary to save a desperate situation—risk well outside the lines of what your client intended.

My mission was to try to retain the Browns for Cleveland if possible, or at least retain the market for the league. The NFL by nature and tradition had experienced franchise movement. This had been true ever since the league decided in 1926 that the Canton Bulldogs, no matter how successful on the field, would never be a gold mine in a small Midwestern industrial city in which Hoovers and ball bearings were the clear priorities. In recent years, Oakland moved to Los Angeles and moved back again. Los Angeles, which had two franchises, had none when the Rams moved to St. Louis in 1994. This was painful for the league—L.A., obviously, is an enormous market. And yet St. Louis raised the bar by providing a new stadium that was the product of a public/private partnership. Every time the bar was raised, the league benefited—to a point. There was still a pretty strong feeling about the need for stability, and avoiding an endless game of musical chairs. The goal of the commissioner was to use the expansion process for new and big markets, and then charge the new owner a hefty expansion fee, and spread the money around. The last thing Paul Tagliabue wanted was owners moving on their own, preempting such a windfall. The Cleveland case, in which I was about to immerse myself, was one of the most difficult the league ever had to deal with.

Modell had owned the team since the early 1960s, when he bought it from Paul Brown, who named the franchise after himself. With the clear exception of the year Modell fired Brown, he had enjoyed decades of respect from Cleveland fans. There was no more loyal fan base in the league than on the shores of Lake Erie. Crowds of more than 70,000 had been the norm for decades. The Dawg Pound (rabid fans in end zone seats) earned a national, if somewhat unsavory, reputation. And it seemed inconceivable that there could be a National Football League without a team in Cleveland. It was like baseball without the Boston Red Sox. Yet that seemed a clear, if lamentable, possibility. Modell's personal fortunes were at a low ebb, and he no longer had the capacity, he felt, to compete with the big boys.

When I introduced myself at the Browns' practice facility in suburban Berea, Modell was pleasant enough. As one of the league's elder statesman, he understood why I was there. And he also understood that he had to speak carefully to me—that all of it would get back to Tagliabue. I explained to Modell that the league wanted a franchise in Cleveland, and wanted me to work to that end. And so I tried to persuade him that the future in Cleveland would prove to be a gold mine. In an effort to persuade Modell to stay, city leaders had placed a referendum on the November ballot. If voters approved, a hefty liquor and cigarette tax would be applied to a stadium fund—an estimated $175 million toward the building of a replacement for the old lakefront facility. It wouldn't be enough—short by about half of what ultimately would be needed—but it was a serious start. Modell was sympathetic, or seemed to be, at first.

As the meetings went on, I could see this approach would be fruitless. Later, I learned he had been to Baltimore several times, where an offer was on the table, an offer that no one in Modell's shoes could turn away. Modell was playing something of a game in the Cleveland media. He seemed willing to consider staying if certain demands were met, but his head was already several hundred miles to the southeast, and had even privately made a commitment there. The same lottery revenue pot that had paid for Oriole Park at Camden Yards would finance a new football stadium. A franchise that wanted to play there would have no responsibility whatsoever to contribute to the pot. In short, he would be home free. A public/private partnership without any private responsibility, leaving the NFL owner free to smoke his cigars without the distraction of ever having to take out a checkbook. In a way, however, all of this was poetic justice. The Colts had been ripped away in the middle of the night from Baltimore years before. Wasn't the city just getting back what it deserved?

Cleveland mayor Michael White, a real fighter, was at the center of an impressive civic campaign to save the Browns for Cleveland. Aside from the ballot initiative, he also held the stadium lease, and the Browns and Modell would have to break it to move. Though it seemed this could be done, the case could get tied up in the courts. White was not at all in awe of the NFL. Though he knew $175 million was not enough, he was not about to raise the liquor and cigarette taxes beyond what it would take to reach that figure. Let the team or the league pay the rest, he said—make it a real public/private partnership. Also, he was reluctant to support the referendum at all without some kind of commitment from the NFL that it was behind Cleveland in the long run, no matter what Modell would decide to do, and without some assurance that a new stadium wouldn't become a vacant white elephant.

My position here was a dicey one, and, as this was my first NFL gig, there was much at stake as I struggled to define my role. On the one hand, I couldn't stand in the way of "progress," and on the other, I (and the league) wanted to preserve goodwill in one of its most loyal cities. When I pressed the Browns owner on the importance of stability, Modell told me, "What you're saying makes some sense. But time may have run out on me. I wish you had been around a year ago."

So now it was my job, clearly, to keep the community hopeful, and lay the groundwork for another franchise in seasons to come. This was a finesse job. The only way Cleveland could be saved for the NFL was by passing the referendum—without the certainty of a team in place. So I became a key player in the referendum push. I made the argument to the public that a new stadium is critical to ensure NFL football for years to come, whether or not it's the Browns. I was arguing infrastructure as much as football. I was arguing the future instead of the past. I suggested, though I really had no way of knowing this for certain, that if the Browns left, the league would replace the team either with an existing or a new franchise.

A referendum is tough enough when a team wants to come to the city, or stay in the city. This was a daunting task to sell it in a situation where failure to keep a beloved team was almost certain. And so—building on ideas I'd developed earlier about pushing my own clients—I helped persuade the league to do something it had never done. In subsequent years, it came to be called the G-3 resolution (a name drawn simply from the place it appears on a document). The resolution allowed the league, interested in preserving lucrative markets, to lend money from shared club seat and skybox revenues to help build stadiums. In doing this, the NFL departed entirely from the stance it took when Al Davis, the Raiders owner, applied for a loan and was told that the league is not a bank. In this case, I helped put together the plan in which the league would front anywhere from $50 million to $125 million—whatever it took—to be sure that Cleveland had what it needed, should the referendum pass. A pretty juicy carrot. Tagliabue, I am certain, was wary of lawsuits, and otherwise sensitive to the singular Cleveland situation.

The referendum in Cleveland passed. And, as expected, Modell announced he would move to Baltimore. The public, as expected, was outraged and felt betrayed. Three months later, the league approved the deal, but with unprecedented baggage. That is to say no baggage. In a compromise I helped arrange, Modell would have to leave the team colors, brown and orange, behind, as well as the team name and its history and records. He had his new franchise in Baltimore, but it would not be the Browns. The Browns would reappear in 1999, at the new Cleveland Browns Stadium, standing precisely where the old one stood. And it would still be the only team in the league—as tradition dictated—to refrain from putting a mascot on the helmets. Stability, after a fashion, triumphed.

Finding the Positive in the Negative

You use leverage wherever you can find it, sometimes in a place you'd never expect. The time of uncertainty in Cleveland turned out to be something of a negotiation advantage 250 miles down Interstate 71 in Cincinnati.

Mike Brown, son of the founder of both the Bengals and the Browns, found himself in near despair. Brown, who knows more about the Italian Renaissance than is necessary to qualify as an NFL owner, was suddenly aware that what he thought was a popular enterprise was no longer so, and his dream of a new stadium seemed dashed.

This realization was the result of a telephone survey of several hundred representative voters. My intention in producing the poll was to determine sentiment about the public funding of sports facilities. It became the model for polling that I used in many cities, and that provided the key document for our success. Polling, of course, is a tried and true campaign method, used for a variety of enterprises. Often it is skewed, to show results that are more positive than reality would suggest. But I wanted polls that reflected real attitudes. I knew that no matter the results, I could use the numbers to our advantage.

I had two expectations in Cincinnati. One was that the poll would ultimately reveal that the public was overwhelmingly opposed to public financing of a new stadium. This wouldn't faze me at all. In fact, it would prove something of an edge—leverage in my conversations with Mike Brown, convincing him of what needed to be done. The second expectation was that in the numbers that had nothing to do with stadiums, I'd find answers to our problem. In short, the polling was the key to everything.

Basic questions came first, questions that had nothing to do with the Bengals. For example, "Do you approve or disapprove of the job the Hamilton County Council is doing?" This was not an innocent, meaningless inquiry. I wanted to know if certain public officials had broad approval ratings—if so, I could use them as spokespeople for our campaign to convince the public to vote for the project. If not, I wouldn't go near them. There were questions, too, about taxes, and about the public's general feeling whether taxes were too high already. It was not until question 18 before I raised the stadium issue.

"There has been some discussion in the county about the possibility of building new stadiums for the Bengals and Reds in order to keep them in Cincinnati. How important is it to you PERSONALLY about the Reds and Bengals staying in Cincinnati? . . . Extremely important, very important, somewhat important, not very important." Only 19 percent answered "extremely important." The poll also revealed that most people, about 7 in 10, would not support public financing of a new stadium.

Mike Brown was crushed. He is a straight-laced guy, totally committed to football. Unlike other owners, who made their money elsewhere, this is a family absolutely committed to the franchise. His father Paul was a pro football legend, founder of both the Browns and Bengals, whose disciplined teachings as coach brought a large measure of respectability to the league. Mike Brown's own world started and ended with the Bengals. Opposition was hard for him to understand. And he took this all very personally.

But it was important to me—always has been important—to be there when the poll numbers come in, because I can interpret them and help turn the thinking around. Yes, 7 out of 10 were against what we wanted. But that was normal. (An Ohio University poll conducted nationwide a few years later about public funding for stadiums revealed similar attitudes.) The Bengals were no worse off than anyone else, which was something of a miracle considering the perpetual misfortunes of the team on the field. The team had been to two Super Bowls (losing to the San Francisco 49ers both times, in 1982 and 1989), but since its founding has compiled the lowest winning percentage of any NFL team, victorious in only about 3 of every 10 games.

It wasn't my job to sugarcoat the results. Brown had to face them. It's like a doctor prescribing medicine. It's my job to present the practical solution. Even so, I tried to inspire and reassure him. I told him our starting point was that we had 3 people out of 10 on our side already, and we hadn't even started the campaign (virtually the same starting point in the Oklahoma City referendum for the MAPS project). All we had to do was convince some people in the middle of the wisdom of our plan. I said, "When you get the new stadium done, and a winning team playing in it, all Cincinnati will love you. But we do need to get that stadium done."

I didn't get the feeling he was buying it. So I shifted to another argument. "It has nothing to do with the personality of any owner. You can see it in the polls—it's a question of the quality of life in the city." I had asked in the poll about many needs aside from sports. Residents were concerned about schools, crime, jobs, kids leaving town to go other places after they finished their education. "Mike," I said, "this campaign will not be about sports."

We talked about a specific financing mechanism, property tax relief, and repair of school buildings. We decided to propose a sales tax that would be paid, to a substantial degree, by visitors—people who lived in other Ohio towns, or Kentucky and Indiana, people who don't vote but who come to town for big events. And, of course, I would ask Brown to contribute the private portion of the public/private partnership, about

$44 million. Without the poll results, I would have had no leverage on that issue. Brown would have kissed off the need to offer part of the financing from the team. But the numbers convinced him that he couldn't expect the public alone to pay for his new stadium. I argued hard about the numbers. I told Mike to put aside the notion of relying on intuition. Intuition will take you only so far—sometimes down a garden path. I don't trust it when hard facts are available. The numbers can set you straight.

During the campaign for the referendum, Brown and I made public appearances together. One of them was at a Young Republicans dinner. I spoke, and went through an hour about the quality of life in the area, and job creation, and a future for kids, and the necessity of improving and expanding infrastructure. I said that residents of Kentucky and Indiana would pay for a lot of this tax when they visited the city. I thought it was all pretty persuasive, but afterward Brown seemed to be in a foul mood. I said, "You seem upset at the process."

He replied, "I'm not upset with the process. I'm upset with you. We just had an hour's speech, and you never mentioned the Bengals once."

I said, "That's precisely the point."

In fact, the marketing literature said, "It's not about sports." I emphasized public schools, property tax relief, the prospect of new jobs, and the estimated $295 million annually pumped into the local economy. Brochures featured a photograph of a wholesome boy, hat tilted on his head, with a milk stain around his mouth. The milk, then, became the carrot, the promise of the right community values. The stick was a moving van in the night: a message subtly but clearly put forth— that if the local population showed indifference to the proposal, the Cincinnati Bengals could become the Cleveland Bengals. It wouldn't take much to lure the team to a new stadium up the highway.

In the end, the majority (51 percent) of those who voted were persuaded that this combination of circumstances was enough to support Brown and the Bengals. However, it has not been a storybook ending.

In the first game at the new Paul Brown Stadium, the Bengals lost to their dreaded in-state rivals, the Cleveland Browns. And, their fortunes didn't improve. Home field became humiliation field, with loss after loss. So much so that an unprecedented phenomenon occurred.

In October 2002, just a year after the stadium's opening, Hamilton County commissioners agreed to seek a legal opinion on whether the team violated the stadium lease by failing to become competitive, and whether a lawsuit against the Bengals would be possible. The team's record in its second year at the new venue was a stomach churning 2–14.

Most observers agree there are no grounds. A new stadium is no guarantee of a victorious football team. The owner of a team still has to hire talented players and coaches. And, if lawsuits were allowed to proceed on the basis of failure on the field, the courtroom agendas would be far more crowded than they are today.

I Walk the Line

I didn't get the chance to save the Oilers for Houston. I came along too late in the process to convince owner Bud Adams to keep his options open, or to help interpret negative poll information for his own benefit. In his efforts to improve his team's fortunes, Adams entertained an attractive offer from Nashville, and widely let that offer be known. Houston mayor Bob Lanier saw a poll (not one that I conducted) that basically said residents didn't care if they lost the Oilers, particularly if it meant building a new stadium. He wrote a letter to Adams, the substance of which was that if Adams had to move out of town, not to let the door hit him in the ass on the way out.

And when Adams read in *Fortune* magazine that I was the NFL's new stadium consultant who would stabilize the league and save certain franchises, including Houston's, he was incensed. For a time, it looked as if I might not be sent there. Bud Adams had his mind made up. I would have counseled him that no matter how he felt about Lanier and the results of the polling, we could have still improved his situation. As a fresh face from out of town, I might have been able to help repair a clearly deteriorating relationship between Adams and city leaders. Fresh faces can sometimes do that.

Paul Tagliabue very much wanted Houston as an NFL market, but Adams, one of the league's most prominent owners, wasn't about to be bullied. He had earned a reputation in the business world as a hard-nosed bargainer—he was chief executive of Adams Resources & Energy (annual sales of $7 billion) for more than half a century. As an NFL owner, he would now put all of his eggs into the Nashville basket. If a referendum for a new stadium were to pass there in May 1996, Adams would move. This did not please Tagliabue. He had another Cleveland Browns situation on his hands. If Nashville were a viable market, then he could exact an expansion price for it, which the league and its teams would share. The relocation fee that he could now charge Adams was peanuts compared to that. Still, the commissioner had no real power to prevent the move. All he could do was try to save Houston as a future possible site for a franchise, and to be certain that it worked out in Nashville. So my focus changed, and I was off to Music City, U.S.A.

Initial polling showed support for a stadium slightly higher than in other cities. This was not a surprise. At the time, Nashville had no big-league franchises, and it hungered for one. Peter King, of *Sports Illustrated,* wrote: "The team is being delivered to Nashville on a silver platter. If Nashville blows this opportunity, it will be a long time before [the city] gets a professional sports franchise, and it might never get one." And yet, more than half of the residents were still against it. There were the usual corporate welfare objections. Here's how it was framed in Nashville: Bud Adams couldn't get the citizens of Houston to build him a new stadium, because the people there got smart. They balked at the idea of making a rich guy richer, because the value of his franchise would increase with the availability of a taxpayer-funded stadium. Nashville opponents argued that if Adams wanted a new stadium, he should build it himself.

This is the thread of a common argument. It is true that the value of a franchise increases when new stadiums are built. But it is also true that there are more winners than simply the owners, particularly in a case such as Nashville, which had never had an NFL team. The dollars that would be fed into the local economy would all be new revenue, which is something I could not argue in cities that already had franchises and were trying to save them. My arguments, as always, transcended football. We would provide infrastructure for downtown development, and the impetus for new businesses.

The bundling effort here was shaped with the visionary support of Mayor Phil Bredesen. There would be money dedicated to preserve the old Shelby Street Bridge, and for I-65 improvements. The stadium, we argued, would create jobs both during construction and when in operation. The new stadium, if a rational deal were worked out, would be a boon to Tennessee State University, a predominantly black institution, that was vital to Nashville and in great need of facility upgrades. To that point, the university had wanted to build a new stadium on campus, but saw the wisdom of a partnership in our effort. President James A. Hefner called it a "golden opportunity." We would pump life into a neglected part of town. In the *Nashville Times,* a publication we created just to sell the project, I wrote, "Over the past several years, in the wake of the rebirth of downtown, city officials and concerned citizen groups have explored various ways to redevelop the East Bank of the Cumberland River—currently the home of an industrial area that many consider to be an unfitting backdrop to the city's central business and entertainment district." This stadium, I argued, was the way to begin this redevelopment.

In the end, of course, Nashville got its stadium and its Oilers, which it renamed the Tennessee Titans, soon to become one of the better teams in the league. Building on that success, Nashville also became an NHL city, with the new franchise the Predators.

And what about the city Bud Adams left behind? Houston is, of course, a place that the NFL did not want to abandon forever. The NFL targeted it as an ideal expansion city. I provided the arguments and materials for a campaign ("It's not just about sports . . . . It's about the future of our community") that resulted in public funding for Reliant Stadium, where, in the fall of 2002, the new Houston Texans took the field.

Get Out of Town

If Modell and Adams, two stalwarts of the NFL, were stubborn and difficult, Malcolm Glazer in Tampa proved to belong in another category altogether. Glazer had achieved almost a perfect rating on the scale of unpopularity. Initial polling showed that 7 percent of area residents approved strongly of what he had done during his tenure as owner of the Tampa Bay Buccaneers since 1995. Glazer was a Palm Beach resident who seemed to Tampa residents as something of a carpetbagger.

Even before Modell, Glazer, the owner of the Bucs who had paid a record $192 million for the franchise, had indicated an interest in moving his team to Baltimore. He also presided over a team that was (until recently) a disaster on the field. Glazer himself is a businessman who has bought and sold a variety of companies. His holdings included the Houlihan restaurant chain and Zapata Corp., the food-service equipment company. The portfolio also included, at times, companies in marine protein, broadcasting, health care, real estate, banking, natural gas and oil, and Internet publications. *Forbes* magazine said he had "an eye for value."

Glazer seemed to be the Gordon Gecko of the NFL, the "greed is good" guy from Oliver Stone's film *Wall Street,* if you can picture Gecko as rumpled, bearded, and entirely unkempt. But, in the end, nobody punched him in the nose. I merely sent Glazer, instead of his team, out of town.

I had argued in Cincinnati that owner Mike Brown should not take negative polling personally. But, as I have explained, every situation is different. And the prevailing attitudes about the owners in the two cities were very different. Malcolm Glazer had every reason to take negative polling personally.

Actually, I didn't send Glazer out of town myself. I asked Paul Tagliabue to perform the deed. I said, "You'll have to tell Glazer his best chance of winning is by going away for a while." The argument was that in his absence the referendum would succeed, and his franchise would be more valuable than it presently was.

Tagliabue objected to the idea. "It will set a bad precedent," he said, and argued for consistency. I replied that the point was not to be intellectually consistent; it was to be consistent only with the idea of winning these referenda. Our position should be that we review everything on a case-by-case basis. The commissioner relented, and called Glazer, who reluctantly acceded to our wishes by going on an extended vacation.

I met with Tampa mayor Dick Greco in the spring of 1996. I explained that we knew that a new stadium was important to the NFL and to the city, but that to sell it we needed to put it into the context of other projects—more bundling. Just the year before a referendum for school spending had failed. So we could wrap the educational needs into our plan. We could also pay for more police cars, more jails, better roads, waste treatment facilities, and flood control.

Having Glazer out of the picture was helpful in many ways but it meant we had to find money for marketing the campaign, about a half million dollars. The only real option was to go to Tagliabue. He said, "We have no budget for this." It's a sentence you hear often in your life, and it's one that you have to learn to answer. I said, "Not having a formal budget line shouldn't stand in the way of us doing what we have to do to get a deal because if the referendum loses, the whole franchise falls apart, and, Paul, you lose the prospect of $300 million in public money." Everybody has a discretionary fund, even the commissioner of the NFL. I urged him to dip into it, and he agreed.

In marketing materials, we emphasized everything but the Buccaneers, and for good reason. I was sitting with Tagliabue in his office, just before the opening of the NFL season, talking about the weekend's games. I said, "If we could control the outcome based only on the stadium process it would be nice if Tampa Bay wins its opener." The election was only two days later. I said, "If the Bucs win their opener, we're doing the referendum as part of the future plans for an up-and-coming team. If they lose, we're building infrastructure." That Sunday, the Green Bay Packers kicked the shit out of the Buccaneers, 35–3. The next day I went on the airwaves in Tampa and talked about infrastructure, and made not a single reference to football. I also avoided another touchy topic.

The polling had showed—surprise, surprise—a distrust of Florida politicians, so I not only wanted to keep them as far from the process as possible, I wanted to turn that negative into a positive. I argued that citizens ought to be in control. From marketing materials: "By voting FOR the Community Investment Referendum, WE get to Decide Where our money goes—Not the Politicians."

With Glazer out of town and certain public officials lying low, and with support of a coalition of teachers, law enforcement officials, engineers, and others, we won the referendum (52.9 percent to 47.1 percent), turning an unpromising situation into an owner's dream—Raymond James Stadium, a state-of-the-art facility that he had almost no hand in.

Open Your Golden Gate—and Drink My Wine

San Francisco—its famous bridge, its charms, its cosmopolitan atmosphere notwithstanding—did not present a pretty picture. The 49ers, though a very successful franchise in the '80s and '90s and a success story from the days of lefty Franky Albert at quarterback, clearly needed a place of their own. Years of deferred maintenance at Candlestick Park had left the stadium in a sad condition, and, with "temporary" bleachers, it never was an ideal venue for football. More than that, ownership was in turmoil.

Eddie DeBartolo, who had come to the city in 1977 from Youngstown, Ohio, and had presided over a team that won several Super Bowls, had gotten himself into some trouble. He was indicted in Louisiana for racketeering and conspiracy in a casino kickback scheme. He was also involved in a family squabble (with his sister) over control of the 49ers, and the real estate involved. Part of the disagreement between brother and sister was about the shopping mall that would become part of a proposed new football complex.

Initial polling of voters in 1997 was discouraging to the people involved. Of all the cities so far, attitudes here seemed the most negative about funding a stadium. This was odd, of course, after so much 49er success. But, as in other places, it never discouraged me. I used the polling information to refine our ideas, and to focus them into a bundling package that would win the day.

I went to the city three days each month, much of the time spent convincing the team officials and city officials to work together. I told Carmen Policy, president of the team, not to pay much attention to the negative poll results, and that if we could come from behind in Tampa

Bay and Cincinnati, where football heritage was not so glamorous, we could surely prevail in his town.

One of our allies was the colorful Mayor Willie Brown—opinionated, flashy, fast-talking, and politically savvy. During an election campaign, he once turned in his Porsche at a friend's car dealership and took in its place an old Dodge Dart. After the election, which he won, he took his Porsche back. This was all orchestrated so he could maintain his image as a man of the people. Willie said to us, "Don't worry gents. You're in good hands. We're going to win this."

Here we put together an enticing bundle of community efforts. Campaign mailers talked about the creation of jobs and the boost to the local economy: $12 million in community development funds, $12 million in affordable housing, $6 million saved annually by training and employing 1,000 people currently on general assistance, $5 million annually for public transportation, and $325 million in economic benefit when the Super Bowl comes to town. Of all this, we hammered jobs the hardest. A brochure said, "10,000 jobs—and the 49ers, too." And, "A proposal that works to put people to work."

We had another big carrot. The 49ers agreed to shoulder much of the load. The team pledged $425 million of its own money to build the new stadium and mall—and the promise of paying back the city's $100 million investment in time. So, the mailer said, "A new stadium. No cost to the taxpayers . . ." The stick: "How long can we expect the best team in major league sports to stay in the worst facility in the nation, particularly with half a dozen other cities clamoring for their own team?"

We relied to a great extent on campaign literature. But we also relied on some unusual inducements to voters. Advisors to Carmen Policy and our campaign decided they needed every vote they could get. Even the votes of the homeless. So they trolled around under highway underpasses, convincing ladies and gentlemen of the street—in exchange for wine and donuts—to register to vote. It might have made the difference. The election was the closest we ever had, winning by only a few hundred votes (50.3 percent to 49.7 percent). But then, as the commissioner often reminded me, it doesn't matter how much you win by.

Paul Allen Asks for Money

By the 1997 season, it was clear that the Seattle Seahawks were determined to find a stadium of their own. But this city presented a problem in three dimensions. The first was that the Kingdome was heralded as a multipurpose facility—the same kind of building that I had once thought was magical in New Orleans. Now, I was obliged to discredit the idea. The second was that the city had gone through an uncomfortable period with then Seahawks owner Ken Behring, who threatened to move the team to Los Angeles before Al Davis beat him to it with the Raiders. Behring was the focus of intense public animosity. The third piece to overcome: the problem of prosperity.

The new owner of the Seahawks was Paul Allen, who with Bill Gates had been co-founder of Microsoft, and whose net worth at the time was estimated to be $21 billion. Why should the public pay a nickel to help build a new stadium for Paul Allen?

Allen, to be sure, wanted to contribute much more than a nickel of his own, but nothing like the total cost of the stadium. He gave every appearance of confidence, inflexibility, and aloofness. He told me, "I'm going to spend $100 million. You do the campaign around that. And I expect it to be won."

The following is from a letter from Paul Allen to the public, which I helped him write, the intent of which was to make him seem like a warm and compassionate human being, which wasn't easy:

June 1997

I'm sure you've heard a lot about the upcoming election regarding plans to build a new football/soccer stadium and exhibition center, and about why I got involved.

Rather than let others speak for me, I thought I'd write to you directly about why I am making a personal commitment.

My involvement began more than a year ago. At that time, public concern about the possible departure of the Seattle Seahawks football team caused a number of community leaders to ask me to purchase the team and keep it here.

Although I was not in the market for a professional football team, I am a native Washingtonian, and I shared public concern over what the team's departure could mean to the state and the economy.

Like you, I know that our community has higher priorities than sports. I've committed my time and resources to supporting higher education, medical research, the arts, and a cleaner, healthier environment. But as this project moved forward, and people across the state joined the effort, I realized we had a unique opportunity to build a new facility that would be about a lot more than just professional football.

As a businessman, I also realized that we had a chance to create new economic opportunities—and to do it the right way this time.

That's why, in the plan you will vote on, the new stadium and exhibition center is designed to be a regional center for sports, culture, trade shows, and entertainment. It will be filled with dozens of events throughout the year, including national and international soccer, and possibly even the Olympics.

. . . Some have asked why I don't just pay for all of the new stadium and exhibition center myself. There are two reasons.

First, I think it's fair that sports fans and others who use the facility help pay for it. Second, I believe the only way to make sure everyone benefits is to make it a fair partnership—where substantial private investment helps build the stadium and exhibition center, but it's owned by the people. As my part of this partnership, I have personally guaranteed $100 million in private investment and a cap on public spending, and I will pay for any construction cost overruns.

I consider myself very fortunate. One of my most important personal goals is to give back to the state and the community were I was born. As a native Washingtonian, I stand behind this plan. I wouldn't commit myself personally and financially if I didn't think it would prove a valu-

able community asset—one that draws people together and enhances our quality of life.

But the most important aspect of the plan is one I've insisted upon since I first became involved: that Washington voters have the final say. I believe we can all be proud of this plan. However you decide, I encourage you to vote on Election Day.

Sincerely,

(Signed) Paul G. Allen

The letter did what we wanted it to do—it had a personal touch, it was passionate, and it set out logical reasons why the burden should be shared, Microsoft fortune or not. In not very subtle ways it pointed out that Allen had his hands full addressing the community's critical medical and educational needs, as well as other quality of life issues, and couldn't be expected to do everything.

Our campaign mailers stressed the versatility of the new stadium, anticipating arguments that would call it an NFL white elephant. We referred to it as a football/soccer stadium and exhibition center, because indeed it would be used for many more events than just the NFL.

The referendum passed, 51 percent to 49 percent. The usual score.

The Problem with Success

In Denver, the Broncos were on a roll, having just won the Super Bowl—perfect timing to ask for a new stadium and get it, or so owner Pat Bowlen thought. We're a shoo-in, he said. No problem. It's in the bag. You can bet on it.

No, Pat, you can't. That's what I told him. "There are many people in this world, even in this city and in this state, who don't give a damn about your Super Bowl trophy." These are the people who worry about whether there are enough women's shelters, and enough good schools, and whether the environment is protected, and if there are enough police or health care workers, and if there are enough jobs to go around. "Pat," I said, "take a look at these poll numbers. They will tell you what you have to do." By this time, I'd had a good track record in the NFL and I knew that the commissioner would back me if I took a hard line here. And I had to take a hard line to convince Bowlen that bundling was his only hope, and that we had to employ the 10-point checklist I developed and used in each NFL city, to one degree or another.

1. It's Not About Sports. De-emphasize, even in triumphant cities, the sports model.
2. Spend To Save. Invest in the future.
3. Compete Or Retreat. There are other places interested in the franchise.
4. Give Your Children A Future. And keep them at home.
5. The Tourist Tax. Put as much of the burden as possible on visitors.
6. Public Invites Private. Investment of public dollars entices private development.
7. Go Downtown. These facilities are the best chance to expedite downtown development.
8. The Generational Obligation. A duty to do what previous generations did for us.
9. The Senior Break. Get seniors behind you (they vote) by having them pay the least in taxes.
10. The Last Best Chance. Each individual project, on its own, will have little chance of passage. Together, bundled, is the most enticing way to present the idea to voters.

"We All Win," said the campaign mailers. Parks, the environment, transportation, troubled teens, women's shelters, libraries, museums. The mailers explained that some of the revenues for the new stadium would be divided among the six metro-area counties for these purposes. We also emphasized the private investment in the new facility. Invesco, the global financial services firm, had bought the naming rights to the proposed stadium, part of $4.1 billion in naming deals in stadiums across the country. Companies had begun to recognize the value of naming rights as a way to raise awareness. Who, for example, outside of the Silicon Valley, where 3Com was based, had heard of the technology company before it bought naming rights to the former Candlestick Park?

The Denver campaign, despite Bowlen's early objections, went very well, and it ultimately passed. All proceeded according to plan until the stadium was under construction, and a newspaper reporter surveyed it from the air. From that perspective, he said, the new Invesco Field looked like a "giant diaphragm." Invesco, fearing the need to explain itself to the socially conservative, considered pulling out of the deal, but in the end decided to keep its name attached, and its financial commitment. They stuck it out because, controversy or not, they would get their name in every newspaper in the land after every game in Denver.

The Virtues of "Home"

On the same weekend in the late summer of 2002, I attended the opening of Ford Field in Detroit and the opening of the dramatically refurbished Lambeau Field in Green Bay. That both of these events came within a couple of days of each other was a happy coincidence. I had worked hard to save two of the league's most historic franchises.

In the campaign to get voter approval in the Green Bay deal, I had used everything on my 10-point checklist, with one addition. Green Bay, of course, would never qualify as a franchise site if a major professional league were started today. True, it is ranked as one of the 10 safest cities in the United States with populations over 100,000. But it barely qualifies with its total of 102,767 residents. It survives as a franchise—and a successful one at that—out of doggedness, loyalty, and enlightened management. It survives, in no small part, because of its distinguished history. From our marketing campaign literature: "Curly Lambeau. Johnny Blood. Herber to Hutson. The Ice Bowl. Lombardi. Starr. Nitschke. Favre. Holmgren." So what I was selling here was heritage. And heritage sold.

Lambeau Field was in great need of renovation. It had no real room for skyboxes, and small concourses. The bathrooms were cramped. Paint was peeling everywhere.

In this case, there was no threat to lose the franchise to another city—the team was owned by the community. But there was a chance the Packers could go bankrupt. Projections showed that by 2003, the Packers would be dead last in the NFL in revenue earned. There wouldn't be enough money to be competitive, and it wasn't possible to be competitive without more stadium revenues.

In Detroit, heritage could be used, but in more subtle ways. Yes, the Lions had won a few championships, but none since the 1950s. It had been a team that at one time or other had great players such as Doak Walker, Leon Hart, Dutch Clark, Bobby Layne, Dick "Night Train" Lane, and Barry Sanders, but the Lions in the last few decades never approached the success of the Packers. In addition, the rich heritage it possessed had disassociated itself from the city.

The 1970s continued a time of general flight to the suburbs and even the provinces, and Detroit was no exception. Along with other Midwestern industrial centers, it had been the scene of race riots a few years earlier. It didn't take much persuasion for the Lions franchise to take a deal in Pontiac in a new 80,000-seat dome. No, the place didn't have air conditioning, and in days before the smoking ban a haze would settle below the billowy roof, but it was far from the troubles of the inner city, and a home where, in theory, the Lions could flourish. As it turned out, however, the Pontiac Silverdome, as it stood, was not the answer. It did not anticipate the eras of luxurious skyboxes and was otherwise economically obsolete. And it obviously did not anticipate a reinvestment in the center city.

In the situation that William Clay Ford Jr. faced, he had to decide between fixing the stadium in Pontiac or going back to the city where the team started. The decision wasn't made until the last possible minute.

As in Cincinnati, there was a need for homes for two teams. Old Tiger Stadium would have to be replaced. Mayor Dennis Archer was convinced that new facilities for both the Tigers and the Lions downtown would signal a rebirth after years of stagnation, and worse. But it would be risky for Ford to move back. He'd built a fan base outside of Detroit. There was considerable convenience for both Lions supporters and for the owner if the team stayed put. Construction and land costs were cheaper, and there was much wide open space. But the lure of the downtown master plan was undeniable.

Pontiac public officials understood that they faced competition. And they came up with a public/private plan that was attractive, but that fell a few million dollars short of ideal. Archer, on the other hand, made up in energy and tenacity what he couldn't deliver with any certainty—that new stadiums for the Tigers and Lions would be in the best interest of both franchises. He wouldn't allow Ford to say no to this deal.

In financial terms, the numbers were very close. For the short term, it would have been more profitable to stay in Pontiac. In the long term, Detroit might be the better answer—if it followed the pattern of other cities. We had the prospect in Detroit of a very complicated deal that would require bringing many strangers to the table—several kinds of public and private funding. Just some of the elements: a county bed tax, a car tax, a public infrastructure fund, City of Detroit general obligation bonds, the Michigan state public infrastructure fund, $70 million from Ford Motor Company to name it Ford Field, and $10 million from the United Auto Workers, who sponsored certain facilities at the stadium. Ford thought he could win a public vote more easily in Pontiac than he could in Detroit. Yet the right thing to do—well, that seemed obvious to me.

There was division, however, in the Ford family. I made my best argument—that Pontiac was nothing more than a regional band aid, and that the real legacy was to be part of downtown development, along with the Tigers' planned Comerica Park. But by our eighth meeting, Bill Ford said, "I appreciate your counsel," as if to say, "It's time for you to back out of it. We'll make a decision as a family." In the end, I think, they always knew where they'd go: back where they, and the Lions, had started.

There was no way I would miss opening day at Ford Field. I correctly anticipated the feeling of pride I felt, even if I didn't think that the CEO of Ford Motor Company would hug me at midfield.

CHAPTER 9

How We Play from Here

The best of prophets of the future is the past.

LORD BYRON

In May 2002, a friend and I drove from my house in Palm Beach County south to a place I hadn't seen in some years. I still harbored feelings about the Miami Arena that I wasn't eager to address. As I maneuvered past trendy Bayside shops toward the Overtown neighborhood, I recalled specifics of the arena's ribbon-cutting ceremony 14 years earlier.

Back in the summer of 1988, I was no longer naïve about politics, and hadn't expected to be carried off on the shoulders of community leaders grateful for my contribution to Miami sports. But I never imagined I'd watch the festivities from behind a construction barrier, like a kid peeking through the hole in an outfield fence.

Now, all these years later, I faced a new barrier. We asked the office receptionist if we could take a look around the building. "It's not permitted without a guide," she said. I asked to see the director. When she went to find him, we noticed the logbook on her desk of upcoming activities—lots of empty weeks, and a few bookings blocked out here and there, and some for Disney on Ice in October. Indeed the Miami Arena had already become a white elephant. A few blocks away was its replacement, the new American Airlines Arena—everything a sports venue should be, with skyboxes aplenty, club seats, and built with a major naming contribution from corporate America. It is the sort of place the Miami Arena would have been if City Commissioner J. L. Plummer Jr. hadn't misdirected millions that had been earmarked for the building to his own district.

The receptionist returned with another woman. I introduced myself and said that I once had a connection with the place. She said, "I'm sorry, but the director is busy. You can make an appointment." We went outside, and were about to drive away. But I had one more idea. The stairs lead to the building's main entrance. Perhaps we could spy the founder's plaque through the glass doors. As we peeked through, in vain, the woman from the office shouted up at us. I thought, gee, I'm going to be kicked off the grounds of my own arena. Instead, she told me she was just going through the files and saw an old letter with my name on it. "Come back in, please," she said.

The director was suddenly available. He took us on a tour that included the playroom built for the kids of single parents of Disney on Ice, and the press room where Jack Nicklaus once put his arm around me and announced, "Rick, we'll go far together." The director told us the arena had seen 15 million visitors since its opening, "but recently it has dropped off." Walking on the main floor was eerie. I thought back to the first basketball games there—the new Heat, which I had fought so hard to bring to town. And then the hockey team. I had lobbied hard for the NHL, though in the end it was Wayne Huizenga, again, who won out. No matter. I was gratified when the Florida Panthers began playing. Now the Heat plays out its seasons a few blocks away, and the Panthers are a few miles up the road in Broward County.

We walked up the stairs to the concession concourse, and arrived at the entrance to section 237. Here was the requisite founder's plaque—a tribute in bronze to, among others, J. L. Plummer Jr., who did everything possible to prevent this arena from being built. There are more than a dozen names on the plaque, but none bearing the initials "R.H."

"Come on. Let's get out of here," I said to my friend.

Later on, feelings of frustration about the Miami Arena gave way to other thoughts beyond the confines of Overtown. The struggle to build the arena and the simultaneous effort to bring Major League Baseball to Miami were turning points not only for the city but for me. Without the Miami experience, I would not have had the chance to take my ideas nationwide, and to work on behalf of dozens of teams and communities that went well beyond the securing of franchises. In Miami we had crafted the public and private partnership and turned the idea into the reality of urban revitalization; my early work here had made it possible for me to become an agent for sports expansion and social change.

And now I could look with gratification on projects all over America, in more than 100 deals that helped turn cities around. I think, for example, of the city a few hours up I-95 from my home. The Better Jacksonville Plan, a more than $2 billion effort, although it embraced sports, also provided for land preservation, neighborhood parks, environmental clean-up, renovation of the city's zoo, library construction, thousands of new jobs, and a host of other benefits. My experience in Oklahoma City had taught me that sports was only one part of a more inclusive and beneficial approach, one that could help address serious urban problems, even despair.

Oklahoma City had been the foremost community symbol, for a time, of terrorism. A few years later, New York City joined the list. No work I can do in Manhattan can blot the memory of the horror that occurred when terrorists steered two hijacked passenger jets into the twin towers of the World Trade Center. Still, I proceed on the deeply felt notion—and the experience of Oklahoma City—that positive energy and vision will make a difference in the difficult restoration effort.

In the days after the September 11, 2001, attack, the mayor of Oklahoma City sent a token of faith to the mayor of New York City. The Alfred P. Murrah Building explosion had burned everything around it, but, miraculously, an elm tree in the midst of it all had emerged unscathed. This symbol of hope became known as The Survivor Tree. The gift from one mayor to another was a bag of seedlings from that tree.

I think of those seedlings as a metaphor, as I expand my work in Manhattan. For me the place had largely been a resource center— headquarters to the NFL, the NBA, the NHL, and Major League Baseball. Now, it has become all the cities I've worked in rolled into one.

New York's Olympian Effort

In the wake of September 11, a great effort has gone into an ambitious idea—securing the 2012 Olympic Games. This is an Olympian challenge when you consider the worldwide competition and the natural worry that officials might have about security in New York.

The first step was to win the vote of the U.S. Olympic Committee, which would choose its finalist to go up against international cities (the final choice is to be made in 2005). Ultimately, New York was selected in November 2002, the judges persuaded by the visionary plan for the city and the games. I have worked primarily on the part that affects the west side neighborhood of the Javits Center, site of conventions and trade shows. It is there that we intend to build the stadium that would host the opening and closing ceremonies, and the track and field events. In a city that has seen the monumental public works of the Vanderbilts and Robert Moses, this would represent the most ambitious urban revitalization effort ever recorded, a more than $2.2 billion public and private partnership.

The economic benefits from the Olympic Games themselves would offset a great deal of the project's cost, based on previous experiences (the benefit to Salt Lake City for the Winter 2002 Games was about $5.5 billion). Moreover, when the venue becomes the new home of the New York Jets, it will represent the city's first natural venue for a Super Bowl, and all of the income such an event traditionally brings.

At the same time as I have been at work on the Olympic plan, I have been involved in a variety of New York area infrastructure projects for the Mets, Yankees, New Jersey Devils, New Jersey Nets, and its soccer Metro Stars. We're also working on developing a NASCAR track for the area. All of these projects are competing for investor and government dollars and attention.

I could probably spend the rest of my professional life just in the Big Apple. But of course I won't.

LA LA Landing

Los Angeles has been a problem for the NFL, and one it hopes I'll help solve. It is by far the largest market in the country without a team. Everyone agrees that Los Angeles ought to be a part of the league, except for key people in L.A. itself. The atmosphere there has been one of passive ambivalence. Politicians perceive the citizens as ambivalent, not as hungry to regain a team as Cleveland was when Art Modell packed his bags for Baltimore, or, for that matter, how Baltimoreans felt after their Colts left for Indianapolis in 1984. The result is that public officials and the business community in Los Angeles haven't wanted to take a risk. This is true even though the economic impact of having a stadium and team there would be more profound than in Baltimore or Cleveland because of the Super Bowls that would surely be hosted over the life of stadium financing.

To complicate matters, San Diego is only a couple of hours down the road. The Chargers need a new home, and the city is balking about spending the money. Public opinion polls on this matter reflect the worst results I've seen about attitudes of the citizenry. One of the options is moving up the road to Orange County, just south of Los Angeles, and building a new stadium there. If the Chargers were to do this, it could improve their circumstances, but also mean the potential loss of much of the San Diego market and largely eliminate Los Angeles itself as a future NFL home.

As you can see, the problems don't get easier. Nor will easy solutions be found in another California city in its effort to build a new home for baseball. The challenge of saving the Oakland A's for the home fans faces a few obstacles. For one thing, the specter of a Major League work stoppage in 2002 (though a stoppage didn't happen) colored public attitudes about making costly commitments, at least for a time, to new stadiums. And, though there has been the threat of losing the A's to other cities, the mayor's priorities have been elsewhere. Jerry Brown, the one-time governor of California and an independent thinker, has pushed housing instead of a new stadium. In theory, that wouldn't be an obstacle to me. I'd bundle a package of projects—new housing, urban rebuilding, public transportation, and a beautiful new stadium. But political attitudes in Oakland have a hard edge. The campaign will be controversial and difficult. But it's always difficult.

The Horrow Principles, and Beyond

All of these new adventures will require my total commitment, just as the efforts in the past demanded every technique I could summon. No matter where I travel or what enterprise I undertake, I rely heavily on certain principles devised from trial, error, necessity, inspiration, and desperation. The following have served me well, and can be a guide for any kind of deal-making.

1. Imagination as Reality

When I think back on how this all started, I am reminded of the importance of dreaming about possibilities. I was naïve and green in those early days in Miami, but I had a tool that my opponents didn't have. I was able to make use of the power of a vision. A vision is almost always, in the end, more persuasive than a defensive stance because it has the capacity to stir the collective imagination, and get everyone to say, "What if?" Instinct and vision are important guides, particularly when those qualities are outside ordinary and sensible lines, or induce blank stares (or worse). Miami was a perfect place to employ them—a city with a profound presumption of failure where a positive voice could get people to pay attention. My inspiration there came from many sources (my father, among them). But in the end, I had to believe in a very personal vision—one that went beyond experience and documentable proof that it was possible, or even sane.

2. Always Do Things a Certain Way. Unless You Don't

It's a rule I never want to break. (Well, of course there's no way to break it.) I prepare to a degree beyond the point required for every presentation, but am always willing, and most often find it necessary, to depart from the script. In Oklahoma City, for example, I went well beyond the prescribed offer to the arts community by unilaterally expanding the potential application of tax revenue. I made the risky decision on the spot, and was willing to ask for permission later. I see it this way: I can turn difficulties into strengths by being flexible and bold.

3. Get Up Off the Canvas

Tenacity is the key. Demonstrating the willingness to pursue the goal, no matter the temporary setbacks. Woody Allen said that 90 percent of success is showing up. I agree with that sentiment. But I have to do more than that. I have to pick myself up and dust myself off again and again. I lost my job four times as director of a sports authority in Miami. But I got it back a fifth time, and found a way to get what I wanted.

4. Bring Strangers, Even Enemies, to the Table

Or the joy of bundling. You can't solve your problems alone. You can't solve them with allies only. The route to full consensus is to find the advantages to every party affected by the plan. In Oklahoma City, I entered a situation where there was a dramatic lack of trust, and where parties competed for attention and dollars. I had to wear away at the differences, to show the common good, and the value of working together so that everybody wins. The same was true in Jacksonville, Tampa, Cincinnati, Seattle, Pittsburgh, Detroit, and many other places. They called me, variously, The Easter Bunny and The Music Man, in my efforts to provide something for everybody. Neither term is a completely positive reference. But I'll take them, as long as the process moves forward and the goals are realized.

5. Finesse the Powerful Ego

When I was in Miami, I thought I'd never see a personality anywhere close to Joe Robbie again. But oppressive people are everywhere. I can't say to myself, "If so–and–so would only move away, my life would be easy." There will always be a so–and–so. Art Modell was an obstacle, but I found a way to get around him. Jeb Bush, at the time Florida's secretary of state, demonstrated the Tyranny of Furniture—putting me in a chair much lower than his to show his superiority. But I sat on the edge of that chair, my back ramrod straight, never giving him the satisfaction from his little game. And yet in another way I play to these egos, understand what they want, and give it to them without compromising my vision. It would not have been wise for me, in my frustration with Joe Robbie, to say, "I graduated first in my class at Northwestern—how did you do, oh brilliant one?" I stay calm. I stay direct. I impress upon the annoying personality what it is I want. And keep at it. I don't take his or her rejection personally, but it's usually aimed at everybody.

6. The Seven-Minute Rule

I rehearse this presentation. I gave my best seven minutes to the governor of Kansas, the mayor of Houston, the owner of the Denver Broncos. No one, not even the most self-centered politician, will deny me that amount of time. And if I can't say it in seven minutes—be persuasive, focused, and specific—then I know I have nothing to say. There are exceptions, of course, to the rule (see point two). In my first meeting with the International Speedway Corporation, I was there to listen and learn. It would have been dangerous to open my mouth, because at that point I didn't know enough, and would have only made a fool of myself.

7. Get Off the Sidelines

There is a tendency among consultants—once they have set the ground rules of a new game—to let the key players duke it out, and to seek the safety of the sidelines. My role is just the opposite. I am, to use another metaphor, a lightning rod. I become the target, the key player, the one who takes and can handle the criticism, sparing my clients the trouble and grief, and freely able to maneuver between parties and deliver sensitive messages. In the case of Oklahoma City, I could tell the arts community that it wasn't favored in the plans. I was doing the dirty work, keeping the politicians free of criticism, a situation that in the end benefited me and the city.

8. Find the Positive in the Negative

In Cincinnati, 7 out of 10 people were against any effort to build a stadium at public expense. I convinced Bengals owner Mike Brown that this was an advantage. We already had 3 out of 10 on our side. All we had to do was convince 2 more out of those 10 to see the wisdom of our idea. Also, we used negative attitudes about how well public officials were performing on an array of other issues (crime and education, among them) to our advantage. That is, we bundled new initiatives with the stadium so that the populace could see that its primary concerns were being addressed.

9. Ratchet, Ratchet, Ratchet

I don't just sit back and wait for the competition to arise, so that the bidding war can start. It's vitally important to play a role in creating the competition. In the case of the NASCAR track, for example, the applications of certain cities (Sacramento and Houston among them) had weaknesses. I wanted Kansas City's effort to succeed, but to do so I had to help the other cities strengthen their presentations. It wasn't cheating or misleading, because their applications became credible, and indeed those cities could have become home to a track.

10. Don't Let Criticism Get You Down

I've always been good at compartmentalizing. That is, I put the disappointment of today behind me and think about tomorrow, as a baseball player must in order to succeed in his next at bat. When I was having all that trouble with Joe Robbie, I focused my energy on a new plan, that $681 nationwide trip to learn about other cities' stadiums. A diversion, yes. But a useful one. Also, when I've been criticized, I avoid carping to others about it during the process. Nobody wants to hear it, and it would make me seem weak and needy.

All's Well That Trends Well

Though the principles above remain tried and true, the ground on which they are based is shifting. The public is becoming much more conscious of both the need for and the costs of new stadiums and arenas as well as other civic projects. These costs continue to rise even when the economy sputters. Therefore, it will be necessary as we address these issues in the future to include a much greater variety of partners than in the past. Big deals in stadium building will require every kind of public and private partnership possible. We'll need the bundling of public projects, the contributions that come from the branding by private corporations (convincing them of the value of attaching their names to these projects), and investments from sports franchises in return for equity. As it is, teams are taking larger risks than ever before, contributing anywhere from 20 to 40 percent of the cost of new facilities with the hopes of making it up in seat licenses (giving a fan the right to purchase a ticket for a specific location) and other revenues. We'll need to do this in large and small ways, and however companies and institutions can contribute. For example, Ford Field's private contribution included not only Ford but also the United Auto Workers, whose brand, although not as prominent as Ford's at the stadium, still gets good play.

Another trend is the proliferation of sports stadiums and arenas in smaller cities. I've worked, for example, on behalf of Birmingham, Wichita, Evansville, and the North Carolina towns of Wilmington and New Bern, where public officials have had the courage to pursue a vision that would secure a professional sports franchise (even if, in most of the cases, they would be minor league franchises). The same principles of inclusion and partnerships work here as well.

Innovation is the essential key. Recently, naming rights for a sports facility in a town in Washington state were auctioned on eBay. And a high school in Midland, Texas, will get $1.2 million from Grande Communications in exchange for putting the company's name on the new 15,000-seat community-owned stadium. A high school stadium! Clearly anything goes now.

Back to Harvard Law School

All of my experiences prove useful when I return each fall to Harvard to help teach a couple of classes in sports law, the course that I helped establish with its full-time professor, Paul Weiler. On a day in October 2002, we staged our annual debate on public financing of new sports stadiums.

As usual, we were in room 102 in Hauser Hall, which is just to the right of the hallway portrait of Oliver Wendell Holmes. The room, not incidentally, features stadium seating. The blackboard had various messages on it this day, including news about the upcoming production of Gilbert & Sullivan's *Trial By Jury* (tickets, $5).

Paul let me make my argument first, holding his in abeyance. Among other points, I argued my five justifications for public involvement—arguments I make everywhere. In short:

1. The facilities generate substantial economic impact during construction.
2. They also generate substantial retail, sales, and development activity surrounding the facility.
3. Major and special events are attracted to a new facility—Super Bowls and the like. Recent Super Bowls in New Orleans, Atlanta, and Miami have each generated over $250 million to the respective local economies.
4. Regions recognize the intangible impact of a sports franchise and corresponding facility on its marketability and potential to attract businesses and new residents.
5. Although more difficult to quantify, franchises and facilities, many community leaders believe, are critical components of image enhancement and community pride.

These arguments have proven persuasive even as an industry of naysayers has emerged. Weiler is one of them. He is the author of *Leveling the Playing Field: How the Law Can Make Sports Better for Fans.* And he is otherwise an eloquent man, for this, after all, is Harvard Law, and no argument you can make will ever go unquestioned.

In his presentation, Weiler argued that we are in an era when governments generally are in great financial distress, and to fund "luxurious" new stadiums is irresponsible. He said that the old model for city and team relationships was enlightened in a way. In most cases, city-owned stadiums charged rent to the teams that played there, a lucrative source of revenue. Now, he says, not only is there no rent, but the citizens of the city are held hostage. And the primary beneficiaries of the arrangement are team owners. In all cases, he argues, their investments multiply in value once they have a new stadium to play in. Their teams inevitably would bring a higher price. He points out that the league revenues in 1960 were $3 million. Now they're $2.2 billion a year. Weiler's numbers in general are impressive, and at least 80 percent accurate.

He offered the local team as an example of the stadium-building model that ought to be prevalent. Robert Kraft, owner of the New England Patriots, built a stadium largely with private money, one of a small number of such cases. The argument goes, then, that if Kraft can do it, then all these billionaires can do it.

In my rebuttal testimony, I agreed that history shows that stadiums and cities earned revenues from teams. But back then, no team made an investment in new facilities. Now, typically, they are investing millions in such projects, and putting themselves on the line financially.

As for the Patriots story, it wasn't that simple. "Robert Kraft," I said, "is an aberration, not a trend." For one thing, he is playing in a large market that has enormous advantage to investors. It is a larger market than in most NFL cities. For another, he got what he wanted by leaving a trail of broken promises. He chose Hartford over the Boston area, signing an agreement with Connecticut governor John Rowland that would provide a new 68,000-seat home for the Patriots. The stadium would become a significant part of an ambitious downtown renewal project. The state would pay all of the $375 million cost, and toss in many other benefits in a deal that some NFL owners considered to be the most lucrative ever offered by a community. The day after the signing, the *Hartford Courant*, in a display of front-page euphoria on behalf of a city that was in serious decline, showed a photo of Kraft and Rowland under the headline "Touchdown!" But the touchdown was called back, if a year later. Kraft had used Hartford as a pawn. As chair of the NFL Finance Committee, he got a loan from the league under the G-3 provision (which has advanced $654 million around the NFL), and then enticed private investors to join his project—which was more lucrative in the large Boston television market than it would be in Hartford. (Later, Kraft paid $2.4 million to the state of Connecticut, a settlement for breaking his agreement.)

Throughout the afternoon at Harvard, there had been a variety of responses and questions from the students—ranging from those who had insightful reactions to the fellow who found it more important to play electronic Solitaire on his laptop than to take notes.

One student, however, got to me in particular, and reminded me why I was there. Before the afternoon's two-hour session even started, he came up to the desk and said he wanted to ask a whole bunch of questions. I told him that I appreciated his enthusiasm, but that I was about to deliver a lecture and had to get ready. "Wait until the class is over," I said. I went back to my preparation. But, out of the corner of my eye, I could see that he wasn't budging.

A few minutes later, he was still there. I looked up at him, and saw the intensity in his eyes, and his eagerness to press his points, as if this inquiry was the most important thing in the world to him. He was poised to write down my responses with a variety of pens in several different colors—just the sort of technique I've always used in my daily calendar. This young man clearly wasn't going away, and he wasn't about to be discouraged by my attempt to ignore him.

I put aside my papers and smiled at him. His features softened for a moment, and then he spoke:

"You don't know me, but . . . "

ABOUT THE AUTHORS

Rick Horrow has been the architect of nearly 100 deals worth more than $13 billion in sports and other urban infrastructure. As president of Horrow Sports Ventures, his signature work has brought together disparate parties to support inner-city revitalization and efforts to secure and stabilize professional sports teams. He has earned a reputation for successfully addressing impossible odds—winning the trust of recalcitrant public figures and team owners and then convincing skeptical voters that public investment in stadiums and arenas is in their best interest. He has also pioneered the public/private partnership and the "infrastructure branding" concept that, to date, has enticed more than $4 billion in corporate funding to cities and development projects. He has been a key player in stadium, arena, and speedway deals in New York City, Los Angeles, Chicago, Miami, Orlando, Oklahoma City, Oakland, Indianapolis, Charlotte, Boston, Denver, Seattle, San Francisco, Philadelphia, Detroit, Cleveland, Jacksonville, Tampa, Buffalo, New Orleans, Houston, Nashville, Cincinnati, Green Bay, Columbus, San Diego, San Antonio, Phoenix, Baltimore, Kansas City, Birmingham, and Pittsburgh.

He has laid the groundwork for college, minor league, and spring training facilities for Wichita, Kansas; West Palm Beach, Homestead, Jupiter, and St. Petersburg, Florida; Wilmington, North Carolina; Columbia, South Carolina; Shreveport, Louisiana; West Palm Beach and St. Petersburg, Florida; Modesto, California; Little Rock, Arkansas; Scottsdale, Mesa, and Tempe, Arizona; Evansville, Indiana; and many other communities. His clients have included the NFL, PGA TOUR, Golden Bear International (Jack Nicklaus), Baltimore Orioles, Cleveland Indians, San Francisco Giants, New York Mets, Great White Shark Enterprises (Greg Norman), Ladies Professional Golf Association, Major League Soccer, Major Indoor Soccer League, and the New York City 2012 Olympic Organizing Committee. Internationally, he has presented sports and facility development options for the governments of Brazil, Chile, Argentina, St. Kitts, and Trinidad and Tobago on behalf of the United States Department of Commerce Business Development Center, World Tourism Organization, International Hotel Association, and the Multilateral Investment Guarantee Agency/World Bank. He also worked for the province of Bahia (Brazil) and the city of Victoria (Canada). His unique "bundling" philosophy—putting together many urban initiatives into one package for voter approval—has resulted in the building of many new libraries, performing arts centers, convention centers, schools, transportation projects, and tourist destinations.

He helped develop the inaugural Sports Law Class at Harvard Law School (where he still lectures regularly as its Visiting Expert). He is the author of *Sports Violence: The Interaction Between Private Lawmaking and the Criminal Law* (1979), and was a contributing author of *The Law of Professional and Amateur Sports* (1991). He is a Founding Director of the National Sports Lawyers Association, and was designated "The Sports Professor" by the United States Office of Patent and Trademark. He is the Sports Business Analyst for CNNfn, and has hosted a weekly television show, *The Sports Business Report,* produced by Fox Sports Net and distributed nationally through Fox Sports/Prime Network/Sports Channel/New Sport affiliates. He is the Sports Business Expert for Fox Sports Radio and has hosted weekly radio show segments, *The Sports Business Minute/The Sports Professor,* aired nationally on Sporting News Radio, ESPN Radio, Prime Sports Radio, and Business Talk Radio. He is also a director of CBS SportsLine, where he contributes a weekly sports business/law/marketing column on the Internet. In 2000, he sold a significant portion of his business to Omnicom Group, Inc., a leading global marketing and corporate communications company with more than 5,000 clients in 100 countries. He and his wife Terri have two daughters, Katie and Caroline, and reside in Jupiter, Florida. For more information, see www.horrowsports.com.

Lary Bloom is the author of *The Writer Within* and *Something Personal.* He edited and was a contributor to *Twain's World.* He has taught nonfiction writing at Trinity College and Wesleyan University, and was a Sunday magazine editor for more than three decades, in Akron, Miami, and Hartford. In addition to publishing award-winning writing, his magazines were noted for initiating many community projects, including Mark Twain

Days, Art For All, the Sunken Garden Poetry Festival, Connecticut Voices, and, in Miami, early efforts to bring Major League Baseball to the city. He wrote an award-winning column in the *Hartford Courant* for many years, and has contributed to *Yankee* magazine and a variety of other periodicals. He writes "Lary Bloom's Notebook" for *Connecticut* magazine, and is at work with Lark Productions on a book about a family farm in Mud City, Vermont, and as lyricist of a musical comedy set in a New England artist colony. He and his wife, Liz Gwillim, live in Chester, Connecticut. He may be reached at larybloom@aol.com.

INDEX

BUY A SHARE OF THE FUTURE IN YOUR COMMUNITY

These certificates make great holiday, graduation and birthday gifts that can be personalized with the recipient's name. The cost of one S.H.A.R.E. or one square foot is $54.17. The personalized certificate is suitable for framing and will state the number of shares purchased and the amount of each share, as well as the recipient's name. The home that you participate in "building" will last for many years and will continue to grow in value.

Here is a sample SHARE certificate:

HABITAT FOR HUMANITY

THIS CERTIFIES THAT

YOUR NAME HERE

HAS INVESTED IN A HOME FOR A DESERVING FAMILY

1985-2005

TWENTY YEARS OF BUILDING FUTURES IN OUR
COMMUNITY ONE HOME AT A TIME

1200 SQUARE FOOT HOUSE @ $65,000 = $54.17 PER SQUARE FOOT
This certificate represents a tax deductible donation. It has no cash value.

YES, I WOULD LIKE TO HELP!

I support the work that Habitat for Humanity does and I want to be part of the excitement! As a donor, I will receive periodic updates on your construction activities but, more importantly, I know my gift will help a family in our community realize the dream of homeownership. **I would like to SHARE in your efforts against substandard housing in my community!** *(Please print below)*

PLEASE SEND ME _____ SHARES at $54.17 EACH = $ $_____

In Honor Of: _____

Occasion: (Circle One)   HOLIDAY   BIRTHDAY   ANNIVERSARY

       OTHER: _____

Address of Recipient: _____

Gift From: _____ *Donor Address:* _____

Donor Email: _____

I AM ENCLOSING A CHECK FOR $ $_____ PAYABLE TO HABITAT FOR HUMANITY OR PLEASE CHARGE MY VISA OR MASTERCARD *(CIRCLE ONE)*

Card Number _____ Expiration Date: _____

Name as it appears on Credit Card _____ Charge Amount $ _____

Signature _____

Billing Address _____

Telephone # Day _____ Eve _____

PLEASE NOTE: Your contribution is tax-deductible to the fullest extent allowed by law.
Habitat for Humanity • P.O. Box 1443 • Newport News, VA 23601 • 757-596-5553
www.HelpHabitatforHumanity.org